# TRUE STORIES

## THE NARRATIVE PROJECT
## VOLUME II

Penchant Press International LLC

# TRUE STORIES

## THE NARRATIVE PROJECT
## VOLUME II

EDITED BY

Cami Ostman
Rebecca Mabanglo-Mayor
Anneliese Kamola

Penchant Press International
Bellingham, Washington

Publisher's Note: Portions of this work are memoir. Names, characters, places, and incidents are products of the authors' recall. Some names of individuals have been changed. Locales and public names are sometimes used for atmospheric purposes. Fictional pieces reflect the imagination of the authors. Each individual author is responsible for the content of their work.

Penchant Press International
PO Box 1333
Blaine, WA 98231
www.penchantpressinternational.com

True Stories  The Narrative Project  Volume II
ISBN 978-0-9998048-2-7
LOCN  2019447756

Cover Design:  Spoken Designs www.spokendesigns.com
Cover Concept:  Kris Roeske and Ingrid Roeske Good

*To those courageous enough
to share their stories.*

*Life shrinks or expands in proportion
to one's courage.*

−Anais Nin

# Introduction

Dear Reader,

I am full of excitement as I write this introduction because I know the excitement of the authors whose names appear on these pages. You hold in your hands The Narrative Project's second volume. This book represents the commitment of twenty-one writers and their coaches, each with a book inside of them longing to get out. These writers made a commitment to themselves and to each other to be accountable, to hone craft, and to work diligently to keep their inner critical voices at bay for nine months as they banded together to write complete drafts of their stories.

When a book idea first comes to a writer, she has a choice. She can let the Inner Saboteur whisper all the reasons she is inadequate or unable to write the book, or she can sit down at her keyboard and open a new document. Often, if she does the latter, the characters in the book begin to speak to her at all hours of the day and night, and before she knows it, she has become the conduit for a story burning to come into the world.

This can happen for novelists and memoirists alike. And once the characters are speaking to a writer, and once she has committed to the process of writing the book, the real trouble starts. Now she has a plotline and characters, but she also still has laundry to do and kids to get to school. She has a full-time job, perhaps. Plus, even when she is writing in flow and the words are plentiful, she has to figure out the structure of the story, the question the story is asking (theme), and the scope of the material. In short, she now has a lot of work to do and skills to build as a writer.

We at The Narrative Project are committed to coming alongside each and every writer to take them to the next level. Some people come into our *nine-month get-your-book-done* program with a lifelong dream of publishing a book, while others come to us with a nagging feeling that they must get a specific story living inside their body out onto the page. However a would-be author comes to us, our passion is to provide structure, along with quality coaching, classes, critique, and cheerleading, so that writers are surrounded by a community which teaches, encourages, and guides them at every step—all the way into the publishing process. Our coaches, all published authors and experienced editors (and all published here along with our students), are also working writers. We know the joys and the perils of the book-making journey. We know that every great book doesn't really represent good writing but, rather, represents good revisions, and that sometimes the path is peppered with roots and rocks one has to scramble over on the way to excellent writing.

And so, even on the hard days—actually, especially on those days when the keyboard seems to sneer or taunt—we say to our writers, "We've got your back. Keep writing." And write they do! The authors published here, some starting with zero words on the page when they joined the program, all completed their nine months with at least fifty THOUSAND words toward their drafts. Some reached double that number. All stretched themselves. All learned how to write dialogue, how to craft a flashback, how to build a character on the page, and how to balance scene and theme. And all of them worked tirelessly to reach their goals.

Here in these pages you have writers experimenting with form, revealing their deepest struggles, discovering aspects of self, and learning to embrace new joy. Both fiction and memoir are represented here. As is the hard-won victory of turning oneself into a *real* writer.

I am proud of these pieces and proud of our team of coaches and editors who supported our writers with honesty and grace along the way. Thank you to Nancy Canyon, Colleen Haggerty, Anneliese Kamola, Rebecca Mabanglo-Mayor, and Wendy Welch for loving The Narrative Project and its mission as much as I do.

Every story matters. Every single story! Keep writing, dear ones.

Your Chief Story Warrior,
Cami Ostman

September 2019

thenarrativeproject.net

# Table of Contents

# A Childhood Lost

## Maggie Andreychak

When I was little, my father used to sit me on his lap, holding me close where I could feel the tickle of his whiskers, smell the fragrance of his pipe smoke. There, in the security of his arms, he read me long chapters of *The House at Pooh Corner*, delighting me as he made up different voices for each of the animals. I loved the times he set aside for just us two. I cherished his readiness to put aside the seriousness of adulthood, his willingness to step into the imagination of a children's book and be swept away by it, and his obvious enjoyment of doing so. I savored the magic and the wonder of those stories until that sad day when Christopher Robin went away.

*How could such a wondrous book have such a sad ending?* The question still nagged at me some six years later, as I sat in the den that Wednesday night before Thanksgiving. I was in the fourth grade that year, well past the days of sitting on his lap, and long since able to read for myself. I was sewing a stuffed donkey—not Eeyore, but one like him—for Hunt's Christmas present. She had been my best friend since nursery school and I loved her fiercely. The electricity in the house had gone out due to a storm, but I was content to be alone in the dark, able to work on my project without distractions or mockery from my three older siblings.

A silhouette appeared in the doorway. I saw it was Becky, my oldest sister. It was a comfort and a joy to have her home from college for Thanksgiving. She had left a void that my sister, Mary, and I navigated cautiously, now that our brother Peter was the eldest in the home. Peter was openly hostile towards Mary and me. We were both afraid of him most of the time.

"You need to put that down and come join the rest of the family in the living room." Becky was usually sil-

ly and playful with me, but tonight her voice was flat. I
didn't know that she had already been told the news. I
didn't even know there was news; didn't know this
would be the last time I would have a "rest of the family."

As we walked into the room, I saw Mama and Daddy, each in their own chairs far apart from one another.
The room was quiet and dimly lit by candles. Mary and
Peter sat at opposite ends of the couch. It struck me as
odd that they would even sit on the same piece of furniture. The mood in the room was serious, perhaps like
the mood in turkey pens across the country during holiday season, as dimwitted birds awaited their execu-
tions. Becky led me to the couch and was holding me
from behind. *Why does Becky have her arm around me?* I
wondered as we sat down between our siblings.

"We have something to tell you," Daddy started.
His tone was foreign, like he already didn't belong here
anymore, and yet his voice was also somehow tainted
with happiness—or relief. "Your mother and I have decided that we need to separate."

Separate? I didn't understand what this meant. I sat
still, letting Becky hold me in place.

"We can't live together anymore so we're going to
try living apart," Mama added, as if reading the confusion in my mind. I'd never heard her sound so sad and
serious. "Your father got an apartment and he is going
to live there until we find a new house to move into."

A new house? I didn't want to leave our house on
the bluff! Our house on the bluff was huge and I loved
it. We'd lived there since I was four, the summer we
moved to Sewanee so Daddy could be the doctor in that
little Appalachian university town where he had earned
his Bachelor's degree. Thoughts of summer times past
flooded my mind, beckoning me to cling to them to
stay afloat. I grasped onto a memory from last summer.

I had climbed on the rock garden on the edge of the lawn one evening, admiring the "pinks" with their feathery, serrated-edged petals, while Daddy "surveyed the estate," as he said, from the patio. Pinks were also known as *Dianthus*, but I could never bring to mind the Latin name. I simply admired the intensity of their colors: bright magenta, deep light pink, white with crimson centers, each variety blooming from the end of a slender, segmented olive-green stalk that seemed too sturdy and too bland for the delicate blossoms. As I'd inspected the flowers that evening, Daddy drained a can of Falstaff beer and handed the empty container to me, while simultaneously grinding his cigarette butt out on the patio where dozens of other butts littered the cement.

"I'll give you a nickel for every cigarette butt you pick up and put in that can."

I'd stared in disbelief. A nickel was a lot of money in an age when five cents would get you a candy bar or a Coke. Then I happily spent the next half hour scouring the rockery and dropping butts in the can, keeping careful count.

After dinner that night I'd chased fireflies with my siblings, delighting in the wonder of the blinking lights that faded in and out of the dark envelope of night. Before going to bed, I'd stood with Daddy on the patio and he'd pointed out constellations to me. I tried to see them, but I couldn't figure out which stars formed a group. He told me their names as he had before, and I tried to see a bear or a belt, trying to remember their proper names, all the while knowing I would have to ask him again the next time we looked at them.

Later in my bed, I'd looked out at the darkness and the stars and listened to the sounds of the crickets and cicadas as they chirped their chorused lullabies for me. I loved the melodies filling the thick night air, the sweet vibrations as if all the warm earth pulsated with their life. The sounds illuminated the quiet, speaking secrets I didn't understand.

I loved the sweetness and simplicity of this place where we were all together. I loved that a birthday meant you got to pick what Mama made for dinner and everybody had to be nice to you. You got to choose the flavor of your cake and frosting and two colors for the decorating icing that she would make into rosettes and leaves and write "Happy Birthday" and your name, and then she would press the leftover buttercream icing between two saltine crackers for a sweet, salty, buttery, crunchy treat.

But it wasn't summer now. Now it was November, grey, chilly and foggy, and my home was being ripped away from me. The fog seemed to have crept into the darkness of the room where we were all becoming strangers.

"This will all work out for the best in the long run," was Mama's refrain throughout the stilted conversation as tears slipped from our eyes. Even Peter, who at 16 was normally aloof or angry, looked scared. "This is just a trial separation..." Her contradicting words washed past me. I didn't know just what they meant but I felt my world being rocked, my body torn apart. My head felt dizzy. I tried to disappear into the fog. Fog was safe, I could hide in it. Fog was cold, yet it cradled me like a blanket. Somehow both the silence and the words kept me bound to the couch, unable to escape.

Every wedding scene I'd seen in the movies and on television featured the bride and groom pledging, "Until death do us part." *Did Mama and Daddy forget about that? And why did Daddy have to live alone?* He looked so sad to be losing us.

"Can I live with Daddy?" I pleaded through sloppy tears. Daddy looked up, his eyes brightening, a little smile starting to form as he opened his mouth to speak.

Mama quickly squelched whatever he was about to say. "No." She looked hurt that I wanted to be with him. "You're too young to decide something like that now."

My temper flared at this injustice, but I quickly tried to find my way back to reason as my heart flailed about, desperate for security, yet I stayed quiet. Silence sat like a turkey butcher on the couch with all of us children. In weak and unsure voices, we each braved our fear and hurt to raise questions to try to change the reality of this unexpected and painful announcement. Our parents responded to us with emotionally stifled answers. I couldn't breathe. If I breathed, I might feel the pain. If I felt the pain, I might break apart. The four of us stared at the couch through our tears, frightened and alone in our thoughts. I didn't know a person could feel this sad. I couldn't understand anything they were saying. I knew I would have to talk with Hunt about this.

But even as I thought that, Mama set down a mandate. "Don't talk to anyone about it yet. We're not ready to let people know. If you need to talk, talk with me or Daddy." *Don't talk to anyone about it yet?* I didn't know anyone whose parents were divorced. I had never even met a divorced person. "And kids, this isn't your fault," she continued. *Why would I think it's my fault?* Were they saying this because it was our fault and they didn't want us to feel bad?

I felt ashamed hearing we were not supposed to talk about the divorce. *It must be really bad.* But then it occurred to me that EVERYBODY in town would know, and almost immediately, because Sewanee had a population of only 1,000; and Daddy, who was the doctor for most of them, was getting an apartment away from our beautiful house. Why did I have to hide something that couldn't be hidden? I suddenly felt so angry at my parents for doing this to me that I knew for certain I was going to tell Hunt. Not on the phone because I might get caught, but the next time we played together I would tell her. She would keep the secret.

The next day was Thanksgiving, so there would be no playing with friends. Thanksgiving was family time, whatever that would mean in light of the bombshell dropped on us. The holiday had always felt pointless to me: no presents or candy, just food and football. I didn't like football or pumpkin or pecan pie. Granny would be there, but even that bright spot was clouded as she was as sad about the news as the rest of us.

Peter and Mary sat in the den watching football. Their outbursts at the events of the game were something like a conversation. In the white and grey glow of the images of players on the TV they found some common ground, some sort of mutual tolerance for each other if not acceptance. I tried to belong with them, but football was simply too tedious for me. The only sport I liked watching was basketball.

Daddy sometimes took me to the basketball games at the University–just the two of us. We sat in the third row, high enough for me to see the action, but close enough that he could respond quickly if a player was injured. Faculty members and students greeted him with respect and admiration. "Is this your daughter?" they asked, as if I were a rare and special thing. I would smile, but then not knowing what to say, let my focus drift off to the power of the rhythmic smacks of the ball against the court, the bubbly cheer of the crowd as it rose and fell spontaneously, the deep voices of command that were exchanged among the players as they drove down court, a flurry of arms and legs, breaking away in surges of speed and suddenly coming to a stop as they would pass or shoot. Sometimes a player might switch into slow motion in a graceful layup where time stood still as I held my breath along with the crowd's collective inhale.

That sad Thanksgiving Day dragged on with the tedium of countless football games. When Friday finally came, cold and rainy, Hunt didn't understand why I didn't want to play at her house. There were too many ears around. Like me, she had three older siblings, with one off at college. "Let's meet at the baseball field," I insisted.

"Now remember, we aren't telling anyone about the separation yet," Mama warned as I left the house.

"I know, Mama. I won't tell her." I savored the deceit as I lied.

The field was midway between our homes. I was relieved to see Hunt and her familiar green eyes greeting me with a question about why I'd asked for this clandestine meeting. We wandered quietly around the field recognizing there was nothing to do in the damp and chilly weather. "Why did you want to play here?" she asked.

I didn't want to speak the news and make it reality, but the misery churned in my tummy. I had to spill the beans.

"I have something to tell you but you can't tell anyone," I said.

"Okay," she said easily. We were both good about keeping secrets, not like so many of the other girls.

"Mama and Daddy are getting divorced," I said.

Her eyes grew wide as her mouth dropped, then screwed into a grin. "You're joking," she said with confidence.

"No, they really are. They told us all Wednesday night. Daddy's moving into an apartment. And they told us not to talk about it yet!"

"Why? How will you get to see him?" The news was as shocking to her as it was to me, I could tell by the tears in her eyes.

"I don't know. They just said they can't live together so they're going to try living apart and it's not our fault." I watched the struggle on her face as we talked, neither of us knowing what to do with the information. And her question confirmed my fear. I would be losing my father. Hunt knew how much I loved him, and I could see her heart was shattered for me.

We went to our homes shortly afterwards. How could we play with broken hearts?

Daddy moved out that day, and the holiday weekend lingered like an injured bird. Our house seemed emptied of life, a mere shell through which we went about our rhythms of meals and homework and bedtime, different only because Daddy wouldn't be coming home anymore. He wasn't welcome there.

Days that felt like a lifetime passed before I was allowed to go see him. "I'm going to visit Daddy tonight," I told Hunt at recess the next Wednesday, feeling the strangeness of the words on my tongue. You're supposed to live with your parents, not visit them. I couldn't wait to see him, but I didn't know how he was going to be. Would he still be sad? What would his new apartment be like? It was his apartment, not my home. What would I do there? My toys and books and siblings were at the house on the bluff.

When I walked into his new, sparsely furnished apartment that night, I wandered around the small space, looking for something to admire. The sight of his pipe and ashtray, his Rx pad, his doctor's bag and his stethoscope gave the place a hint of familiarity. We didn't know how to act with each other. I felt torn apart. I didn't know who he was, and I felt that I didn't belong here.

"This is where you'll sleep when you come over," his words echoed in the emptiness.

"When you come for dinner next week, you'll get to meet Elfriede." He said her name proudly—el-free-da—as if she were something special. Elfriede was Daddy's new girlfriend. She was the reason he left our family. I wasn't sure I wanted to meet her. Would she change him? Change who he was to me?

"She's a nurse, and she's from East Germany," he went on. I knew a little bit about Germany from Social Studies: East Germany was a communist country; West Germany was free. I knew enough to know that East Germany was unknowable, separated from the free world behind a wall. Was my dad dating a spy? Did she know things about him I didn't know?

The following Wednesday Mama dropped me off at Daddy's apartment. "I'll be back to pick you up at eight o'clock, or you can call me if you're ready to come home sooner," she said.

"I won't want to come home sooner," I retorted, still resentful that I couldn't live with him. I kissed her goodbye anyway. I felt sorry for her after witnessing her recent crying jags. My tough mother had been collapsing night after night, sobbing without caring who saw.

When I entered, the apartment was thick with steam and the smell of potatoes.

"Hi there Maggie Lou!" Dad's familiar greeting rang out as I jumped into his arms. He seemed happy and for a moment I felt he was the man who had read to me at bedtime and taught me about the stars.

But then he said, "This is Elfriede." There was a flourish to his tone as he led me to the kitchen and showed me his trophy. She was very short and very fat, not very pretty, with breasts that looked like watermelons. I had never seen breasts that big before. It was hard not to stare as my mind tried to make sense of them.

"*Hallo Meggie, it's nice to meet yoo. Your Daddi hast zed zuch niez tings about yoo.*" I had trouble understanding even these simple words, as her accent was so thick and heavy and foreign. And once they registered, I wasn't sure what to say. *Well of course he said nice things about me. I'm his daughter. He loves me.*

"*Doo yoo vant tsum cookies?*" It helped that she was holding out a plate of cookies, but they didn't look like any cookies I knew. "*Ah made tsem fur yur daddy today. Yoo kahn haf one befoor tze dinner.*" I was never one to say no to a cookie, so I reached for one—even though I felt it might be a betrayal to my whole family.

"Thank you," I said.

"*Bitte schoen,*" she responded.

"*Bitte schoen* means you're welcome," Daddy explained. I took a bite of the cookie but all I tasted was flour and nuts. I didn't like nuts in baked goods. Cookies should have chocolate or sugar—or both. I chewed, feeling the bland mound of dough sucking the moisture from my mouth. I wanted to spit it out.

"*Tzer goot?*" she asked.

I tried hard to swallow, and nodded the requisite "yes." Being polite was always favored over being honest.

The evening turned into a misery as I could hardly understand a thing she said. I was embarrassed as I had to ask her to repeat things again and again, while my father remained rapt by her every word. I resorted to offerings yesses or nos or weak smiles as I guessed at what she was saying. She seemed very nice, but I wasn't sure where either of us fit in Daddy's storyline.

Daddy helped her in the kitchen, where she roughly cut the pot roast into half-inch slices, and ladled coarsely skinned potato halves into a bowl and blessed them with an ENTIRE stick of butter. Her presentation wasn't tidy like Mama's dinners, where meat was sliced in quarter-inch thick slices and fanned out on a platter in perfect unison. Daddy and Elfriede bumped into each other—on purpose—as they moved around the kitchen. When he kissed her and hugged her, I saw how he was a sexual being, and the realization scared and confused me. I felt further disenfranchised from my dad because, that night, I became scared of what I didn't know about him.

I went home after my visit with Dad and his new girlfriend. No cicadas sang to me as I tried to drift into sleep that night in my bed in the house on the bluff. No stars shone through the shroud of coming winter outside my window. No moustache brushed my cheeks when I said my goodnights. My cherished quiet moments alone with my father slid from my grasp like a foggy wraith through the night. The security of his love was an unfinished story, a book with pages torn out.

Daddy had been my refuge. Now the sense of security he used to provide me was as foreign as his girlfriend's tongue.

I rolled onto my side to cry in my pillow, clutching my stuffed Winnie the Pooh. I tried to recall Daddy's lyrical tone from when he used to read to me, but all I could hear was Piglet's piping voice: *What do you want to do today Pooh?* I remembered then how the *House at Pooh Corner* ended: with Christopher Robin leaving the animals, never to return.

I would move to another house before the pinks came up in spring, before summer nights brought fireflies out to dance along the bluff again. I wouldn't pick up cigarette butts for a nickel each, or try to learn the constellations, and I would never get back to the security of my father's lap and to the wonder of those voices and their adventures in the Hundred Acre Woods.

# Honeymoon with HIV

## Jessie Blair

I married Randy because he was my best friend. But there was more to our choice to get married than friendship—or even love. We met at our church, a conservative congregation where Randy had confessed openly that he was gay. He was thirty-two and had only been with men up until we started seeing each other, and he'd lived with the guilt of sin and the shame of letting God down for years. When we fell in love, the leaders at the church saw our relationship as Randy's way out of his turmoil. They pressed us to get married. A man like Randy, inclined toward men but who fell in love with one—only one—woman, should marry the woman he loved. Quickly. Before he fell back into temptation.

Also, we both wanted children. But I especially wanted them—like a hunger that can only be filled by the one thing you crave. And since we loved each other fiercely, it wasn't hard to make the decision to wed— full of hope and with plans for a family as quickly as we could make it happen.

The day after our wedding, Randy and I hopped a plane to Tucson, Arizona for a two-week honeymoon of travelling around in the southwest of the United States. I was only twenty-five and had never been on a commercial airplane before. Nor had I ever been married for that matter, so I was so excited. We travelled from Tucson to Flagstaff and saw the Grand Canyon, then drove through the Painted Desert and the Petrified Forest. We continued into New Mexico to see Taos, then to Old Albuquerque, and back to Tucson, later taking a side trip into Nogales, Mexico. The mix of

Native American, Spanish, and English cultures capti-
vated us, and we fell in love with the desert. The oth-
erworldliness of the orange-mauve sunsets, the
flowering cacti, and the tall saguaros gave us a feeling of
being somehow spiritually connected to the earth and
yet isolated from other human beings. We wandered
through our honeymoon excited about the life that lay
ahead of us.

The only thing that soured the trip was that near
the end of the two weeks Randy fell sick with nausea
and fatigue, capped off by a terrible cough and some
kind of intestinal disruption. I was worried enough
about him that I took him to the Emergency Room at a
hospital in Albuquerque. But he was given antibiotics
and we were sent on our way. We didn't think much
more about that hospital visit because the medication
seemed to help in the following days—and we were
young.

After our honeymoon, we settled into a routine. I
played the part of a happy monogamous housewife
with a part-time job as a secretary in an office. Randy
went to work as an accountant for an insurance broker-
age company. We got a grey and white cat that we
named Snuggles, and I began to look forward to the day
Randy and I would have a child together.

Then, about three months into our marriage, Randy
felt ill again with similar symptoms and said he was going to see his doctor. I didn't worry, assuming he had
some kind of bug that was hanging on. The doctor
would give him another round of antibiotics and Randy
would get better.

But Randy came home a week after his appointment
and stood in the living room beside the couch looking
upset. He gestured for me to have a seat. "I have something quite serious to tell you," he said. "The doctor
took some tests when I went to see her. I need to talk
to you about the results right away."

My mind raced as I sat there, wildly searching for what could be so upsetting about his tests.

"What is it?" I blurted. I could feel it was bad.

"I've been diagnosed as HIV positive." As he said this, I saw the fear in his eyes.

I stared at him, my emotions roiling from fear to anger to disbelief. I suddenly felt like I was in a surreal landscape where I didn't recognize anything around me. Was my husband really telling me this?

"Oh no, Randy. AIDS?"

He shook his head. "Not AIDS, Jessie. HIV."

I was shaking. "What's the difference between HIV and AIDS?" I asked.

"HIV can become AIDS but it isn't AIDS yet. It's AIDS only when T-cell counts go below 200," he continued. "My T-cells are still over 1,000."

"What's a T-cell?" Again, I was just filling space.

"They're white blood cells that fight infection."

I was quiet for a few minutes as I tried to take this in. The silence helped me come back into my body.

We sat in our silence together for a long time as I tried to understand the information he'd given me, what it meant, and what this would mean for us as a couple.

The next day I thought about going up to the church, but I didn't. I was afraid someone would say Randy deserved this, given his sexual choices. Instead, I called an AIDS Hotline to talk to someone, anyone. I wanted to hear that I was going to be all right, that there was hope that my husband wasn't going to die within the next year. The woman I spoke to on the Hotline was a nurse. I broke down crying and couldn't stop. I bemoaned the fact that I could no longer plan on having children. She was very kind and patient.

"You sound like you're in shock," she said.

It never occurred to me that I was in shock. I'd just kept living, moving, breathing over the past twenty-four hours even though I felt weighted down as though HIV was a huge monster sitting on my chest restricting my deep breaths and distracting me from everything I tried to do. That giant monster threatened to take away everything positive, stable, and loving from my life. HIV had Randy and it wouldn't be letting him go. I needed her to toss a weapon to me, so I could wage my own battle against HIV. Any weapon.

"With the antiviral treatments we have available now," she told me, "people with HIV are living a long time—for over 20 years sometimes."

I'd never heard about the new antiviral medication. I still thought HIV meant certain and rapid death. The nurse had tossed me the weapon of hope I needed. I caught that hope with both of my hands and brought her close like body armor.

But I wanted to know if 20 years was really the norm and how many HIV positive people were living that average lifespan. I wanted to know if we could still have children. And if he would be around to see them grow up. She said she didn't know the exact statistic for years of survival or if children conceived by a father who had HIV would contract the virus, but she was willing to get back to me with that information. I was skeptical; sometimes when people say, "I'll get back to you," it really means, "I don't really want to answer that question and I'm too lazy to look for the answer."

After we got off the phone with each other, I went to work that day and did my best to appear as though everything was normal. Looking back on it now, other people probably knew something was wrong but didn't want to ask, and I felt inhibited to talk about Randy, especially to people outside my small social circle—my family and people at my church.

I ran on automatic for several days. Every movement came from muscle memory. A full week went by and I hadn't heard back from the nurse at the AIDS Hotline confirming my skepticism.

*See, nobody cares or has the time to answer questions,* I said to myself.

But about eight days later, I received a large envelope from AIDS Committee Toronto, an educational agency. Inside was a copy of an article about a procedure that I could undergo at the University of Milan that would allow me to get pregnant with Randy's child without contracting HIV. The nurse included a note that noted the average lifespan of HIV positive people was 19 years and included the sources of the statistic.

I felt renewed hope and energy and finally had the courage to call my parents and my friends to share the news with them that my new marriage was being threatened by a terrible disease. Overall, everyone was as supportive as they could be, although they didn't know what words of comfort to offer me. My feelings were very raw at that point in time and I was almost inconsolable most days. It didn't take much to stress me out. Little did I know then that stress would be the catalyst for a complete transformation.

I lived with some small renewed hope for Randy's survival after getting the package from the woman at the hotline. Perhaps we could still raise a child together. Then, about two weeks after Randy had told me the news, I decided to call the AIDS hotline again to talk to the nurse about the fertility procedure in Milan. A different nurse answered my call. When I told this one what I was thinking and about my circumstances, her voice became terse.

"You're not thinking things through carefully," she insisted. "It's irresponsible for you to consider bringing a child into such circumstances. If Randy dies, your child would be fatherless. You would become a single parent. I'm a single parent myself. It's a hard way to live."

By the end of the conversation, I felt shaken up, and I retreated deep inside myself. I felt guilty for having even thought—dared to hope—for children with Randy.

The shreds of what remained of a vision of a family fell to the ground along with my heart and my soul. It was the last time I would call the AIDS Hotline.

A couple more weeks later, I went to AIDS Committee Toronto, an organization that educates people about HIV and AIDS, to check out their resource library and do research about nutrition and quality of life for HIV patients. I just wanted to be in an environment where being a partner of an HIV person wasn't an anomaly. While I was there, I saw that people could make an appointment with a counsellor. I was feeling at loose ends, so I made an appointment.

When I met the counsellor the next day, a middle-aged man with salt and pepper hair and kind eyes, my energy was very low. I didn't even look him in the eyes. After the introductions, I sat on the small sofa in his office and started talking in a monotone voice.

"I've been married for four months. Last month my husband was diagnosed HIV positive."

"I'm so sorry," the counselor said kindly, "HIV is difficult to live with."

"Yes. And hardly anybody in our community understands what we're going through. They try, but because my husband is gay, they have a hard time wrapping their minds around our marriage in the first place."

The counsellor nodded his head in agreement.

"I feel so confused and alone," I continued, looking down at my hands. "We want to have children but with the HIV that's not going to happen."

"Have you thought about adoption?"

"I have thought about it, but then children wouldn't be our own." I so desperately wanted the whole experience of being pregnant and giving birth. And I wanted to raise children that would be ours—that would have Randy's common sense and my sense of humor. That had been our plan.

He nodded his understanding.

"How are you and your husband getting along?"

I lifted my eyes and looked at him. "Things have been rocky between us since his diagnosis," I admitted. "I'm upset all the time and he's been irritable."

"You know, it's okay to cry about this."

"I know, but I've cried so much. I just feel numb now."

The counselor's soft eyes gave me permission to simply sit there in his office immersed in my pain. There were simply no words for my grief and worry. For Randy, and for myself.

The antibodies that form when HIV is introduced to a person's body could be detected in 1994 only after a person was infected for at least 6 weeks. Up until the time of Randy's diagnosis, we had been having unprotected sex. We were already concerned that I was infected.

My thoughts were running like a caffeinated hamster on a wheel as I got ready to go to the Free Clinic to be tested six weeks after Randy's diagnosis. Would I be okay? What if I had HIV too? If I did, then I couldn't be a mom no matter what. Would I live long enough to take care of Randy? So many things to fret over. On the subway, from the stop near my home and all the way to the clinic, my mind raced. On the train, I stood and held tightly to the handrail even though there were seats available. I'd chosen the Free Clinic instead of my doctor because I didn't have to give my identity at the Free Clinic. If my test turned out to be positive, there wouldn't be a record. Not that that would help me.

As with all medical clinics, there was a sitting room for patients. I walked in, took a number and a seat, then waited to be called by the intake worker. When I was called, they directed me to another room where they drew my blood. Then they asked me to take a seat in a different room and told me to wait to talk to a sex educator. I gripped the arms of the ugly blue chair where I sat and became aware of my jaw feeling clenched. My breathing felt shallow and my mind raced while my life was being held in the balance. Finally, one of the sex educators met me and told me what to expect from the HIV test, what the antibodies meant, and how to have safe sex. Everything seemed so matter-of-fact to her. But this conversation was about life-and-death to me.

The next week while I waited for my results was one of the longest weeks of my life. If it turned out I had HIV, I knew I would find the strength to move on in life albeit with disappointments that would run deep. I curled up on the sofa to read and sip hot tea on the cold fall morning before I was to go in and get my results. Snuggles came and lay next to me, purring and looking up at me with emerald colored eyes against her smoky grey and bright white fur. She was so beautiful. Her cuddliness made me smile and I talked to her as I pet her gently, telling her about my worries. She would occasionally answer me with her raspy voice, a sound that put me in mind of an older woman who hangs out at the neighborhood bar chain-smoking and drinking. She helped to soothe my high-strung nerves.

When it was time, I stood once again on the subway train gripping the handrail so tightly that my knuckles were white from the tension. All I wanted to do was wake up from this dream and hope that it was all a nightmare. I could hear my own heart thumping inside of my head as I approached the building. This was the moment of truth. Would I need to start antiviral therapy too or would I be negative? But even if I were negative, I still had decisions to make.

I entered the clinic, checked in with reception and took a seat in the waiting room. A middle-aged woman with long, brown hair called my number. My face drained of all its color as I followed her into a private room where we sat down.

She seemed to take forever to situate herself across from me before she announced, "You are not HIV positive."

I took a deep, long breath then, and as I breathed out, my body went limp as all the pent-up tension released at once. I felt tired suddenly, and my eyes filled with tears. I was so relieved.

"Oh, thank God!" I said. "But how did I not get the virus after being repeatedly exposed?"

"Nobody really knows," she said, shaking her head. "Some people just don't get it. We don't know if that's because some people are immune or what. It's one of the mysteries of the virus right now."

I nodded sadly, and she must have seen how much pain I was in because she asked about my marriage. I told her Randy was gay and that the church had pressed us to get married—though we'd agreed easily because we loved each other. I told her I wanted children but that was probably no longer in the cards because he was HIV positive. She stared blankly at me.

"I'd divorce him and get another partner," she said flatly. "You don't need that kind of stress in your life."

I felt my eyes narrow at her insensitivity. I'd never once thought about getting out of this short marriage of mine. First of all, divorce was discouraged in our faith. But besides, Randy and I were soulmates as far as I was concerned.

"I don't want to divorce him," I said to the woman.

"It's up to you. I'm just saying that you're better off without him." She spoke this definitively. I was annoyed by her insensitivity.

"I don't agree with that," I said with more confidence than I felt, unwilling to let her opinion stand without resistance. "Randy and I are still friends, companions, and very good for each other."

"You could have better," she declared.

I walked away from that conversation in an angry mood. I thought to myself, what is the purpose of getting married if at the first sign of hardship a person bolts out on the other person? That's not the type of marriage I wanted or needed. Nor was it the kind of person I wanted to be. Other people may not take that vow seriously, but I did. And abandoning my loved one in his time of need was not my idea of being loyal.

I told Randy what happened at the clinic.

He didn't seem as upset by the nurse's suggestion as I was. "The decision is yours," he said.

I looked at him full of appreciation. I loved Randy. And no matter how our union had been influenced by others to start with, I had committed my life to him. I had a feeling that moving forward we would be often misunderstood. As we marched ahead on this journey together, even the church would wonder about our commitment to one another and would suggest that perhaps I should get out of the marriage. But the fact was that I wanted to share my future with Randy, and I hoped for a long life together.

I asked Randy for a conversation a few days later. And I started by saying, "I know what the church believes—about how your being gay is a sin. But I love you and I plan to stay in this thing with you no matter what. I think we'll need to think outside the box—both for our relationship and around this diagnosis you have. I think I'll need to leave the church to pull this off."

Randy looked at me with his intense eyes. He'd been through as much as—no, more than—I had. "Okay, he said," and he looked at me piercingly. "If you're willing, I'd like to make our life together work, too."

I nodded in gratitude. I didn't know then that we would have to walk away from our community and forge a new definition of partnership and marriage. I only knew that whatever happened, we would be in it together.

# Pepe

## Sarah Buel

Pepe was a handsome old black and white tomcat who lived at the neighboring apartment with a woman who loved him dearly. She had just had a baby.

I was the single woman who lived next door. Pepe knew I loved him. After the baby came, Pepe began to come over and wail at my apartment door around 2:30 or 3 a.m., just after the bars closed.

Pepe was a cat. He had no money to be out drinking at the bars.

But doesn't this story sound familiar anyway? His woman who loved him had just had a baby. And he began to show up at the door of the single neighbor woman after the bars closed, crying to be let in.

What a dog!

No. Pepe was a cat.

Like all handsome old tomcats who are accustomed to being loved by the ladies, he knew how to find the codependent single gal who couldn't bear to hear him cry. He could sniff out the one who would rise from her slumber, stumble to the door half-awake, and let him in at 2:30 or 3 a.m. in the morning, after the bars closed, and not even be mad. That gal this time was me.

I knew his woman who loved him. I liked her. I respected her. I wanted her to like and respect me. I knew she had just had a baby. This was not like me, to let another woman's tomcat on the prowl into my apartment when he came crying to my door after the bars closed. And yet I did. Over and over again.

I was powerless. I could not say no to handsome Pepe.

Every night after opening the door for him, I would stumble back to bed, Pepe following close behind. I would lay down, and he would jump up on top of me. No "hello, how are you doing." No "I missed you, baby." No small talk of any kind. He would just follow me back to the bed and jump on top of me where he would knead my breasts with his paws, purring loudly. For about a half an hour. And then when he was done with me, he would jump off, and then stand and wail at the door to be let out.

Once again I would get out of bed and groggily stumble to the door—by now it was 3 or 3:30 a.m.—and let him out.

Night after night this happened.

I was tired, and I was not okay. I need my sleep. I can't have my sleep interrupted at 2:30 or 3 a.m. every morning for half an hour, and still be okay during the day. I have responsibilities. I need to be sharp.

Obviously, if I could not say no to the tomcat who belonged to another woman who had just had a baby, the cat who came wailing at my door after the bars closed in the wee hours of the morning, if I was willing to let him in to jump on top of me for a half an hour and then willing to get up when he was done with me, to stumble to the door to let him out again, I was not okay.

My not-okay-ness and my weariness only increased as a result of these nightly interruptions to my sleep.

Pepe was not forcing his way into my apartment. I would get up willingly and let him in. Even though I was not okay and my not- okay-ness was daily increasing after these nightly visits, I somehow still had enough sense to know that I was at fault, and that I could not blame Pepe for my exhaustion. He could not open the door to my apartment himself. Even if I had given him a key.

That handsome old tomcat knew that he could come wailing at my door at 2:30 or 3 a.m. in the morning after the bars closed, and I could not say no to him.

My inability to say no to a handsome old tomcat, who belonged to another woman who had just had a baby, when he came to my door to have his way with me in the middle of the night, was disrupting my life.

I had to face that I had a problem.

I was powerless over this unhealthy cycle with the old tomcat, and my increasing weariness was making my life unmanageable.

I needed help.

Because I had a history of allowing handsome old tomcats and dogs (most of whom stood on two legs), to exploit my codependency, I was already in a support group. I was already trying to learn to set boundaries and trying to learn not make the same mistakes with Tom, Dick, and Harry that I had made with Steve, Scott, and George. Trying to overcome my codependency. Trying to learn to say no.

At my weekly support group, I screwed up my courage, and I raised my hand.

I told them all about Pepe. That Pepe was a handsome old cat and that I loved him. That I could not bear to hear him cry. But I was tired. So tired. And in my weariness, I was ashamed. Because I knew that Pepe could not get in my apartment by himself at 3 a.m. Even if I gave him a key.

They laughed at me.

Yet in their laughter, I heard not judgement, but recognition and acceptance. Often, through acceptance, one finds courage.

Shame flourishes in isolation. Through sharing with others the shame of not being able to say no to the handsome tomcat Pepe—to my obvious detriment—and then hearing the loving laughter of my fellow support group members (who understood how difficult it is to say no to a handsome tomcat to whom you once said yes), a newfound courage replaced my shame.

It was not easy, to lie in bed that night and hear the handsome one cry out in the cold (California) night outside the door for me, and not rise to comfort him. Hearing his plaintive wailing, and being guilt-stricken that I was not comforting him as I had allowed him to become accustomed to, I worried. Would he think I didn't love him anymore? I did not sleep that night either. Or the next night, when he tried again.

But I had my support group, even though they lovingly laughed at me. And the memory of their laughing faces gave me courage. Alone I had been powerless, but they had given me a new-found power to say no. To a handsome old tomcat.

I stood strong, lying in bed. Now, night after night, I did not rise to his pleas outside my door, and finally, Pepe came no more to my door at 3 a.m.

I could sleep through the night again, and no longer had to drag myself wearily through the days. I felt better. Manageability was returning to my life.

Perhaps Pepe returned to spend the whole night with his woman, who loved him, and the new baby. Perhaps Pepe found another codependent single gal who would let him in after the bars closed. I know that I went back to sleeping through the night.

Our relationship changed. Sometimes when I had a moment to sit out on the deck in the afternoon, Pepe would come and say hello to me. It was not the same. But it was what it needed to be.

# My Brother Visits—An Excerpt from *Struck: A Memoir*

## Nancy Canyon

"Yo, Nance," a voice calls out.

The lookout tower shakes, pinging guy wires and rattling windows. Jack and I step out onto the catwalk and peer over the railing, surprised to see my brother's grinning face looking up from the landing below. For some reason, out here in the middle of the Nez Perce National Forest where I'm on fire lookout for the summer with my husband Jack, his presence seems weirdly out of place. Maybe not as much as Mother's did when she visited with her new beau, Charlie, but still....

"Oh, my God! Bruce!" I squeal.

He climbs the rest of the stairs and, winded and coughing, steps out onto the catwalk, looking around vigilant-like, as if he's still on patrol in Vietnam.

"Right on, man!" Jack says and reaches for his hand, shaking it heartily.

"This is a surprise," I say, wrapping my arms around his massive girth and squeezing tightly.

He returns the love, burying me in a suffocating bear hug, mumbling something about hanging around for a while. There's a vague reference to needing to lie low, then a smirk. Then more hacking, and a request for a glass of water.

Jack and I look at each other questioningly. I turn to go inside to get Bruce a drink, wondering what he means by "lie low." Lots of Vietnam veterans walk into the woods after they return home and are never seen again. I hand him the water and he downs it in three silent gulps. I can see in Jack's stance that, though he's open to my brother being here, he's skeptical: there's no room in our 16'x16' fire tower for an extra body, especially one as large as my brother's.

"Stay as long as you like," Jack says.

"But where will he sleep?" I say.

"In the woods," Bruce says. "I brought gear."

I nod. "Come on in, then. Are you hungry?"

"First things first," Bruce says. ""Gotta set up camp."

And just like that, he turns, taking the tower stairs agilely despite his heft. I watch from the catwalk as he hikes down the road, backpack slung over his wide shoulders. He enters the forest where the road rounds out, right before it heads downhill toward the stream that we collect drinking water from. He's not the same man who joined the Marines in '66 at the age of eighteen. Though I'm happy he's home, there's a distance between us now that wasn't there before. A darkly shadowed abyss I'll need to cross in order to reach him; perhaps it's the horror of war, the story he'll tell us one day.

It's getting hotter outside as the day draws on. I drink a glass of water and wipe my mouth with the back of my hand. Waving away a fly, I lean over the fire finder and jot down the daily weather details in the log book. Jack's outside studying the forest through high-powered binoculars. Bruce hasn't left the woods all day. By the time he emerges, Jack has traded places with me and I'm leaning against the catwalk railing facing west, perusing the territory where a few lightning strikes hit the week prior. Nothing!

I lower the binoculars and see Bruce waving at me from the road. I wave back, thinking the forest is a fine place for him to sleep. Good even, given so many returning vets need quiet hermitages of sorts to recover from the trauma they've experienced.

Soon, we're all sitting around the green picnic table eating Cream of Mushroom soup and Wonder Bread—

which has become our standard meal these days. His hair is curlier than mine, and redder. He wears it cut close to the scalp, military style, though it has grown out a bit, making the curl more obvious. His beard, which is bright red in patches, is scruffy; his face freckled and plump. He finishes his soup and lights up a cigarette. Jack hands him a beer and the two of them step outside to commiserate.

I clear the table and wash dishes. Between the two of us, I'd say he got most of our Irish heritage. I have a smattering of freckles across my nose, but he's completely covered. Mom says we're Irish, English, Scottish, and Welsh. Oh, and there's a little bit of German in there, which explains his hirsutism, I guess. Pennsylvania Dutch too—which also happens to be Jack's mother's heritage—shoofly pie, hot bacon dressing, hard salted pretzels, cabbage and bratwurst—yummy!

Outside, the two of them sit side-by-side on the catwalk. Feeling antsy, I pace between stove, counter and table, wiping down surfaces in an agitated manner. My brother has been at large for such a long time, hardly staying in touch even while on R&R. We worry about him constantly, not knowing his whereabouts until he shows up unexpected. Thus, my shock at seeing him standing on the tower stairs. And my relief.

I know how it will go soon, me scolding him for something even though he's older by three years. My sister does the same with me, scolding me even though she's four years younger. Come to think of it, we all scold each other. They say you treat the ones you love the worst. I think we treat each other the way we've been treated. I look toward the woods, imagining his campsite: small tent and fire ring. We'll have to remind him that he can't light a fire. The woods are growing crisper by the minute. I can smell the warm pitch and feel the dryness baking the air.

Dad told me that Bruce got an honorable discharge from the Marines for medical reasons—alcoholism and obesity—which is much better than a dishonorable discharge, which would have happened if he hadn't volunteered for Nam after he went AWOL from Camp Lejeune. He couldn't handle being ordered around in boot camp. And ridiculed: "Give me 100, Sergeant Sponge."

Long before boot camp, Dad's constant put-downs for not acting like a man pushed Bruce over the edge. I once overheard them fighting; Bruce cried that the reason he enlisted in the Marines was to prove that he was a man. And then to be mocked in front of all those other men in boot camp...shit! But we all had to get away from home somehow. Those last few years living on Madelia Street: Dad's drinking, our parent's fighting, our step-brother moving in with us, and the ongoing sexual abuse, was all too much to take.

After two stints in Nam, he arrived home from Bangor, and proceeded to tear around in the '55 Chevy Dad took away from me and gave to him. Bruce flew into rages easily, slapping people across the face, drinking too much, getting in bar fights, breaking out windows, and getting tossed out onto the sidewalk, landing on his ear. We were shocked to see his once 5'8" frame, usually a lean 175 pounds, now clad in bulky farmer overalls and an X-large T-shirt.

Our mother's fear of obesity could be likened to her fear of the wind. I think her fear of fat came about because of my grandmother's weight. She's dead now from the strokes that paralyzed her left side, but Mom hasn't forgotten Grandma's excess poundage, and is always vigilant about not gaining an extra ounce. And, she's critical of anyone who does—including her daughters. And now her only son.

It's odd to be so afraid of fat, especially when Mom's so thin. In the photos of her pregnant with my little sister—Dad's real daughter—she appears anorexic in her pin curls, plaid shirt, and pedal-pushers, which she says she wouldn't be caught dead in now-a-days.

Since obesity is Mother's *numero uno* fear, she pulls every ounce of fat off the chicken legs and thighs and pares dense white fat from steaks and roasts before she cooks them. Roasting is my favorite way to make chicken, and eating Mother's Southern Style chicken breaded in salt and peppered flour, and baked in the oven with a cup of butter drizzled over the top, is akin to dying and going to Heaven. And fattening as hell!

And Bruce's favorite meal. He regularly requests Mother's chicken for his birthday dinner, which is coming right up. Too bad he missed Mom's visit, as she brought her famous chicken along when she and Charlie drove up the mountain to visit. Bruce could have eaten his fill that night. Of course, he would have had to interact with Charlie, which wouldn't have been pretty, I'm sure of it!

Bruce steps out to use the john and returns with a .22 rifle balanced in his right hand. He lifts it, cocks it and shows me how he's filed the hammer down to a hair-trigger. He runs his hand over the polished gunstock and grins. I nod, agreeing that the wood grain is beautiful. He seems content, turns and sets the .22 rifle in the corner behind the door.

Jack hands him a homebrew, which I hope doesn't loosen the light hold he has on his Marine instincts. I go back to cutting brownies from the baking pan, ignoring my anxiety.

The men wander out onto the catwalk and take a seat facing the distant heat-wavering prairie. I follow them, carrying the plate of sweets for us to share. Jack doesn't waste any time rolling a *bomber*. Again he claims the bomber is his own invention—a nice fat joint that will get the two of them plenty high. Jack passes it to me and I wave him away. Someone needs to tend to the forest, don't they?

I head back inside to start dinner. I don't feel like getting high around my brother, no matter what. The last time we smoked together we were living in Spokane. Bruce was still a Marine then and home on leave. Somehow it got back to the Corps that we'd smoked pot and soon we decided we better stay below the radar. Nothing ever came of the whole fiasco; except for Dad's satisfaction when he found out what we'd done and that he was right about me; I really was a *crumb bum*.

I open chili and spoon it into a pot, stirring it over the gas flame. It's clear to me that Nam took it out of my brother. It's a horrible war, complete with napalm, Agent Orange, gooks, monsoons, and jungle rot. "Rot," Bruce says, "ate away my feet inside my leather boots. No matter what you do, you can't get rid of it. There's no way to stay dry while wading through a rice paddy, you know?"

I imagine rice paddies and the wet steamy jungle rigged with mines, and I think how the war turned my brother's personality explosive. Once, while on leave when I still lived at home, he said, "Never wake me in the night. I sleep on the floor with a knife under my pillow. I could kill you in an instant."

"Come and get it," I say, and serve up the canned chili and Rye Crisp in green Melmac® bowls. Bruce denies the offering at first—a hand lifted and a *no thank you* shyness written in his eyes.

"Go on," I say, "there's plenty. I opened two cans."

He mumbles his thanks and takes the bowl of steaming chili. After dinner, he heads back into the dusky woods below the tower. We don't follow him down to see how he's got his camp set up; just give him the space to do whatever he needs to do. We hear the sound of a shovel once in a while, but no other sound comes from the woods except the high-pitched chitter of a Douglas squirrel.

The next morning Bruce says he's heading out on foot to town. I remind him it's a fifty mile round trip. He shrugs. My stomach tightens. He may never come back, that's the way he is. "You're coming back, right?" Bruce shrugs and turns, ambling away.

My brother was beaten by our real father. Mom said that that was the reason she left him. I was only two at the time—Bruce was five. I wanted to know if he'd ever hurt me—or her, for that matter. She shook her head no. "He loved you very much." I've never told her this, but I'm thinking of finding him some day. Especially since Dick (I've decided to call him by his real name from now on) won't give me the time of day since Mom divorced him too.

The silence is final with Bruce gone from the mountaintop: no shovel, no hacking cough, no wind, just a light breeze and clouds building on the horizon. Jack is mad at me because I didn't want to do it this morning. I think, although I may be wrong, that twice a day is too much sex for one person. I mean, I'm not conceiving again until the mass in my belly is gone. Besides I'm too sad to give him anything more than a hug right now. The possibility of surgery is always on my mind. The doc said I will have to have exploratory surgery when we come down from the tower. He said that it's probably not cancer, because I'm young. But, to tell the truth, I'm more worried about my brother than myself at the moment. He'll probably sit in a bar in Grangeville tonight, swilling beer or bourbon—my flesh and blood downtrodden by two dads and a stupid war.

Once I asked Bruce if he could remember our real dad and he shook his head no. That's nearly all we said that afternoon, sitting next to each other, time stretching out in one long awkward silence. I finally looked at him and said, "I love you; you know that don't you?"

He smiled a little. That was after the shrapnel had injured his head and arm, after he recovered from losing his whole battalion. He healed, so to speak, from his physical wounds, but he was the sole survivor, receiving the Purple Heart for bravery. A medal for surviving carnage, which is hard to imagine.

"Why are they sending you back?" I'd asked him.

We were silent again, our hearts swollen as road kill. He smiled that smile that always seemed to say he was amused by a secret he kept. I thought it meant he couldn't say how sad he felt. Or maybe how uncomfortable he was with my prying. Or that he had orders, that's all there was to it. Back to the bunkers, to the Asian piss beer, to his team of buddies. Back to the gooks, rifles, snipers, explosives, helicopters, and napalm, for God's sake. Back to the booze. Back to being beaten and struck one more time.

While he's gone, we call in a potential smoke. The plume is far out on the prairie and turns out to be a manufacturer. Still, we are on edge, the fire danger being extremely high right now. We scan the territory almost constantly and still we're afraid we will miss something. As the afternoon heats up, I become increasingly anxious.

Jack says, "Fuck! Your brother can take care of himself. He's been to war, you know."

"I know," I say, and I do know, but it's becoming more and more clear to me that what he survived in Nam is more shocking than we know. "Someone needs to help him," I say. "He's always scratching at the shrapnel. I want to ask him about it, but you're right, he doesn't want to talk about it."

"Shit, just leave him alone. He's a grown man!"

I give Jack a killer look, lingering on it for a while to make sure it sinks in deeply, but like all weary warriors, I decide to retreat. "It's just that Bruce is different now. He's antsy, close-lipped, a vagabond at the mercy of the wind. He's no longer the guy who bought me a necklace for no reason at all, or bragged to his buddies about his pretty sister, carrying my picture in his wallet."

"He's only been here three days," Jack says.

I nod, recalling how mad Bruce was when he first returned from Nam. He cornered me in the laundry room, angry because he thought I looked like a hippy with my frizzy hair and granny glasses. Hippies protested Vietnam, so to him I was a war protester who didn't support the troops. Who didn't support him!

"I'm not a protestor," I said.

Still, he backed me into a corner and as quick as a snake, struck me hard across the face. I cried, covering my bloodied lip with my hand. Mom ran downstairs, shouting, "What have you done to my baby?"

He backed out of the laundry room, looking ashamed, though still raging, "She's a goddamned war protestor."

I sigh, wondering now how long he'll stay with us. Or maybe he won't come back from town. I wring my hands, feeling beside myself with worry. Then the tower shakes and I hear his boots on the stairs and a sense of relief washes through me. I feel giddy like I did when my runaway cat returned home. He pops up onto the catwalk and lumbers in the door with a large bag of groceries. He drops the sack on the counter. "Ciao!" he says.

"Oh my God! How'd you get to town and back?"

"Hitchhiked." He grins mischievously and says no more.

I nod, wanting to say something like, *Hitchhiking is dangerous*, but I keep my mouth shut. Really, he should be the one protecting me. He's the trained killer. I remember him holding my hand and taking me for walks in the woods at our step-grandparents' house. The ground was spongy with thick moss and gave as we walked. For some reason, the give was so frightening to me at four years old, that I started to cry. Perhaps I thought I'd fall through the surface, down into the center of the earth. "It's a long walk," I say. "You must be tired."

"We walked all day through the jungle," Bruce says. "Patrolling, you know. I'm used to it."

"Of course," I say. But I don't really understand, since it isn't clear to me what happened in Nam. In some ways, I'm not sure that I want to know.

He unpacks the bag of groceries: hotdogs and buns, potato chips and beer.

"Right on, man!" Jack says.

I'm not okay with our real father hurting my brother. If we ever meet, I'll tell him that. Even though he never hurt me, I can imagine the shouts and thumps and cries, and how I could have become as jumpy as a beaten dog whenever he was around. Mom did say that she hid Bruce in the closet when our father returned from his trucking trips. And then there is the questionable behavior of our step-father. I don't know if he abused my brother sexually or not. Someday, I will ask Bruce. I look up at him.

Bruce grins. "Penny for your thoughts?"

I grin back. "I'm glad you're back." I want to ask him where he stayed last night, but I bite my tongue. After all, if he gets in a dangerous situation, he knows how to kill someone with his bare hands. This is a terrible thought, but also, he knows where to sleep, how to survive on very little food, and how to outrun the enemy. I've been trying to learn how to do this my entire life.

"There are cows in the creek upstream," Bruce says.

"Yeah," I say. "We boil our drinking water now."

He takes a seat in the green chair, frowning, wiggling one foot, tapping the other, lighting a cigarette, smoking in short bursts. The cabin turns hazy. I begin to cough.

Mom is a fiend for Winstons. Grandpa loved his Camels. And Dick smokes a pipe on occasion, packed with vanilla flavored tobacco. I'm the only one in the family who doesn't smoke. Well, a little weed now and then. I finish writing in the log book, recording weather from earlier this morning, the smokestack we called in by mistake, and how there's little else to note today, other than a very dry forest and clouds building along the horizon.

Flies circle near the ceiling above the fire finder, a continuous lazy loop in the center of the room. It's another hot one. I hear a distant plane. Some days it is all we hear and then there are days when people actually wander up the road to the tower, committing to the 45 feet of stairs to pay us a visit. It always makes me nervous. We don't know these people from boo!

"I need the outhouse," I say, and head down to the ground. As I cross the road, I can see the path leading into the woods to Bruce's camp. I want to sneak down the trail and see how he has it set  up. I should have done that while he was gone. I hurry to the outhouse, opening the door to the dark hot stink. Flies buzz. I wave them away, my worry turning to spiders climbing through the hole from beneath the seat. I become vigilant, keeping spider watch, forgetting all else.

# Transitions

## Cathie Collins

My son, Ryan, is transgender. He was born with female parts, but his mind does not match the parts. He came out to me when he was twelve, stating that he didn't feel comfortable with who he was. "I'm not a girl. I never have been. I can't look at myself in the mirror. When I get my period, I feel like I'm dying inside. I need help." That was all I needed to hear. I could see his unhappiness, and I didn't want that for my child.

This started our transition journey.

After three months of counseling, my husband and I understood that Ryan was indeed consistent, insistent, and persistent in his male identity. These three words are the hallmark of a child who has a mismatch in their gender identity and birth sex. Once we had this clarity, our next step was to seek out health care professionals who could medically help Ryan with his transition.

One very positive thing I can say about Ryan's transition is that our community has never met us with hostility or blatant negativity. I know that there are those around us who don't agree with our "allowing" Ryan to transition, who don't believe transgender is even a thing, but no one has been overtly antagonistic (at least not to our faces). Even so, what's hard is that when you have a transgender child, you are always coming out, in a sense. There are times when Ryan will have to let someone know he is trans even if he passes as a male because of the circumstances. Visiting the doctor is one of those times.

Our pediatrician is a young, nice-looking man who I'm told has a large family. He and his wife are devout Christians who foster children and have adopted several. My armor was on as we went for our visit. I was prepared with speeches and had brought some medical articles that could inform him about gender dysphoria and treatment. When we were called back to the room by the nurse, she asked why we were here today.

"We are here to talk to Dr. Potter today about the possibility of Ryan starting on hormones to suppress puberty. He is transgender and puberty is causing him to be very anxious."

The room went quiet. The nurse's eyes widened for half a second before she pulled back and put on her nurse poker face. "Um, okay. I'll let Dr. Potter know and he'll be in here in a second." She managed a tight smile and hurriedly left the room.

"Well, that went well," Ryan joked. "I think she is really open-minded and completely onboard with all this."

I laughed, but mostly out of anxiety. "It could have been worse," I said. "At least she tried to hide her surprise." Ryan nodded.

Dr. Potter entered the room a few minutes later. I knew he had been briefed by his nurse, and I was a little relieved he already had a heads up. At least if he disagreed, he would have been able to get hold of his derision a little bit before entering the room. He read over the letter from Ryan's therapist, nodded his head a few times, and said, very matter-of-factly, that he was supportive and wanted Ryan to feel comfortable discussing anything with him.

Ryan and I exchanged a glance of happy surprise.

However, Dr. Potter told us, because he did not have experience with this, he did not feel comfortable prescribing hormones without a consultation with a pediatric endocrinologist. Should that endocrinologist prescribe hormone blockers, he would be happy to have his staff administer them, and felt comfortable following the plan of care set by the specialist.

We got in to see the endocrinologist within the month.

When Dr. Soros entered the room, you could almost feel the positive energy she exuded. She was a small, cheerful, energetic, open woman who took a great interest in Ryan. From Romania originally, her thick accent only added to her exuberant presence.

"You are my first transgender patient, Ryan! I am so happy to know you, and we are going to do everything we can to help you," she said.

Ryan's introverted personality usually doesn't respond well to people who are so overtly extroverted, but I was happy to see he was taken with her friendly demeanor and complete acceptance and respect. She listened attentively while we discussed Ryan's history, asked pertinent follow-up questions, and then did a thorough physical exam. I marveled that we'd found such support and kindness in our small rural area of Appalachia.

Dr. Soros also didn't feel she had the experience to prescribe hormones for her first transgender patient. She was excited about Ryan being her first, however, and said she was going to do all she could to help. She assured us that she understood Ryan's dysphoria and agreed that stopping his menstrual cycle was a priority. She wanted to contact other colleagues to discuss Ryan's case, however, because she just needed some guidance. A week later, after she received that guidance from Cincinnati Children's Hospital, we were to begin Lupreolide®, an injection given every three months, which essentially stops puberty. Children who are not transgender are given this for precocious puberty (puberty that starts too early). As a mom, of course I worried about the effects of the injection, but I learned there are no long-term effects in stopping puberty. If someone decides they don't want to take the hormone anymore, puberty will just restart. The fact that the effects can be reversed allows time to ensure that the child is, in fact, consistent, insistent, and persistent with their identity.

The cost of Lupreolide®, without insurance, is approximately seven grand for one injection. If a person needs an injection every three months, that gets expensive. The medical insurance we had when Ryan began the injections paid all but one hundred fifty dollars. We were lucky to have this insurance, and an excellent endocrinologist who went out of her way to ensure that our insurance covered this. We received the first injection in the mail, and went to our pediatrician's office to have it administered. I tried to talk Ryan into allowing me to give him the shot, since I am a nurse and more than capable of giving injections, but he laughed at me and said, "OH Mother! You're hilarious! How about we leave this to the real professionals, okay?"

Teenagers! I love them.

The first injection went smoothly, and after the first month, Ryan's periods stopped. He was overjoyed. Trans men say one of the worst things to go through is having a period, as this is such a female experience and reminds them they are not the males they want to be. By month two on the Lupreolide®, we began to see other changes in Ryan. He was beginning to smile more, talk more, and just seemed actually, genuinely happy. This glimpse of what could be bolstered my confidence and made me realize we were doing exactly what we needed to for our child.

The second injection did not go as planned. Lupreolide® is a powder that has to be mixed in the syringe before it is injected. It comes in a kit with specific instructions as to how to mix it. In fact, several parts of the instructions state in bolded capital letters: *Read Instructions Carefully Before Mixing.* This time, it took a long time for the nurse to come into the room. She walked in, and very matter-of-factly, stated, "Well, the syringe broke. You will need to get another one."

I was stunned. "Why did the syringe break?" I asked.

"Well, I guess it was defective or something. It just wouldn't mix right."

But since I was a nurse, I knew exactly what happened. Someone did not *Read Instructions Carefully Before Mixing.*

"Wait a minute," I said. "I can't just get another one of these. They cost a lot of money and our insurance company won't just give us another one before the next dosage is due."

After some back and forth, I finally asked to speak to the office manager, and we were able to obtain a new dose. The doctor's office paid for the new injection. Because of this debacle, Ryan was now convinced that perhaps it actually would be best if I administered the injections from now on. Not only could I *Read Instructions Carefully Before Mixing,* I was also able to capably administer an injection.

We continued on this road for the next year.

When Ryan was 15, our endocrinologist let us know that she was moving to Boston in May, and we had two choices: we could start over with another endocrinologist in her current practice (something that did not feel comfortable to any of us, considering we would literally have to start over with someone who did not have any experience with transgender kids), or transfer to Cincinnati Children's Hospital's Gender Clinic. We were able to get an appointment there the following month, but Cincinnati is a four-hour drive from our house, so we became commuters to Cincinnati for Ryan's care.

Our first trip to Cincinnati was nothing short of amazing. It was like finding a whole family of people who understood exactly what we needed. There was a counselor named Sarah who talked to us first. She was bubbly and excited and made us feel like we were at the right place, doing the right thing. She talked to Ryan first, then talked to all of us together. Melissa, the nurse, came in next, and did a physical and took a thorough history. Ryan was smitten with her. Melissa was a cute young woman with big blue eyes and a sweet smile. She laughed at all of Ryan's jokes, and told him he was her favorite patient because he was so funny.

After the nurse left, Dr. Conard came in to visit with us. She was friendly, unassuming, and very approachable. She made us feel as if we could ask anything, and gave us such clear, understandable information. She wanted to continue the Lupreolide® for another three months, then see Ryan again. I felt validated by the whole experience. Ryan felt validated. We went home happy, and I realized on the drive home that I was finally feeling more comfortable with this journey because we had found an understanding support system. I hadn't even realized what I'd been longing for.

Three months after our first appointment in Cincinnati, when I was expecting to receive another Lupreolide® refill, our insurance decided they were no longer going to pay for the injection. I called Cincinnati, in a panic. We were due for a new shot, and now our insurance wouldn't pay. They asked if we could come for an appointment the next day. We made the drive, and Dr. Conard decided we could go ahead and just start Ryan on testosterone.

Testosterone is the hormone that would begin male puberty, and with escalating doses, eventually would overtake the estrogen that Ryan's body naturally made. It was also around fifty dollars for a 10 ml vial without insurance, which could last us months—a far cry from the $7,000 for one dose of Lupreolide® to keep puberty at bay.

This decision was a big one. No longer were we "watchfully waiting" to see if Ryan's decision was firm.

Taking testosterone was a more serious step. Some of the effects of testosterone, unlike the puberty blockers, would be permanent—vocal changes, growth of the Adam's apple, muscle development, and, most alarming, possible sterility. Dr. Conard asked Ryan if he had any interest in harvesting his eggs for the future in case he decided he wanted to have children of his own. Ryan was adamant—no, he did not want to do this. I was more skeptical. At fifteen, I would not have cared about the possibility of not having children either. How could anyone make such a decision that young? But even if Ryan had wanted to harvest his eggs, the process for harvesting is invasive, as well as expensive (insurance does not cover this, of course, as with most other transgender treatments, I was finding).

I was worried enough about the permanency of this outcome that I pressed the issue. Dr. Conard explained that, while sterility is most definitely a possibility, studies show that it may not be as final and permanent as the other effects. There are actually many trans men who, later in life, decide they want children and are able to successfully conceive with temporary testosterone cessation. I expressed my relief, but at this point, Ryan looked me squarely in the eye and said, "Mom, I don't want to have a kid. If later on I decide I do, I will adopt, or get a surrogate or something. My body is not female and to have a kid would be the most female thing ever. I would rather die than have that happen to me."

His words stopped me short. He would rather die.

I'd been reading about trans kids who had committed suicide. Without the right support to fully express who one is, despair can lead to depression. I didn't want that for my child. I would do whatever it took to stand behind Ryan.

So we decided that beginning testosterone was the best option at this point. Ryan was 15, after all, and continuing to suppress puberty was about to be an issue anyway. You cannot keep a teenager prepubescent indefinitely, wondering if things will change. I knew now Ryan was firm. Consistent, insistent, persistent. Ryan was all three... incontrovertibly.

So, September 15, 2015 was "T-Day." This was a momentous occasion, celebrated by going out to dinner and then for cake afterward. Ryan was now a kid who was on the road to becoming who he truly was meant to be. After the celebration, Ryan went upstairs to his room. A few minutes later, he appeared with a beard and mustache drawn on his face with black marker. "This stuff works wonders!" he exclaimed. We all laughed until we cried.

While the administration of the first injection of "T" was a significant occasion, it was definitely more dramatic than it should have been. Ryan was extremely afraid of needles. His shots of Lupreolide®, every three months, had taken hours of mental preparation for him each time. Even after he had "pumped himself up," it had been at least a twenty-minute production for me to finally get the needle into his hip. Here is how a typical injection session would go:

*I wipe the site with alcohol.*

Ryan: You're sure that's where it's supposed to go, right?

Me: Yes, Ryan. I made sure I got the correct spot.

Ryan: Okay. Well, make sure you count 1-2-3 before you stick it in.

Me: I always do.

*I take the cap off the needle.*

Ryan: Whoa, buddy, why are you being so quick now?

Me: I'm just taking the cap off the needle.

Ryan: okay. Make sure you count 1-2-3 before you stick it in.

Me: I always do.

*I place my hand on his hip to stabilize the muscle.*

Ryan: Hey! Why are you not counting!

Me: I'm not going to count 'til I am about to put the needle in.

Ryan: Well, stop going so fast!

Me: I'm not.

Ryan: Okay. Make sure you count 1-2-3 before you stick it in!

Me: Okay. 1...

Ryan: Wait! You're ready?? I thought you weren't going to go so fast.

And on, and on, and on. Twenty minutes later, after the injection is administered:

Ryan: That wasn't bad. You got a Band-Aid®˒ right?

Me: Yes. *I stick a Band-Aid® on the non-existent bloody mess he believes is now present on his hip.* Now I need a nap. I'm exhausted.

Ryan: Don't be so dramatic.

So now instead of every three months of this, we were going through this script every other week. A few months in, when I mentioned the process to Ryan's therapist, she told Ryan he needed to start mentally preparing himself to begin giving injections to himself unless he planned on living with me the rest of his life. He turned green. I joked that I wasn't sure which made him more sick: the thought of having to give himself injections, or the thought of living with me forever. Either way, Ryan began wrapping his mind around the idea of doing self-injections.

Testosterone is a magical hormone for a transgender male...in only three months we began to see changes. The first changes were not so fun...acne. Lots of acne. And a lot of mood swings. I had to remind myself that we had basically halted the teenage hormones for a year and a half with the Lupreolide®. Now we actually had a teenager with hormones. I had to watch what I said, because anything could be misunderstood or taken as an insult.

Me: How did you do on your math quiz today?

Ryan: I don't know.

Me: Was it easy?

Ryan: *About to burst into tears.* I said I don't know! You know I'm bad at math! I probably did horrible! So what now? Am I grounded?

Me: *Deep breathing...counting to ten. Staying silent.*

It was not fun—but it was also, as I said, magical. Along with the mood swings and acne came the decrease in breast development, which pleased him greatly. And, within a short four months, the vocal change. All of a sudden, there was a manly voice in our house— sometimes. If you ever watched *The Brady Bunch*, and remember the episode where Peter's voice changes suddenly, that's what happened with Ryan. For a while, his speaking was a constant source of comedy in the house. He would have a deep voice, then all of a sudden it would crack and go really high. We are a family that likes to rib each other, so the constant vocal changes were fun for us. That is until Ryan would get super sensitive because he was now a pubescent teenager. You never knew what was going to happen if you laughed. He might either smile or laugh in return or have a meltdown because you were taking great joy in making fun of something he had no control over.

Ryan was in the thick of his vocal change when he tried out for *Grease* in the spring of 2016. The drama teacher said he sounded like a young Frankie Valli, just not consistent enough for the actual Teen Angel part. No matter... Ryan was happy bossing people around backstage in his role as the stage manager. The longer he was on the T, the more his confidence increased. We had seen glimpses of more peace of mind when he had started the Lupreolide®. But now it was as if there was an entirely different person living in our house. And essentially there was. Ryan was happy now. He was friendly (when he wasn't in a teenage funk, of course), conversant, funny, and very confident in himself and his abilities. I tried to associate in my mind the child before transition and the child after, and there was simply no comparison.

About six months into Ryan's T journey, he finally decided he wanted to try and inject himself. This was big. Super huge! Brimming with confidence after administering his first injection into a mannequin at the nursing school where I worked, he now felt confident to try it on himself. At this point, Ryan was receiving his dose of testosterone intramuscularly (in the muscle) every other week. The needle for an intramuscular injection is long, usually an inch to an inch and a half. It is intimidating to look at. I was skeptical that he would be able to do this, considering our usual injection ritual had not changed since we started. But I was more than happy to let him try.

He drew up the correct dose like a pro. Then it was time to find the site. Because he was administering it to himself, he would be using the thigh muscle. He found the site, and made me mark it with an "X" to make sure he hit his target. Then he cleaned the site with an alcohol swab, uncapped the needle...and we sat there...for an hour. He would get close to his leg with the needle, but every time he was about to inject, he would pull back.

"1-2-3...Oh my god, I can't do it yet. That was just a practice run," he said.

"Ryan, this is practice run 20," I replied. "Why don't you let me go ahead and do it? We can try again next time. You did great getting to this point." I was trying to be patient, but it was getting harder the longer we sat there.

"I'm going to do this. Don't rush me. 1-2-3...Oh my god. Okay. Okay. Okay."

I'm not sure what made him finally decide to do it, but he did plunge the needle in after counting 1-2-3 for what seemed like the 800th time. I was so surprised he did it, I audibly gasped. Big mistake. My gasp so startled him that he let go of the syringe. It just dangled from his leg, needle fully embedded under the skin.

"Ryan, don't let go!" I shouted. My shouting didn't help the situation either.

"Why did you make that noise? Did I do something wrong? Oh my God! It's just stuck in there!"

I grabbed the syringe to right it and had him reach down to push the hormone into his leg. When he pulled out the syringe, a bead of blood collected on his skin at the site. "Band-Aid®! Oh God! Band-Aid®! Now! It's bleeding! Band-Aid®!" I placed the bandage on the site, and then proceeded to praise him like he had just found the cure for cancer.

"Ryan! You did it! Wow! This is so great!"

"Yeah. Except it would have gone better if SOME-ONE hadn't freaked out. I mean, what was that?"

"I was just so surprised it happened," I said. "I really didn't think you'd be able to go through with it!"

"Oh, thanks. Thanks for all the confidence and support. Next time, I'm going to do it by myself so you won't get all freaked out that your kid can actually accomplish something."

I just love teenagers. I've mentioned that before, right?

When injection time rolled around again two weeks later, Ryan determined that he would be administering the injection by himself without me present to freak him out. He drew up the T, and headed upstairs to his bathroom. He exuded such confidence in his ability to complete this task that, despite a nagging feeling that he should still be supervised, I sat still. Fifteen minutes later, while in the kitchen washing dishes, I heard a "thud" from upstairs. I ran upstairs and opened the bathroom door. Ryan was sitting on the bathroom floor, syringe and needle lying next to him. He was pale and had the most confused look on his face. "How did I get here?" he asked.

"I think you passed out, son," I replied.

A look of understanding came over his face, and he said, "Yeah. I just remember sticking myself and then getting tunnel vision. I guess I freaked out when I saw the needle just sticking in my leg."

"You do know that you're not doing this by yourself anymore until you can do it without passing out, right?" I waited for him to blast me with his teenage ire, again accusing me of being unsupportive.

"Congratulations!" he said. "You have your job back!"

And since then Ryan has refused to inject himself. He now has shots every week, given subcutaneously. This type of injection does not go as deep and is a much shorter needle. He acknowledges that they are most likely easier to inject, but will not do it. I guess he will be living with me forever. But at least he will be happy with who he is.

# The Bud Adventure

## Saskia Davis

October 1973

I was almost there. I'd spent the last year preparing to travel the world. I'd sold all my belongings, quit my job and closed my home in Oakland, California. I would be gone indefinitely.

To handle the stress of travel, I'd adopted a spiritual discipline designed to build faith that I would be protected and provided for. Meditation was part of it. Another part involved making decisions and taking action on the answers that came after consulting within. Another part involved asking for help and then, looking for it, pretending to assume it would come. Since I'd begun the practices in the safety of my ordinary life, the risks had been relatively small, but they always had proven worthwhile. When I traveled, though, I expected the stakes would be bigger. Now that I was starting my journey, this fledgling faith was all I had. I wondered if it would be enough.

My travels were to be open-ended. Before leaving, I'd driven to Washington State to say good-bye to my family and friends. I was to have the perfect send-off. My friend Bud had invited me for a cruise through the San Juan Islands on his fishing boat. I'd just arrived at the boat on which David and Betty, Bud's brother and his wife, lived in Port Townsend. We'd planned for Bud to pick me up from there, but when I arrived, David had disappointing news.

"Bud went to Friday Harbor yesterday," he said. "He told me to ask you to meet him there."

Feeling let down, but trying to be a good sport, I ferried over to San Juan Island. By afternoon's end, I'd searched all the island's docks. Frustrated, I thought, *There just aren't that many marinas! How can I be missing him?* Then, having almost given up, I noticed a small fishing boat tied up to the private dock of a waterfront house. With renewed hope, holding my breath, I rang their doorbell.

"No," said the matronly woman who answered the door. "That's my husband's boat. But why don't you come in? Maybe we can help you find him. We've just finished dinner. Have you eaten? We have plenty if you haven't."

"No. No thank you," I said.

"You haven't eaten yet, have you?" she said, smiling. "I insist. Come in and have a nice piece of fried chicken and some salad, at least."

Uncomfortable with such instant cordiality and hospitality, I hesitated. *But I do want help finding Bud*, I thought, and *I don't want to be rude. Plus, she's right, I haven't had dinner, yet.*

"Well, okay," I said, feeling shy. "Thank you."

As we chatted, it turned out I'd already checked all the moorages they could suggest. Having established that, she began asking me about myself. When I said I was an R.N. but was taking time away from work to travel, a frown furrowed her brow.

"How old are you?" she asked.

"Twenty-nine," I said.

"Oh my goodness! I thought you were a teenager!"

Suddenly, I saw myself as she had: jeans and leotard, sandals, backpack, and long tasseled, blond braids fastened with Native American beaded thongs.

*Oh!* I thought. *Now I see why she was so bent on feeding me and helping me find Bud. She thought I was a teenager and she was trying to take care of me!*

Her cordiality stiffened and the climate inside the house seemed to plummet. She never said, "You tricked me! You let me take care of you when you're plenty old enough to take care of yourself." But in my mind, those words rose in a cartoon bubble over her head.

It was awkward, but what could I do except thank her and say goodbye?

I found a coffee-house with a phone to call David.

"Bud called just a little while ago," he said.

"That's a relief!" I said. "Where is he? I've checked all the marinas and I can't find him."

"That's because he's already underway, again. He's headed for Port Hardy at the north end of Vancouver Island. He wants you to meet him there."

Instantly exasperated, I said, "No!" That's asking way too much!"

"Why not?" he asked. "You have the time and it could be fun!"

He was right of course.

I took a moment to ask for Guidance.

*What shall I do?*

I heard. *Go.*

Soon, with the help of Treble, an island woman whom I'd just met in the coffee-house, I had a plan: Park in the Customs parking lot next to the ferry dock on the U.S. side of the border, ferry to Victoria on Vancouver Island as a foot passenger and then take another ferry to Vancouver on the mainland. From there, take a plane to Port Hardy.

The next morning at about 9:30, a floatplane—with me aboard—taxied to the dock of the Port Hardy Hotel. Several blocks walk down Main Street beneath brilliant, red and gold-leafed maple trees took me to Port Hardy's marina. It was a working marina: No pleasure boats here, just an endless expanse of catwalks lined with fishing boats, large and small.

"Hi, I'm here to meet my friend, Bud. He has a small fishing boat," I told each person I met. "Have you seen him?"

"No." No one had.

After a couple of hours, walking the docks, I was invited to lunch on one of the boats, a big purse seiner. I welcomed the invitation. *I've never been on a seiner before. It'll be interesting and I won't have to walk away from the marina to find a place to eat and rest my tired feet*, I thought.

At the end of a surprisingly delicious lunch, I thanked the Captain. With a few of his crew, we were standing next to the boat's moorage.

"Where will you stay, tonight?" he asked.

"Bud will be here by then. I'll stay on his boat," I said.

"Well, in case he hasn't shown up, you can have my quarters. That boat," he said, pointing across the cat-walk to another seiner, "belongs to my friend. He's away and I'm taking care of it for him. I'll sleep in his cabin. You can have my quarters. And none of my men will touch you."

I thanked him, though I felt certain Bud would arrive before then.

At day's end, Bud had not shown. By then, I'd made so many passes past all the moorages the fishermen were beginning to seem like friends. Many had teased me, joking about how a guy could be so dumb as to jilt me. Winking, a few had invited me to stay with them. I'd laughed with them, though I'd interpreted their winks as signals of invitations not to accept.

Earlier, I'd checked out the town's one hotel. It was full for the next week. I was stranded. Even if I was willing to give up on Bud and leave, there was no available transportation until morning.

The Captain's offer had sounded genuine. He'd said he would sleep on another boat and he'd promised my safety in front of witnesses. With no better options, I made my way back there. It was dinnertime. He and his crew were headed into town to a restaurant. I was invited along. Before leaving, he introduced me to his tiny cabin and showed me how to lock the door from the inside. Then, he gave me his key.

After a tasty steak dinner, replete with light-hearted banter, one of the crew dropped me back at their boat while the others stayed on at the restaurant. Grateful for the blessing of this safe place to spend the night, I let myself into the Captain's quarters and locked the door. Exhausted, I stripped off my jeans. Then, leaving my leotard on, I unrolled my sleeping bag on the captain's bunk, turned off the light, and crawled in.

No telling how long I'd been asleep when there was a loud thud as the cabin door hit the wall behind it. Alarmed, I was on my feet with the lamp turned on practically before I was awake.

The Captain stumbled in. Having lost his balance when he'd kicked in his own, locked door, he fell at my feet. After bouncing back up, with one hand, he switched off the lamp while grabbing at me with the other.

I switched it back on. He switched it off. Again and again, we worked the lamp until it broke.

The room was black. And now, I was blind.

His heavy breathing broadcasted fumes of bourbon and beer.

His rough hands pawed, groped, grabbed at my leotard. In the small space, there was no getting past him.

I could hear the scraping sound of his zipper. His pants brushed me as he kicked them off.

My heart pounded.

Over and over, he grabbed me.

Screaming and shoving him hard, repeatedly, I started for the door, each time, only to be grabbed again.

*Those other men must hear me screaming! Where are they?*

Finally, bear-hugging me, he heaved my writhing body onto the bunk and landed on top of me. His boozy breath gagged me. His stubble sandpapered my skin as I rocketed my face side-to-side. With one hand pinning my wrists above my head, he tore at the crotch of my leotard with his free hand while forcing my legs apart with his knees and trapping my ankles with his big feet.

Defeated and defenseless, I gave up. Resigned to being raped, I prayed he would not beat or maim me.

His voice was a husky growl. "If I go through with this, are you going to tear out all my hair and gauge out my eyes with your fingernails?"

Suddenly, the terror I'd been holding at bay overcame me. I could hardly speak. Meekly, oh so meekly, I managed, "No."

He paused for a few seconds. Then, he sprang off and crashed to the floor.

"Oh," he said, "Oh, what have I done? Please forgive me! I don't know what came over me. Please, please forgive me!" He sounded horrified at his own actions.

Confusion overcame terror, then gave way to relief as I heard him fumbling with his clothes on the floor.

Finally, anger erupted. "Get out! Just take your clothes and get out!"

Still apologizing, he left.

Shaking, I made my way to the door. The lock was broken. The door hung askew. I fit it into its frame, hoping it would hold. Then, I pulled on my jeans.

I'd just crawled back into my sleeping bag when a knock came.

"What?" I barked.

"Can I please come back in and get my pants?" said a very contrite Captain.

"Yes, get them and take them with you!" I snarled.

*Wow! That was so close!* I thought as I crawled back into my sleeping bag for the third time that night. *What do I do, now? Pack up and leave? But there's no place to go. There's only one hotel and it's full. So, what do I do?* It was a circular riddle and I was weary of chasing my tail.

I asked myself, *What would you do if you had faith?* Answer: *Meditate. Trust the answer to come.*

The cabin was too chilly to sit for meditation, so I snuggled deep into my bag instead.

I knew I'd slept because I was awakened: knocking: soft, insistent—different from the Captain's knock.

I got up and crossed the small floor. Careful to keep it from falling, I opened the door. The night's chilly breeze hit my face.

Beyond the tall man facing me now, oceans of stars glittered in the cobalt Heavens.

"I'm Tito," he said in a stage whisper, his Greek accent strong. "I'm First Mate on this boat. Miss, we don't have much time. The Captain will be getting up soon."

"Yes, I recognize you from last night at dinner. What time is it? And what don't we have much time for?" I asked.

"It's ten after four," he said, turning to the moonlight to see his watch. "I'm so sorry, so very, very sorry about what the Captain did to you. You must get away from here before he wakes up. I have a place I can take you. It's out of town on the other side of the island. A logging camp. My good friend is the cook there. He'll keep you safe. Will you come with me?"

"That's okay," I said, skeptical. "I can just gather up my things and leave the boat. You don't have to take me anywhere." I didn't know where I would spend the rest of the night, but I didn't want to leave Port Hardy. *What if Bud shows up and I'm not here?* Would he leave, again before I got back? *And besides, why would I trust this man?*

"No! It's not safe for you to be anywhere around here when he wakes up," he urged. "I've already talked on the phone with my friend. I told him what happened to you and said you're my girlfriend and that I need him to keep you safe. I trust him, especially if he thinks you are my girlfriend. We'll be putting out to sea this morning, and he can bring you back to Port Hardy this afternoon. Please, please come with me."

Although I was not keen to trust him or anyone else, he was offering an answer to the conundrum I'd been trying to solve before I meditated.

*What shall I do?* I silently prayed.

*Let him take you. It will be all right,* I heard.

Remembering my faith discipline, I thought, *Less than a few hours ago, the Captain was going to rape me. But just when I thought for sure I was a goner, instead, he stopped and apologized. That has to count as a miracle. If ever there was a time to practice faith, this is it!* "OK," I said. "It'll take a few minutes for me to get ready."

Belching and bumping across Vancouver Island to the lumber camp on the West side, Tito's old Chevy pickup truck was a bare-bones version of its younger self. *Apparently, muffler, shocks, and heater are luxuries that can be done without,* I thought, hunching against the cold.

Repeatedly, Tito apologized for his Captain. Finally, I asked the question that had been burning since he'd wakened me: "I screamed and screamed. Obviously, you heard. Why didn't you come then?"

He swallowed. "I'm—I'm so sorry I didn't," he almost whispered before pausing, then, swallowing again. "I—I couldn't... He is my captain, my boss. I need my job to support my family. I'm taking you away now in secret; he doesn't know."

*There it is,* I thought: *I was surrounded by men who could have intervened, but didn't dare for fear of losing their livelihoods.* I didn't like the answer, but I couldn't change it, and it made sense when I tried to see it from their perspective. I would try to let it go.

"Thank you, at least, for the risk you're taking now," I said." He didn't respond. We rode on in silence to the camp.

Inside the camp's big kitchen, Estefan, the cook, was rushing breakfast for a mess hall full of lumbermen. Having greeted his friend in Greek, Tito introduced me in English.

Briefly breaking the rhythm of his work, Estefan nodded, saying in hesitant English, "I'm honored to meet you." Then, he returned to his grill and again spoke in Greek to direct Tito to the bunkhouse where I would stay.

It was one of many identical barracks. Beneath screened windows, end-to-end narrow cots, each tightly made up with a wool blanket, lined the walls. I unrolled my sleeping bag on a bare one. In case I needed to make a fast getaway, I would sleep with my clothes on.

"You'll be safe here. All the men are at breakfast. They won't be back before they go off to work," said Tito. Then, assured I was situated, he said, "Goodbye."

Although this was supposed to be my safe haven, alone in this light, wide-open space, I felt exposed and vulnerable. *I am not alone, I am safe, protected and provided for in every way*, I repeated like a mantra. And I fell asleep.

Time had passed. As I was waking I could hear the slow, quiet breathing of someone standing over me. Was I about to be assaulted again? A scream rose in my throat. Telling myself, *Don't let him know you're awake*, I held back.

As I concentrated on breathing the same rhythm I believed I'd been breathing in my sleep, I was relieved to feel myself being gently covered with a blanket. *It has to be Estafan*, I reasoned. As gratitude began to replace fear, the sweetness of his gesture was not lost on me. *Should I thank him?* A few, eternal moments later, while I was still trying to decide, I heard soft footsteps moving away. Something creaked across the room. I slit an eye open just enough to glimpse him lying on his own cot. Feeling a tiny bit guilty for having played 'possum, I continued feigning sleep until once again, it took me.

The next time I woke, I heard moaning. Opening my eyes, I saw Estefan, rigid on his cot, holding his jaw.

"Estefan, what's the matter?" I asked, crossing the floor. I couldn't understand his speech, but I didn't need to. I could see immediately that he needed help. His dark red, swollen jaw radiated pain.

"Estefan, you need a dentist! Do you have one?"

"No." He groaned.

"Is there someone I can call for you?"

"No."

"Then, I'll find you a dentist. Where's the phonebook?" I asked.

"No phonebook," he said. Still moaning and holding his jaw, he got up, signaling me toward his truck. We would simply have to go into town to find him one. I'd never driven a pickup before, but we got to the dentist in Port Hardy safely. Having delivered him into competent hands, I thanked Estefan for taking care of me and I said goodbye.

I resumed walking the docks, relieved to be back where Bud could find me. I thought, *Surely, within the next few hours, I'll find him.*

Feeling discouraged when that hadn't happened, I realized I needed to meditate. In the warmth of the Indian summer sunshine with a salty breeze cooling my face, I found a tree to sit against in a grassy area not far from the marina. I craved deep stillness. I needed to allow my being to resonate with the Divine. Opening to the silence within, I let it take me. Afterward, I found myself reoriented from anxiously waiting for Bud's arrival to reveling in the recognition that I was safe in this moment and my every need was being provided for.

Refreshed, I returned to the docks. I was met by 81-year-old Ted, just ready to board his boat with an armload of supplies. A mighty smile overtook his face as he offered me the floor of his boat to camp on for the night.

Having told him I'd be taking the bus out the next day, I awoke in the morning to a feast, an extravagant,

Swedish smorgasbord. He meant to send me off in style. Such a generous gesture, it brought me to tears.

But then, another new friend, Brian, enticed me to stay still another day for Canadian Thanksgiving dinner.

During the bus ride back, realization of Grace began to dawn. I saw with increasing certainty that Divine Order had been in play. Missing Bud and the cruise had made room for a vibrant kaleidoscope of opportunities to deepen my faith. The miracle of the aborted rape, being rescued, and being in the right place at the right time for Estafan had been among them.

As Grace had provided for me, my faith had deepened. Or had my deepening faith been calling forth Grace? Or was it both? However I looked at it, as a discipline, faith was proving itself to me.

Back in Port Townsend, I missed Bud yet again! But I finally learned why: While he was on his way to Port Hardy, his father had died. So, he'd returned to be with his family in Spokane. He was where he needed to be. And, clearly, so was I, as I had been all along.

# Redemption in the South Pacific

## Wendy DiPeso

I open my eyes. They feel gritty and dry, drawn towards the open canvas flaps where the bright sun lights the dim interior of the army tent. This luminescence hurts my eyes, so I focus instead on the ballet of the dust motes reflected in the light. I hear distant explosions and the pop of gunfire. Where? Disjointed memories like pictures on a broken film reel tell me I am in an army field hospital tent in New Guinea. Corporal Jane Smith, age twenty-four, with the Women's Army Auxiliary Corps or WAC. It is September 1944 during WWII, but I am not here in this hospital because of a battle wound.

A glass bottle hangs from a metal pole by my cot delivering fluids through rubber tubing to the needle in my arm. I resist the urge to pull it out. My belly aches, and I roll into a fetal position, closing my eyes. I want oblivion. The ache in my belly eases but not my sense of loss. I smell the metallic scent of blood—my blood—stirring a memory I wish to forget.

When I was fifteen, The Christian Science Practitioner had prayed for me because my periods were so heavy, sometimes lasting almost a month. Finally, Mimi took me to see Dr. Aaronson. He told Mimi I had something called 'fibroids' and that I needed to eat more green leafy vegetables and less meat. "If she's not better in eight to ten months, come back," he had said.

They went into the next room. I hurried to dress wondering, *Why are all doctors men? Why can't women's privates be seen by women doctors?!*

I heard Dr. Aaronson's voice suddenly drop, so I paused to listen through the door, which stood ajar. "She'll never have children... no problem conceiving... but her uterus is tilted... won't be able to carry children to term."

I felt a tingle up my spine. I knew he was talking about me, but I didn't know how to take in his diagnosis. Then, I could hear anger in Mimi's voice when she answered him, "I refuse to believe my daughter can never have children."

When she said this, my gut relaxed. For one fleeting, forgiving moment I felt Mimi had taken my side, was my champion, loved me. Such moments were rare and I wanted to savor this. But then she said, "I will not live with the shame of having an idiot daughter who can't even have children. God would not do that to me."

My face stung and flushed as if slapped. My gut tensed again. Unable to think, I gathered myself up and stepped into the next room pretending not to have heard. I saw pity in Mimi's eyes—though it might have been pity mostly for herself.

On our way home, Mimi said, "Don't tell anyone we were at the doctor's." She made me recite from Christian Science: "Divine Love always has met and always will meet every human need." I said the words, but I didn't feel loved. Mimi had always been ashamed of how my brain seemed to mix up letters and numbers, my frequent migraines and bouts of trembling. And now this.

For me, life without children would mean a life without love. For Mimi it was one more reason not to love me. In that car ride home, I finally understood: Mimi didn't care what I felt. She only cared about what other people saw. I turned my head away from her and focused on the sound of the rumbling car engine.

Like waking from a dream, the sound of boots on the dirt floor pull me back to the present and I open my eyes. "I see you are finally awake." It's Sergeant Walsh, a woman in her early twenties with a tiny nose and hazel eyes that sparkle in humor. The Sergeant wears a sheen of sweat on her face from the heat. Like all the army nurses in the Pacific theater, she wears a khaki uniform with long sleeves, calf high boots, and a wrap around her hair. When Army nurses and the Women's Auxiliary Army Corps first arrived in the Pacific in January 1944, the women's uniforms were skirts and heeled shoes. The ravages of malaria quickly taught the military the importance of providing the women with pants, long sleeve shirts, and mosquito netting. These precautions didn't protect me, and that's one reason I'm here now.

"Blue Nose, you've done the Army a great disservice," she says, looking at the glass bottle of fluids and making notes on a clipboard.

I catch the sound of jest in the Sergeant's voice. Everyone calls me "Blue Nose"; a reference to my oversized nose and a vain habit engrained from Mimi to make it look smaller by tilting my head up. That, combined with a slight, affected European accent—also promoted by Mimi—and my own shyness made people assume I felt superior to them. My comrades, determined to bring me down a notch, gave me the nickname. As we've gotten to know each other better, this moniker has become a term of endearment and I don't mind it. I'm not sure what she means by "disservice," but I hope she's kidding about this too.

"We need this cot and this space for injured soldiers, not WACs who can't keep their legs crossed." *Ah, the miscarriage*, I think. That's the other reason I'm here. Of course she doesn't know the *whole* story. Sergeant Walsh pulls back the covers and I begin to shiver. Blood has soaked the menstrual pad and a layer of padding underneath my bottom. I feel a mixture of gratitude and embarrassment, as she quickly and efficiently cleans my bottom and replaces the padding.

"Thank you," I manage to say and am rewarded by a silent smile and nod.

As the covers are replaced, the doorway to the tent darkens momentarily with the entry of an army doctor. "Captain Rogers," his name tag reads. He is tall and, like most of the malnourished troops, thin. His white coat streaked with a light brown stain on one side, evidence of others suffering war's circumstances.

"Sergeant Walsh, what is our patient's condition?"

"I haven't taken her vitals yet, but I can see she needs a heavy dose of humor."

Captain Rogers bunches his heavy eyebrows, his eyes serious. He takes my pulse, then glances at the nurse, "Has she had anything to eat today?"

"No sir," I croak, my mouth pasty.

Captain Rogers walks around to the other side of the bed. I lift my left arm for him to apply a blood pressure cuff, and shiver when the cold band is wrapped around my upper arm.

"How long have I been here?" I ask.

Captain Rogers, stethoscope in his ears, does not reply. Removing the blood pressure cuff with a grim expression, he writes some notes on the clipboard. He takes my temperature, prods my belly, and notes the new bleeding. He sends Sergeant Walsh to the dispensary with a note. Then pulling up a chair, he folds his thin lanky form into it. Elbows on knees he focuses his tired eyes on mine.

"You are one sick little lady, but with rest and treatment you are going to be okay. We just received more Atabrine®. I am going to give you a large initial dose to be followed by small doses daily. It will turn you yellow and may cause other side effects such as nausea, but it'll take care of the malaria. It's important that you take this medication. Agreed?"

I nodded numbly, aware that some of my fellow soldiers refused to take the medication. The side effects were significant, and the uncommon side effect of sudden, violent rages was enough to discourage many GIs.

"You've also lost a lot of blood from your miscarriage. I am ordering an extra ration of meat. If this were not a combat hospital, I would not discharge you for a week, but I don't have that option. Tomorrow you'll be moved to your tent. For the next five days, stay in your bunk except for meals. The bleeding should stop in a day or two. If the bleeding becomes heavy again report immediately back to the hospital. Here is the name of the Commander's cook." I take the piece of paper. "His name is Corporal Lawrence. Every evening at 5:30 pm I will see that Corporal Lawrence meets you behind the Commander's tent with a piece of cooked meat."

Captain Rogers makes me repeat his instructions to be sure I understand, then helps me take a drink of water. "Why are you doing this for me?" I ask, "Meat is hard to come by."

"You're my patient. Meat, medication, and rest is what you need to recover. I expect you to follow my orders." Captain Rogers rises from his seat, compassion in his eyes.

"Thank you, Doctor," I say as he leaves.

I shiver again, this time from the fever, new sweat breaking out on my brow. I pull the thin wool blanket up higher around my chin as another visitor arrives. It is the Christian Science Practitioner, Private Helena Janssen.

"Jane dear, you have been asleep for a day and a half!" She takes the chair recently vacated by Dr. Rogers, and, wearing a mask of cheer on her freckled face, sits with legs crossed as if wearing a skirt instead of Khakis.

*Why does Private Janssen always call me "Jane dear," just like mother?* I think to myself. I wish she would leave me alone. But I say nothing.

"I came to see you yesterday, but you were still not awake, so I prayed and then left. You must accept that your current condition is not real, it is error born of a lack of understanding. You will be restored, just as Mary Baker Eddy was taken ill and recovered through understanding that God takes care of us all. When we experience less than perfection, we need to change our thinking to accept God's truth." She says this all by rote. I know because I've heard it all many, many times.

I'm so tired. I want to sleep. It takes energy to speak, but I feel compelled to respond. "You forget, I grew up attending a Christian Science Church. I read *Keys to The Scriptures* by Mary Baker Eddy as a child. This is familiar to me." I think maybe if I remind her I'm already indoctrinated she'll leave me alone.

Private Janssen sits up straighter. "Well, now's your opportunity to apply to your life what you learned as a child. Once you're back with your husband you'll be able to conceive again."

"I can't think about that right now." I turn my head away, willing Private Janssen to leave.

"Rest. You'll be restored in time and then you can get on with your life again with Corporal Smith."

Clarity crashes through my exhaustion, sweat, and grief. The truth of my situation tumbles out of my mouth—and with it my vitriol and accusation toward her for her part in this fiasco. "He... raped... me," I spit out, looking at Private Janssen squarely.

Her eyes are wide, as if she isn't sure how to respond to my anger. As if the word "rape" disturbs *her* more than the experience of it disturbs *me*. "Be that as it may... I just wanted to take away your shame at finding yourself... violated."

Despite my weakness, I raise myself on one elbow. "I was a virgin. He forced himself on me. I didn't even know this man, and you told me I had to marry him to avoid '*error!*'" In fact, I don't know how she convinced Corporal Smith to marry me after I'd confided in her about the rape. Or how she convinced the Chaplain to perform the ceremony. Nor do I really know why I agreed to the marriage either. Except that I was in a foreign country in 1944 during a terrible war that was decimating the whole world. And I was only 24. And that I was traumatized and trusted my spiritual practitioner to help me understand what to do in a crisis. But I quickly discovered that marriage to Corporal Smith was nothing more than sanctioned sexual violence resulting in this miscarried pregnancy. My mistake was listening to Private Janssen.

Private Janssen rises, her eyes wide under furrowed brow, clearly unsure of herself for once. "Once soiled you could never marry, Jane. Never be happy. Marriage to Corporal Smith was the only answer I could see. 'Divine Love always has met, and always will meet every human need,'" she says, raising her chin defiantly.

I fall back exhausted. "There's nothing 'divine' about Mr. Smith. Please Go Away," I say dismissively rolling my back to her as far as the intravenous drip allows. Private Janssen is silent. I hear the scuffle of her footsteps receding quickly and I wish I could feel triumphant for standing up for myself. But I don't.

Days later I lie in my bunk in the late afternoon. Heavy rains from the night before have left the air damp but free of dust. The bleeding is just an intermittent dark brown now. The malarial sweats and chills are less intense. I am stronger. I've written a letter that will go out to my parents on the next flight which asks them to pass on an enclosed letter to a lawyer to help me get an annulment. I know Mimi will break the seal and read the letter intended for the lawyer. And I know she will blame me for everything. I sit up, swing my legs down, sliding my feet into my boots. *And Mimi will find a lawyer to protect her own reputation*, I think. I lean over to lace my boots. Mimi may never change, but I can. I haven't had a migraine since leaving home—even after being raped. Even after getting malaria. Away from Mimi's constant criticisms I can think.

I stand, take a deep calming breath and square my shoulders. "I have no intention of allowing Corporal Smith his conjugal 'rights'," I say aloud, though I am alone in the tent.

It is almost 5:30 pm. At 6:00, the sun will set as if a light switch has been thrown, casting everything into darkness. Time to head over to the Commander's tent for meat. I feel a sense of gratitude to Captain Rogers, recently transferred away from us to a field hospital closer to the front lines. And thankful for the commander's cook, who continues to provide me with meat indefinitely.

I step out of the tent and into the mud just as some of my fellow WACs are returning from their daily assignments. Looking to my left I see Corporal Smith among them and I shudder. His unit has just returned from a combat mission. His helmet hides his blond hair but not his steel blue eyes.

Corporal Smith is smiling and teasing Carol, one of the other WACs. A blush spreads over her tanned cheeks. He can be charming when he wants to be. No wonder no one believes me when I tell them that his charm hides a chasm of insecurity, or that he is a dangerous predator.

Corporal Smith looks up, and I see his eyes take in my thin waist and facial expression. His smile fades. He approaches, taking off his helmet, clutching it under his left arm.

"Jane, I just heard what happened. I'm sorry," he says. And if I didn't know better I would believe he cares.

The other WACs file past into the tent behind me, averting their eyes, pretending not to hear.

"You're sorry?" I said, "You looked pretty happy just now."

A look of surprise flits across his face at the sarcasm in my voice. "Oh, well, it means we can try again." He grasps my right hand firmly and starts pulling me away from the tent. "Right now, in fact," his eyes are hungry and I feel a sudden cold rage in my gut.

"No!" I pull back, freeing my hand. I am weaker than when he caught me alone near the edge of camp and raped me back in June. But now I am angry, and a tent full of WACs is only a few feet away, listening to every word exchanged.

"Jane, you're my wife. It's okay now that you're my wife and I..."

"No. I am not going with you. I almost died from that miscarriage."

"Ok, then maybe you need time to recover. But," his eyes grow bigger and hungrier, "you can give me a blow job. That will do for now."

I don't know what a blow job is and I don't care. "Stay away from me," I demand, backing away from him even farther.

Corporal Smith starts to look alarmed, as if he can't imagine what is bothering me. His entitlement is just that unconscious. "Jane, what's wrong?"

"I'm having our marriage annulled. As long as you're stationed in the same camp, you are to keep your distance." I say this with a strength I didn't even know I had.

"You can't make me stay away. I need you. I love you." His voice and eyes have transformed from predator to a two-year-old's pleading. But I know this is just one more of his strategies to get his way. I feel nothing but cold disgust as he drops to his knees in the mud and puts a hand around the ankle of one of my boots.

"Please, I need you. Don't make me stay away."

*How many women has this worked with?* I wonder. I also know he's capable of overpowering me, but with the tent full of WACs listening in, he won't do that now. Right now, he'll put on this puppy dog performance that will make me look hard-hearted to those who don't know the whole story. "Take your hands off me," I say, glaring. Corporal Smith lets go as if struck, shrinking back. I march away to my dinner of meat without looking back.

A few days later I return to my duties as a draftsman, making blueprints for new airfields and installations. At breakfast I hear other women in the camp mutter "slut" under their breath as I make my way through the chow hall. Corporal Smith's good looks and ability to charm has the rest of the camp fooled. They look on him with sympathy and no longer see me in an amiable light. I am a pariah now and people leave the table when I approach, and I wonder if Corporal Janssen is right, that I will be without love. That I am damaged. But be that as it may, I will not be bullied by Corporal Janssen, Corporal Smith, or the Christian Science doctrine.

October of 1944, we are transferred to Leyte Island in the Philippines. A new platoon joins the camp, part of our enormous invasion force under the command of General MacArthur. It is Sunday and I am not required to do any drafting that day. I am out on a walk, feeling good about the work I have been doing in the war effort. I come across a wood-built church. Other soldiers are filing in and I follow, knowing that there will be music, my passion. As I enter, a young Sergeant serving as usher to help people get seated looks up at me and smiles. His kind grey eyes catch the light and seem to twinkle behind his spectacles. He has a strong jaw in his handsome angular face. He directs me to a seat and then sits down next to me. The services are starting.

There are no hymnals but the gathered souls, myself included, enjoyed singing "Onward Christian Soldiers" and "Shepherd, Show Me How To Go" by heart during the service. I am keenly aware of the presence of this handsome young man sitting beside me and surprised by the fluttering of my own heart, though I dare not let myself hope for real love, or even gentleness. Most good men have not been interested in me with my large nose, mouse brown fine hair, and small head. At least that's what my mother would have me to understand.

Robert Anderson from Minnesota introduces himself after the service. I noticed he does not include his rank. We are standing outside the church now. I see other soldiers greet Robert with an air of affection that goes beyond the required military respect.

We stand by the church for almost an hour talking and during that time, I learn he's heard about my marriage to Corporal Smith. He asks me about it and I feel safe enough to recount my story in detail. He listens, watching my face as I speak. His eyes seem to take it all in. To take me in—without judgment.

"I'm sorry," he says when I finish my story.

"After the war I hope to get a job drafting blueprints. The doctors say I can't have children," I tell him. "No one will want to marry someone who can't have children, much less someone who has been married before." I don't know why I'm telling him this, but when I say it, I see the corners of Robert's mouth curl up slightly, as if he might smile.

"You could be surprised," he says.

The war ends soon after Robert and I meet. Before Japan's surrender, Robert asks me to marry him, and full of hope and love I say yes! But because my marriage to Mr. Smith is still not annulled, we will have to wait till we are both stateside to marry.

Then, on Christmas Day, 1945 Robert B. Anderson and I are married. In a sweet ceremony at Mimi and Papa's home. And I dare to hope happiness is meant as much for me as for others.

It will be eleven years and four miscarriages later before Wendy is conceived. On the afternoon of her birth, holding her in my arms I marvel at the reality of her existence. "You're real. You're here," I say to her suckling contentedly at my breast. "How in the world did I go from being so wretched, to so loved?" I think about Mimi and Private Janssen. "It wasn't just that I met your wonderful father," I tell my sweet little Wendy.

Real love doesn't come from the appearance of beauty, or talent, or intelligence. It doesn't come from repeating doctrine or believing in an ideology. It wasn't until during the war, when I had no expectation of love from others that I started to see, value and love myself. Others then started to value and love me too.

Author's note: This story is based upon actual events as recounted to me in letters and spoken word from my mother Jay Anderson.

# Living Large in Lake O

## Lula Flann

Caddie hummed as she peeled off her whitening strips, cautiously layered on concealer from chin to straightened bangs, smudged ivory matte highlighter beneath her plucked brows, and lined her jade-colored eyes with liquid gel. Moving quickly, she dotted peach blush at exactly the spots the Sephora technician had instructed if she wanted to minimize the baby roundness of her cheeks. The entire effect was polished off with a light dusting of shimmer. She stabbed the fat diamond studs Willie had given her for their last anniversary in each ear as she caught the time out of the corner of her eye.

"Damn." Even though she'd completed her regimen in a record 35 minutes, she'd still be five minutes late meeting Willie. He'd hate that. And he could be mean-spirited and mean-mouthed. She wasn't sure which attribute bothered her more.

She dumped out the contents of her ceramic catch-all jar and rifled through the heap of junk jewelry, searching for the shiny onyx bracelet he'd gotten her last Christmas. It was hideous, but he liked it when she put it on. With one final look in the mirror, she stood sideways and appreciated her silhouette. If her breasts were just a little higher... a little firmer, they would fill out the sweater better, but what could she do? As she exited the bedroom, she glanced at her change jar on the dresser. It would take a million years to save for an enhancement surgery at the rate of a few pennies and quarters a day. But she would get there. And then she would be more confident she could hold her husband's attention.

Pulling up to the Lake O'Grill, she tossed her keys to the valet and gave him a wink, a smile, and a crisp $10.

"Take care of that baby—I'm borrowing it from my pop-in-law, and I need to get it back in one piece!"

She didn't usually valet the car, but today it felt good. That was another thing that would torque Willie. He had a problem with her using cars his dad borrowed from the dealership. His own father didn't have a problem with it, though. Her father-in-law, Arnie, did fairly well for himself at the local used Mercedes dealership. It had everything he wanted in a retirement job: flexible hours, the chance to tell tall tales, the opportunity to meet pretty women, management that was willing to look the other way when he borrowed a car for the weekend, as long as you met your monthly quota. Willie, though, was judgmental about his father's behavior. So Arnie and Caddie didn't talk about the fact that Caddie sometimes drove a borrowed car from the dealership. And Willie always left Caddie to finish their Thursday lunches on her own while he went back to the office, so he would be none the wiser today. It made her life easier to keep him happy, but she also believed she was entitled to a little fun.

Willie waited for her at their favorite table by the back window which overlooked the lake. For once he was not looking at his watch. She bent down, kissed him on the neck. He liked that. He smiled at her and motioned to the chair next to him.

"Sit here by me. I've got some good news."

That explained it, something was distracting him from the fact that she was ten minutes late. He smiled when he saw her, and she noticed that he'd bothered to take his jacket off. Usually he wore an all-business grimace in the middle of the workday and rarely even removed his jacket for their quickie lunches. Now he looked uncommonly relaxed. He rose from his chair and pulled out the seat next to him with a flourish. Goodness. He must have really good news.

Willie signaled to the server and placed his arm around Caddie's shoulder as the waitress approached. "What would you like to drink, sweetie?"

Left to her own devices, Caddie would often have a beer right about midday, but she wouldn't normally order one when she was joining Willie on his lunch break, lest he give her that look that said, "That midday alcohol is exactly the reason you can't drop the extra five pounds." And he was right of course.

"Just a Diet Coke for me." She tilted her head and twinkled her eyes at the sleek young thing who nodded back at her and handed her a long, leather-clad menu. Then she turned to her husband to see if his gaze was on the young woman too.

"And you, sir? Can I get you something to drink?"

Willie shook his head. "Nothing for me, but make that a rum and Diet Coke for the lady."

Caddie raised her sculpted brows in mock astonishment and shrugged with complicity. "OK, then! We must have something to celebrate."

Willie shifted his chair to a slight diagonal, pulling Caddie's hand into his own.

"The commissioners called me into the boardroom this morning and offered me the administrator's position on a full-time basis."

Caddie gave a sharp squeal, dropping Willie's hand and exchanging it for a full-body hug. "I knew it! I knew they'd have the sense to see you were more than just the interim guy!"

A smirk lit his face, giving it a self-satisfied sheen.

"I'd heard they might make the decision this week, but I didn't want to get your hopes up." He looked in her eyes. "I told you I'd make good." Willie shifted in his seat and took a quick sip from the cocktail in front of Caddie. Intent on the delicious details of Willie's announcement, she hadn't even noticed it being delivered. He swallowed and spoke again. "And that's not all. You know this job comes with a raise in pay."

Caddie nodded. As Willie had waded through the tedious application process and prepared for the numerous rounds of interviews, they'd talked about how the extra money would be spent—on saving for a down payment for a home.

"They offered the job to me at a higher grade than we even thought they would. Twenty percent more."

Now Caddie took a drink. She felt warm. She was pretty sure an actual glow was starting to creep from her collar bones to her hairline. She'd never doubted him, even when she'd been bored to tears by him.

Her husband cleared his throat again. "I got you a little something. You deserve it for standing by me, for moving here with me from Boise, for putting up with my dad's weirdness. For being you. I can't thank you enough."

She felt misty down to the spaces between her toes. In that moment, scenes bounced like so many campfire embers in front of her eyes. The time she first saw Willie giving the foreman at the cannery hell for a safety violation that could have meant quick dismemberment for any one of their friends working alongside them on the line. The time they hunted their first elk together and came up with nothing except reasons to lavish stinging witch hazel all over each other's numerous mosquito bites—and laughed so hard they'd cried. The $50 Victoria Secret gift certificate he'd given her when they were dead broke. That he thought she would look good in that teensy, sheer sheath of lace. All these flitting memories made her touch her hand to his now.

"Sweetie." She breathed the word into his ear and ran her hand up his thigh. For the first time in a long while she felt a glimmer of sexual attraction toward him. *I've let too many things get me down and pissed off,* she said to herself. *I should cut him some slack.*

Willie handed her a flat, rigid package, wrapped in sky blue foil, tied with a slick white ribbon. Caddie pulled her hand from his thigh to take the package in both hands and turned it over before peeling back the cellophane tape from the giftwrap.

"I wrapped it myself."

Caddie batted her eyes while her fingers felt their way down the edge. "I noticed the perfect corners. Of course you did. Thank you!"

Tapping his butter knife on the table, he leaned into her and nuzzled her ear. He was really sweetness itself, she thought.

"You can just rip the paper." Willie lifted his eyebrows at her slow progress. "I've got something else for you after that."

"I'm almost finished. Just hold on a second." Caddie rounded the third corner and reached into the package, drawing out a Manila envelope tightly sandwiched between two cardboard sheets. She shook it, hearing metal upon metal. Caddie raised her eyebrows.

Willie took the envelope from her, flipped open the fastening clip, slid a glossy sheet of paper out of the pack as a pair of keys fell into her lap.

Caddie looked at the real estate flyer for a 3-bedroom lakefront condo. Looked like it was just on the north side of the same lake they were lunching at today. She cocked her head at him. A wave of excitement flushed through her. And then a concern.

"I don't understand. This looks like Jim's place. Are they moving?"

Willie sat back and templed his hands.

"That's right. He's been transferred. I told him we'd take it. They're giving us the option to buy it on contract. You loved it, remember? There's a gas fire pit on the deck. There's a room you can reserve in the complex where you can hold parties. There's a rooftop pool."

Caddie caught her breath. The housing market was crazy. They'd been wandering through open houses every weekend since they arrived and this kind of thing was something she'd not dared hope for. But excited as she was, something gnawed at her, too.

"You already signed the papers?"

Willie's eyes slid away from hers. "Last week."

"Before you knew you'd gotten the job?"

Willie ignored her question and produced another sky blue packet from his interior jacket pocket. "I got this for you too."

Caddie bit the inside of her cheek. She knew questioning his thinking would cause a ruckus. Besides, he usually came through for her, didn't he? But she had watched men come and take away her parents' new TV set and their stereo system when she was a child. She and her sister had had to pack everything that would fit into two American Girl suitcases and move into their grandparents' house when they'd been evicted. She liked to have things nailed down before taking financial risks. And he knew that.

"Go ahead. Open this one." He pushed the envelope closer to her.

Caddie frowned and slid her manicured nail under the seal. It was another envelope, she could tell that. She was wary. All of a sudden, the last thing she wanted was for them to spend more money. Willie was talking at her but he seemed far away. He jiggled her knee.

"You'll love this. I did research, so I know he's good. He's right around the corner from your dentist. I know you've wanted this forever. I checked your calendar, and I've set up your consultation appointment."

Caddie no longer felt misty. She felt clammy, all the way from the crown of her conditioned hair to the arches of her feet. She looked from the glossy brochure in her hand to the stubble on Willie's chin back to the brochure. The words printed on the brochure were

fuzzy, as were Willie's words. She caught a few sylla-
bles, though.

"...Know you're not happy about the way you look
in certain clothes ... See that jar on your dresser every
morning ... Know you've been saving your pennies..."

She bounced her head up and down, mostly to keep
from grinding her teeth. Her eyes smarted, and she
knew there had to be a way to halt the tears that
dripped onto her lap. In an instant, she hated him more
than she'd thought possible. In a nano-second, more
scenes as thick as snowflakes on a wet Anchorage
morning piled up before her eyes.

The anniversary evening he'd lit up a cigarette right
across from her during their fancy evening out, even
though he knew her asthma had been acting up. The
homemade card he'd made for her with a black heart
cut out of construction paper and a tear right through it
when she'd disappointed him by staying out later than
he thought she had a right to after her cocktail shift
ended. The day six months after they were married
when he'd informed her she might be getting herpes
because he'd had a fling while away at school. The
thousand times he'd picked up his cell phone and started reading text messages while she was talking—as if
she weren't there at all. Now he was giving her a clear
gift of disapproval with this coupon to surgically alter
herself.

She opened her eyes wider and looked at him closely. He was still talking. Still. Talking.

"I knew you'd be happy to finally get your boob job,
but you don't have to cry."

Caddie squinted her eyes and the fat droplets
seeped out the corners. She swallowed. Hard. A low
hum of acquiescence was her only outward response.

He squeezed her hand, released it to check his
watch, then turned back to his soup.

"I've got to get to the office, but you take your time. We can talk about all the details tonight. You can start looking on Craigslist® for boxes for our move. We can give our 30 days' notice right away; would you mind sending off that email? Of course, I'm going to be in high gear back at work, going through the full on-boarding process, catching up on all the areas that the commissioners thought could be put on the back burner until they had a full-time administrator in place..." He took a breath and seemed to notice her silence. "Are you okay, honey?"

Caddie nodded again, stared out the floor-length window at the lake. A wind had whipped up short whitecaps on what had been a bright winter afternoon. The water had turned the color of iron. She coughed into her napkin and waved him goodbye.

"Just fine. Just thinking about how often we'll be able to take in this view," she waved vaguely at the lake.

He kissed her on the cheek, and walked whistling to the exit.

Caddie had always wondered what it would take to make her happy; life on the lake? handsome man? handsome home? She still didn't know the answer to that.

But. She understood now what it would take to get her out the door.

# I Would Die for You

## Ingrid Roeske Good

*Your fragility is also your strength.*
—Pina Pausch

I remember our large family home with explicit detail and lucidity.

Until I was eight years old, my family owned and lived in a white multi-story heritage building with bright, red-trimmed windows. It was three stories high, had a large yard and a garage for my father's white f85 Oldsmobile, with its red interior. My family lived entirely on the main floor. I LOVED this house the way only a child can love a place, with a belief in wonder, enchantment, and a great sense of awe.

The floors above our living area housed three suites on the second floor, and two more suites on the top floor. The basement also provided two tenants with living space and had a large separate room which had a manual washing machine. The entrance was located on the main level of the home. There, in the grand wooded foyer, sat a refrigerator. All of the tenants were welcome to utilize the great white appliance. My family had our own refrigerator in our suite. Although there was always the exception, everyone who resided in 1155 Nelson Street interacted quite harmoniously.

I recall my colorful upbringing and the many diversified souls who contributed to it. I learned the Japanese art of Origami at the age of four from our Japanese tenant Akiko. She had shared a special secret with me: if we made a thousand cranes, all our wishes would come true. I recall rushing up to Akiko's suite each day and working together to add to our collection, and then counting and recounting how many cranes we'd completed. Akiko would smile and hug me tightly. "Tomorrow we continue, little one," she would say sweetly in her broken English.

Johan, another of our tenants, was my first crush. He was easy on the eyes and had charisma oozing from every ounce of his being. He always had an exquisite woman by his side and included my family and me in his inner circle of friends. He spoke of travels to foreign lands and I asked Johan often to tell his stories of his adventures to Africa, which he readily did—and with flourish.

The tenants who encompassed my childhood enriched me, and even then, I knew that.

I especially loved an elderly husband and wife, whom I referred to as Mr. and Mrs. Santa. Mrs. Santa's wrinkled cheeks were a consistent rosy color and her eyes twinkled with a certain magical joy. Mr. Santa was a tad thinner than you would expect and had a laugh that stemmed from deep within his inner belly—and was most likely a result of all of his enthusiastic use of "liquid cheer."

Mr. and Mrs. Santa and I had a weekly gift-giving tradition. Much to my sheer delight, they would covertly throw chocolate bars, or tiny wrapped gifts brought home from the local department store bubble gum machine, down to me from their second-floor window. I would look up from the back yard grinning from ear to ear and holler, "Thank you!" My mother was not one to accept gifts from others and would not have approved of her daughter receiving little presents from the neighbors, so the Santas and I kept our ritual to ourselves. I didn't mind keeping it a secret. But sometimes my mother heard me yelling my thanks up to the second floor.

"Thank you for what, Ingrid?" she would yell back from the kitchen.

"Nothing Mamma," I'd reply, as Mrs. Santa would send a wink my way. She often concluded our exchange by blowing a floating kiss off her palm to her adopted granddaughter. I pretended to grab it from the Heavens and hold it close to my heart.

There are completely blank periods of my memory during that time. For a long time, I didn't remember that a week prior to the fire, I came home from school to a "For Sale" sign speared into our front lawn. At this time, I was starting to build a life outside of the house with school and my friends. I ran into the house and hollered, "Mamma, Papa are you here? What's that For Sale sign doing outside? Did someone put that on our lawn by mistake?" I hoped it was a mistake! My mother stopped what she was doing in the kitchen to look over at me. I was confused and upset. My heart trembled with anxiety as I searched my mother's face.

"Your father has decided it is time to sell this house and move closer to his work and our church." She said this matter-of-factly.

"We can't move!" I wailed. Mamma shot me a stern look, which would translate into any language that our conversation was over. I ran to my room and slammed the door. I felt suddenly and utterly bereft at the idea of moving and knew I would miss everything: my friends, the park across the street, the tenants who loved me, and most of all the house! My anger turned to sorrow, and that afternoon I hugged my pillow tight and wondered why my parents had not even told me of their plans to move? This was a betrayal.

My sorrow at the idea of leaving my beloved house was already heavy when, the night before the fire, my mother had a dream predicting the blaze. From my bed I heard her hesitantly relaying her premonition in her mother tongue of German to my father. "*Bernard, Ich hatte noch einem meiner Träume schon wieder. Da war ein Feuer.*" My parents both thought I was asleep.

My father responded softly speaking Germlish, "*Du bist nur nervös* my love, because we sign the papers for the sale of the house tomorrow. Just get some rest, and everything will be fine in the morning." I heard my father kiss my mother for reassurance, and then heard them both prepare for bed.

I fell asleep that night and awoke the next morning with terrible sadness, knowing the sale of our home would be made that day. And that night, I knew this would be one of my final sleeps in this grand and beautiful place.

Then, I awoke to the screaming of a taxi driver passing by, "Fire–Get Out!" And before I knew how I got there, I was standing beside the grand maple tree in front of my blazing home, waiting. The paramedics were wheeling out covered dead bodies to transfer them into an ambulance. I was shaking terribly, feeling small and vulnerable with a frenzy swirling around me. As I stood waiting, alone, terrified my parents were among those lost, I saw a stretcher halt right beside me. A sheet covering the jumping, jittering body. The sheet fell to the side to uncover Mrs. Santa's body. My face contorted and I tried to pull away from her. I thought she was still alive because she was moving. Did the firemen know that she was still moving? I wondered why they didn't help her.

Time seemed to stand still and as Mrs. Santa was wheeled away, a fog came over me. I scoured the crowd like a wild animal looking for my mother or father. "Why am I standing here all alone? Where are my parents?" I asked into the air. Were they trapped inside the fire? Where were all the other people who lived in the house? Akiko? Mr. Santa? The others? How did all this happen? Was anyone going to make it out alive besides me?

Later, I would remember beginning to scream, "Mamma, where are you? Where are you Papa? I'm here! I'm here! I'm here!" Tears coursed down my cheeks, when suddenly a police officer took me by the arm.

"Let's move you away from all this and we will try and find them for you" he said in a deep and reassuring voice. The officer put his arm around me, but I struggled to stay planted by the tree. I wanted my parents to be able to find me. I screamed loudly and fought to remain in the spot right there where I knew I could be seen. But the police officer gripped my forearm and pulled me away from the madness towards his police car down the street, away from the paramedics as they transferred the rest of the bodies of my beloved neighbors into the ambulance. The officer placed me in the back seat. "I'm going to go look for your parents," he told me. "You'll be safe here. I'll be back soon."

I tried to open the door of the police car but was unable to get out. It was locked! I sobbed uncontrollably and began banging on the glass windows, first with my hands until they were red and hurt and then leaning back on the seat and kicking the glass with my bare feet.

It seemed to me that a lifetime went by without anyone hearing my trapped cries. Finally, a blue uniform approached the vehicle. The door opened and a female officer spoke to me in a soft and even voice.

"It's okay. We've found your mother, and she is on her way over." I felt exhausted as I heard my mother yelling in the distance.

"Ingrid, I'm coming. I'm coming." I looked up through the open car door to see my mother running as fast as her legs could carry her, her nightgown rubbing in between her legs. I pushed past the officer and, still barefoot, ran sobbing into my mother's arms.

"They made me move, Mamma, they made me move away from the tree."

My mother knelt on the ground, cradled me in her arms, and rubbed my back gently. I felt warmth there with her now. But we still didn't know where Papa was.

"*Es ist okay mein schatz*, everything's okay my dear. Stay here in the police car, and I will come back for you. I'm just going to find Papa." I saw her look over to the police officer, who nodded.

"But I haven't done anything wrong, Mamma. I want to go with you." I was thinking that the only reason a person would be put in a police car was if they did something bad. I wanted my mother to know I hadn't broken any laws. But Mamma was gone, and I remained alone, confused and tired, waiting for her to return with Papa.

I saw the assemblage of the distinct, frightened faces of my community lining the entire city block. The masses collected in front of the roaring blaze, a chaotic frenzy of individuals seeking friends, family members and pets. People screamed out names in hopes of reuniting with their loved ones. Grief and resignation enveloped the street as the morning's darkness turned into light.

More time passed and I recall my mother returning, telling me through an exhausted haze that she had found Papa, though he wasn't with her now, and they would be going to Berta's apartment next door, where we would be safe. Berta was also from the old country and this familiarity brought a crumb of comfort to me.

Mamma and I met Berta at her apartment door. The elderly woman invited us to enter.

"*Danke* Berta, you are too kind."

"I will make us something to eat and drink," said Berta.

I couldn't believe that anyone would want to eat after the events that had just taken place. But no matter what the circumstance, the German manual clearly states you can never leave a Germanic home without a good meal, so we would get one whether we wanted one or not. And we would eat it because you could also never decline a meal, as this would also be considered rude.

All I wanted to do was sleep. I was exhausted. My mother sat and looked out of the apartment window with tears rolling down her ash-covered face. I walked over to take a look at what she was witnessing. Embers still burning from fallen timbers of our once cozy home, firemen still hosing down certain areas and people rummaging through the rubble to see if there was anything worth salvaging. A bulldozer had come from somewhere. The operator stopped the machine.

"I think I've uncovered a body," he yelled out. We could hear his words through the window.

My mother pulled me from the window and directed me towards the table where Berta was serving scrambled eggs swimming in butter. Rye bread, cold cuts and more butter blanketed the table. A teapot steeped tea.

"*Ess meinen Lieben. Trinken sie den tee, es wird sie beruhigen.* Eat, the tea will calm you."

My father joined us some hours later and we eventually made our way to my aunt's house as the smoldering continued and the losses were calculated as devastating.

I lost the horrific memory of that night for many years. Life immediately after the fire was a whirlwind. With true German grit, my parents regrouped and made sure I didn't lose a beat in my education. I missed no school and don't recall any attention given to making sure I properly grieved the loss of everything—and everyone. The whole event went deep underground in my psyche.

But then forty years later, my mother was diagnosed with dementia and was in the process of losing her own memory. This is when I stumbled on an article about the fire in her belongings. I was cleaning out her closet in preparation for moving her from her home to a safer living environment when the slip of a newspaper clipping slid onto the floor. I picked it up and read it. And visions of the fire came flooding back.

Three homes had burnt down and the "Police evacuated more than 1,000 other people from nearby low-rise apartment buildings at the height of the blaze. At least 90 firemen with 11 pieces of equipment attended the fire, which was still merciless three hours later," I read. "Fred Roeske, 46," my father, "the owner of 1155 Nelson, said he was awakened by cries of fire in the street. As soon as he realized it was the house next door, he sent his wife out and ran up-stairs, knocking on doors to wake the tenants. 'Then I went back down and threw some of our things out. By this time there were flames leaping from the house next door right through our window,' said Roeske."

When I read my father's words, suddenly I remembered everything.

I recalled the image of my long-time next-door neighbor, Caroline. She was a frail woman who could always be found cradling her cat, Ms. Ruby Tuesday. Her clothes were on fire as was her flesh; I remembered how Caroline refused to jump because she couldn't find Ms. Tuesday, and when the police officer tried to help her, she slipped out of his grasp and fell to the ground. I'd seen all of this as I'd waited for my mother to find me.

Holding the newspaper clipping in my hand, I sat down on the floor in the doorway of the closet, piled high with boxes of my mother's things—things she would no longer need—and I finally cried. I cried for Caroline and Ms. Ruby Tuesday. For Akiko. And both of the Santas, for they were both lost in the flames. I now remembered finding that out sometime after we were safe at my aunt's house. I cried for the loss of our home, our beautiful house. And I cried for my own little self, so traumatized that I couldn't hold on to the memory of that night. And finally, when I'd spent many tears on the past, I cried for my mother in her current state and her dementia, which would mean she would soon be forgetting who she was. And as I cried, I could almost hear Mrs. Santa saying, "Ingrid, here is a little gift for you. The gift of memory." And quietly, so my mother wouldn't catch me, I whispered, "Thank you."

# Nevertheless, She Persisted

## Lynn Goodman

After decades of struggling with addiction to opiates and heroin, at forty-six, I was clean. I was working on fishing boats in Alaska as a biologist. I loved being at sea, and I'd finally found some measure of peace out on the water. And I loved my job. Then one day about two years after I started, I fell on an icy dock, and sustained both a concussion and a soft-tissue injury to my lower back. Shortly thereafter, I was sent home to Ohio to recover, and there I spiraled into a deep depression.

Landlocked and miserable with pain, I longed for the peace that I felt out on the water. I wasted hours surfing the net or playing games to distract myself from my circumstances and trying not to give in to the urge to go score dope, the only way I really knew to deal with pain and grief. Then, one day, while scrolling through Facebook®, I came across a post from a friend about something called "Spartan Race®"—an athletic obstacle course race. I clicked the link and lost myself for the next few hours in a free e-book that insisted that, with sufficient mental fortitude and an indomitable will, I could overcome anything. The book contained stories from people with far worse injuries than mine who had competed in Spartan Races®, in some cases with prosthetic limbs or while on crutches.

I knew myself to be capable of incredible stubbornness and I was inspired by the people featured in the Spartan material. The thought occurred to me that maybe something like this would give me a goal to shoot for. The races were tough mental and physical challenges: maybe training for one would help me lift myself out of my depression. If people with missing limbs could manage these races, surely I could as well.

There was a group from The Wounded Warrior Project that went to every race. Most of them had been badly injured in combat. Through Spartan Race®, they found community, purpose, and some measure of healing. I needed all of these things.

But it was the story of a guy named Chris Davis that inspired me the most. He'd weighed 700 pounds at the beginning of his journey. Then he started walking, and later had bariatric surgery. When he was down to about 400 pounds, a coworker suggested Spartan Race to him. He signed up without knowing what he was getting into. Once he'd researched it, he decided that he was probably going to die. But he went anyway, and he finished that race. Later, the founder of Spartan Race invited him to train with the team at their headquarters in Vermont. Chris worked hard and blogged about the experience. He became part of the Spartan team, and inspired others to sign up for the races. I read his blog and even talked to him over email a couple of times. I could really feel how the Spartan Race had changed his life.

Spartan Race is one of several such obstacle course races now available around the world. The races are grueling, and come in three different lengths and difficulty levels: The Sprint is approximately three miles, the Super is about eight to nine miles, and the Beast is around 14 miles. Each of the races combines difficult terrain with barriers or tasks that must be overcome. If you fail an obstacle, you are required to do 30 burpees as a penalty.

Burpees, it turns out, are pretty brutal. You put your hands on the ground, throw your legs out behind you, do a complete pushup, draw your legs back in, then jump with your hands in the air. I did a lot of them while training, working up to three sets of 30. They were the bane of my existence that year. However, considering my past, if burpees were the worst thing I had to worry about, I was doing pretty damned well.

The whole idea of completing a Spartan Race® intimidated me, of course. I'd never run any sort of race before, so I wondered if I was crazy to even consider it. But as I read, I became convinced that this was a goal worth striving for, whatever it took in terms of physical training. I wanted to get my life back, and was willing to push myself to my limits to get there. The Spartan Race® was the perfect vehicle to take me where I ultimately wanted to go—back to sea.

I discussed the race with my physical therapist. I asked him to put me into a work-hardening program to get myself ready both for the race and to return to the boat. He agreed.

For the next few months, I was in the gym four hours a day, four days a week. I worked my ass off; my therapist said he should make me his poster child because he didn't normally see anyone putting forth the level of effort that I did. I could see why, too—others, who were ostensibly at the PT clinic for work-hardening, seemed to spend more time staring at the TV or drinking coffee than they did working out.

Not me. I went at it as hard as I could, relishing the soreness at the end of each session.

I lifted weights and carried heavy boxes across a mini obstacle course designed to mimic my job at sea. I pushed sleds piled with weights and worked on balance trainers. I did endless planks, bridges, and V-ups. I ran as hard as I could on the elliptical trainer and tortured myself on the climber and, of course, did my burpees religiously. And I grew strong. Other patients even started to tell me that I was inspiring them.

When the time finally came for me to be discharged from physical therapy, I felt ready for anything. Physically, I knew that I was strong enough for a race. Mentally, too, I was in a much better place than when I'd begun training. My depression had eased up. So with all of my progress, I made plans to return to work and started looking around for a Spartan Race® to enter.

There was only one within a reasonable distance of home: seven hours away.

But it was a Super.

I was disappointed, since I'd been aiming for a Sprint. I was completely daunted by the prospect of an eight-mile obstacle race. But Spartan Race® emphasizes the necessity of mental toughness above all else, and I'd bought into the Spartan mentality by now, so I signed myself up. A woman I'd met in an online forum for Spartan women invited me to run with her team, and I accepted.

The race was held at a ski resort in Virginia a couple hours from my mom's house, so I invited her to come along.

"Sure!" she said. "Won't that be fun?"

I booked a room at a relatively cheap motel not too far from the resort.

After driving down the day before the race, we went out to look at the course and figure out where parking and registration were, and to check on my volunteer shift.

I'd signed up to stuff race envelopes in return for my entry. A few hours' work was well worth the entry fee, and my shift was scheduled to begin shortly.

"Would you like to volunteer, too?" the woman working the booth asked Mom. "We still have a few openings."

"Sure!" she responded enthusiastically.

"Great!" said the woman, giving her paperwork to complete. "You get a free entry for volunteering. Would you like to use it this weekend or some other time?"

Mom laughed.

"Oh, come on, Mom, you should train for one of these," I teased.

"I'm over seventy years old," she said.

"No excuse, Mom. I doubt you'd even be the oldest woman to finish one of these."

More laughter.

We collected volunteer t-shirts, then headed off to work our shift. We stuffed entry numbers, forms, and headbands (also displaying the entry number) into envelopes for each racer. After a couple of hours, the envelopes were finished, and they let us leave.

We hadn't gotten much of a look at the course, only the part at the beginning and end near the shared start/finish line. Many of the most difficult obstacles were grouped together right before the finish, and the terrain was exactly what you'd expect from a ski resort—steep hills covered in dirt and rocks. We were able to take a quick ride on a chair lift to get a general look at things, but I still had no real sense of what I'd gotten myself into, only a vague dread that I might have bitten off too much this time.

We ate dinner at one of the excellent restaurants at the resort before heading back to the hotel.

"So, are you excited?" Mom asked.

"I guess," I replied. "More nervous, though. I'm kind of worried about being able to finish this."

"I have confidence in you," she replied. "You've trained hard. You can do this."

We finished our meal and headed back to the hotel. Mom crashed almost immediately; I was too wound up to sleep. Eventually, I did drift off and was awakened a few hours later by the alarm.

I dressed in my race gear: compression pants and socks, a painfully snug sports bra, a t-shirt, and my trail runners. Then we headed over to the lobby for a very mediocre breakfast.

I did the best I could with the offerings on hand, eating some hard-boiled eggs and a couple of waffles covered in peanut butter. I wanted to make sure that I had enough fuel to keep me going, though I had a small pack containing a water bladder, electrolyte tablets, an assortment of energy gels, and lightweight, high-energy snacks for the course.

We drove up to the site and I picked up my race packet and donned my number and headband. Then I said goodbye to Mom, leaving her to watch the race from the line, and went to locate my team.

I didn't actually know any of the people on my team. I'd talked to a few of them online, but hadn't met any of them. I went to the spot where we'd agreed to meet and located them after a short search. All of them were at least twenty years younger than I was and looked very fit. This didn't help my anxiety level.

Our start time was coming up, and we were herded into the starting area with a lot of other people. When the gun went off, I began to run. Very soon, we were on an incredibly steep hill, and my pace slowed. I started to have difficulties breathing and realized that I'd left my inhaler behind, which sent a wave of panic through me. I have mild exercise-induced asthma, and the lack of that inhaler was going to slow me down significantly.

I called to my teammates.

"Hey! I forgot my inhaler. I need to slow down. Y'all just go ahead, don't worry about me."

And with that, I was on my own. The depression I'd been fighting in the previous months was all but gone, but self-doubt was certainly a companion. The next hours were intense, to say the least. At one obstacle, I fell off the monkey bars and felt a sharp pain in my shoulder. I ignored it, did my thirty burpees, and moved on, trying not to think about what life would hold for me if I further injured myself after all this hard work. I hiked up and down double-diamond slopes, ran when I could, crawled through mud on my belly for what seemed like miles, missed sticking my javelin (it went into the target, but fell right back out), did another thirty burpees, and kept going.

Then, just as I was wondering why I was putting myself through all of this, I ran into Chris Davis, the man with the weight-loss story who had inspired me, out on the course. I introduced myself to him, reminding him of our email exchange.

"Hey!" he said. "So good to meet you! I'm really glad you made it out here!"

"Great to meet you, too!" I replied. "I'm really inspired by what you've accomplished."

"Thanks," he said. "These races saved my life."

"They weren't kidding about how challenging they are," I said. "I'm tired already, and there are miles left to go."

"You got this," he said. "I have faith in you."

And somehow, his faith buoyed me. I smiled and continued the race, grateful for his words of support.

The day was hot, the sun merciless. I refilled my water at the water stations spread out across the course and added electrolyte tablets each time. At one point, I saw a young, healthy athlete being carried off the course with cramps and dehydration and was glad that I was well-prepared.

A little later in the race, I hooked up with a young woman named Sandy who had also been separated from her team. We helped each other over some of the obstacles—a time-honored tradition in Spartan Race—and kept each other moving, urging each other on as we struggled through the course.

Eventually, we came to an obstacle which required us to carry a log down a hill and back up again. I picked one up as instructed and started down the incline. The log was heavy, and I had to stop every twenty or thirty steps to put it down. I made it to the bottom but, of course, the climb back up was much harder. My shoulders ached and my legs wanted to give out, but I just kept going, even if I only progressed a few steps at a time. When I completed the task, I was overjoyed and filled with pride.

At the end of the log-carry was a water station where Sandy and I joined other racers. We drank our water gratefully, and I refilled my water bladder yet again, adding electrolytes and passing a few of the tablets out to others who needed them.

When we finished drinking, the volunteer pointed at what might have been the steepest hill yet.

"Climb up that hill."

Sandy and I looked at each other. We were both covered in mud, and I could see lines of pain in her face. I had no doubt that they mirrored those in my own.

"We don't have to do this," she said. "We could just skip it—go around it, I mean. Come on, who's gonna know?"

I thought about it for a millisecond.

"I can't," I replied. "I need to finish this."

"You can still finish," she urged. "We'll just...take a shortcut."

I couldn't believe after how hard she'd worked so far that she would even suggest this. Skipping part of the course went against everything that Spartan Race® was about. The whole point of the race was to test ourselves—physically, yes, but also mentally.

Still, in that moment, I was sorely tempted. I was tired, already sore, and worried about what lay ahead.

*I could just stop*, I thought. *I won't collect a finisher's medal—but no harm, no foul. There is no reason to put myself through any more of this.*

Then I remembered that the mental game was the real obstacle. It is in these moments of decision when you either fail or refuse to give up. I thought about the days and weeks of physical pain I'd endured after my injury. Then I thought about the withdrawal pain I'd endured when I came off the drugs I'd been addicted to for so long. *If I can do that, I can do anything for a few hours*, I thought. *I'm tough enough to finish this.* I was gonna need every bit of that toughness; I felt physically spent, and wasn't at all sure how the hell I was getting up that mountain.

"Well, good luck," said Sandy. "I'm out." And she walked off in the direction of the finish line.

I started up the hill, where there were a couple hundred racers. On one side of the slope, people climbed up; on the other side, the line moved down. Many people were sitting down to rest. From the bottom, it appeared to be several miles of near-vertical terrain covered in loose rock. After a few minutes, I stopped to catch my breath. A young man climbing near me was looking a bit haggard.

"I hate to ask, but do you have any energy gel or anything?" he asked.

"No worries! I have some extra stuff in my pack," I replied. I dug through my pack and handed him an energy gel.

He took it gratefully and said, "My leg's starting to cramp. I dunno about this." His head hung down, and his exhaustion was evident to me.

"Here," I said, handing him a couple of electrolyte tablets. "You should put these in your water."

"I don't have any," he replied, but took the tablets and chewed them up.

I handed him my straw. "Have a drink with those," I urged.

He took a long draught.

"Thanks a ton," he said. "That might just get me through this."

We both started back up the hill.

Shortly thereafter, everyone around us suddenly stopped in their tracks to watch a group of people making their way down the other side of the hill. They were wearing combat fatigues, helmets, and gas masks. I knew this had to be the contingent from The Wounded Warrior Project whom I had read about. Nearly all of them were missing at least one limb, some more than one. Most of them sported prosthetics, but one soldier carried, in a sling on his back, a guy who had no legs and only one arm. As they passed, the other racers applauded, pausing to give them the respect they were due.

Suddenly, my own aching limbs seemed much less of a burden, and I knew that there was simply no way I would quit. I would finish this race no matter what it took.

At the next water station at the top of the hill, I refilled my water bladder again, then headed back down to the final group of obstacles. I tried to get over a wall, but didn't quite make it. Thirty more burpees. I failed miserably on the rope climb; I could barely grip the rope at that point. Burpees again. And then I fell off another wall with a traverse of bricks that stuck a little way out from the surface. I did my burpees, but it took me a good ten minutes to get through thirty. I had almost nothing left to give.

Finally, I headed for the last obstacles: a gauntlet of "gladiators" wielding pugil sticks, followed by a leap over flames. I probably looked every bit as completely undone as I felt, because the "gladiators" merely touched me with their sticks as I passed. I forced myself to run and somehow gather enough power to leap over the fire.

And finally, there was the finish line. I barely remember crossing it. I staggered and struggled to keep myself upright as someone said, "Good job!"

When I looked up at the man holding my medal, it was Chris Davis. We hugged as if we were old friends. I was overjoyed to see him again, and it meant a lot to me that the man who had inspired me to go on this journey was the one handing the finisher's medal to me.

I thanked him and moved on to where Mom was waiting for me with a look of pure awe on her face.

"You did it!" She grabbed me and started to pull me in for a hug, then pushed me away. "Maybe you'd better shower first," she said, laughing. "You're a mess!"

We stopped to collect my finisher's t-shirt, then took a couple of pictures by a wall they'd set up to celebrate the race.

In the shower, I discovered that there wasn't a single spot on my body that wasn't covered in mud. I stood under the cold water scrubbing for a long time, enjoying the relief of the cool water on my skin. Mom had bought me a Spartan Race® beach towel, and I made good use of it once I was finally clean.

Afterward, I emerged from the shower tent and found Mom again, collected my hug, and went to get my complimentary beer.

"Cheers!" said Mom, hoisting her own beer.

"Salut!" I replied. "Tastes like...victory." I grinned.

"You must be absolutely exhausted," said Mom, laughing.

"You have no idea," I replied. "I can't believe I made it."

"I never had any doubt," she replied. "When you really want to do something, you just don't give up."

For the next few days, I found myself in excruciating pain; my legs would barely hold me. Getting up and down from the toilet was particularly difficult. Every time, I wanted to scream. On a few occasions, I believe I did.

There was a time when I'd never have tolerated such pain; I'd have begged a doctor for relief or looked for something on the street to make it stop. But those days after the race, I reveled in my agony. The pain reminded me of what I'd accomplished, of my refusal to give up, of the sure knowledge that I possessed the mental fortitude to overcome anything I chose to.

Spartan Race's® tag line is "You'll know at the finish line." They don't lie. That finish meant more to me than any other single physical challenge I'd ever undertaken. I had pushed myself beyond what I thought I was capable of, and somewhere on that mountain, I came to understand that the real challenge is not the hills or the obstacles, but maintaining the will to keep pushing forward no matter the cost.

The experience meshed with what I'd learned about quitting dope: physical withdrawal sucks, but the real trick is winning the mental game. Your mind is adept at justification, denial, and sabotage. It is necessary to be vigilant against these enemies, and not to give in because it's easier than toughing it out.

I learned a lot about myself on that mountain, especially that I have that will, and will never back down before reaching my goal once it is set. I took that knowledge with me, knowing that someday I'd need the reminder of the value of perseverance. I hung my finisher's medal in my bedroom, in a place where I'd see it every night and every morning. When I returned to sea a few weeks later, I took it along, a reminder of the struggle that I had overcome.

# The Man on the Street—
# The Marlboro® Man

## Mary Lou Haberman

**1971 - My Twentieth Year on Earth**

That Saturday morning in Lincoln fit my way of being just fine. I slowly woke up, slid out of bed, and slipped into my comfortable attitude of stroll. It was like, "Oh, okay, well, here I am again." I wandered through my bedroom, then strolled the perimeter of the tiny living room. Suddenly, my roommate hollered from behind the closed glass doors covered by heavy paisley curtains. These curtains were only closed to keep wandering eyes from witnessing what she claimed was "the best sex." I thought her sounds were silly and at the same time, I admired her boyfriend's grunts and groans. He sounded invested in what he was doing.

I wondered when would they would just stop and get out of there. I was hungry for solitude after the "Wild West" party last night to which I had gone as Calamity Jane and ended up naked on my friend's front lawn. My hobby horse had had it for the night. So much for the Wild West, eh?

I added a dab of left-over coffee to the multi-layered stain already growing in my cup and tiptoed outside and down the steep wooden stairs to the screenless front porch. Even at this hour—7 am—the sickly, sticky humidity reminded me it was deeply and seriously August. August held all living creatures hostage in Lincoln, Nebraska.

After tripping down the porch steps, still a bit hungover, stretching my arms over my head and taking the first few steps onto the street, my stroll turned into a lolligag into the neighborhood. I had nowhere in particular to go.

Out of the blue, there was a man lollygagging toward me. Much like me he was clearly aimless. At twenty years old, my automatic assessment of any man's suitability as a lover would hold at bay what little common sense I had. So as we got closer, I noted his handsome, tanned face, bushy eyebrows and black curly hair that hung down just below his ears. His tight, beltless, faded blue jeans matched the whitish short sleeve shirt he wore untucked. He was weirdly casual and stiff at the same time. In an odd way, he was colorless. I admired the way his face suggested a dark beard. His glinty eyes lacked sparkle. When he looked directly at me, those eyes landed on my gaze just long enough for my reliable assessment of suitability to fully switch on. So far, so good.

We exchanged mumbled words, "Uh, hi."

"How are ya?"

"Where ya' goin?"

I was glad to see he smoked—even if it was Marlboros®. I amused myself by wondering, *Is this the real Marlboro man?* I knew for sure he was a man and that was enough at the moment. Then, he asked, "Where do you live?"

It was an innocent enough question and I, clueless, invited him home. For coffee and a cigarette, of course. There was nothing like a Tarryton® with a cup of stale coffee on a Saturday morning with a Marlboro® man during August in Lincoln.

I invited him up to come back to my apartment, where my roommate and her boyfriend were still probably still going at it and, at the same time noticed my forest green Volkswagen® bug across the street, sitting paralyzed by the humidity as it rusted in silence. The unique silence of those heavy August Saturday mornings in Lincoln.

The man followed me across the sad excuse of a front yard where the wilted weeds were tired of trying. We went through the porch and up the stairs—me like a horseless savior and he like a homeless puppy. "Uh, what's your name?" he asked when we were inside. I told him and turned to get the coffee. He cleared his throat with that disgusting sound men often make in the morning, and then with tears in his eyes, told me his paycheck had bounced and he needed to buy a bus ticket to get home because his brother had shot himself to death and his parents needed him. I didn't think to ask what his name was because as soon as I knew his plight, my assessment of his suitability evaporated, and I immediately assumed the helper role. I made empathic murmurs and obeyed my new instinct: "I can help, let me help, you need help."

We sat silent on the tattered, pocked green couch in the living room. I don't know how the man and I ended up on the floor, but we did. Well, I do know how. I was hungry to be noticed, hungry for affection, even skin hungry.

He lay on his back, and I put my arm over his chest—in an embrace of sorts. I glanced over to gaze into his eyes. His head was turned away, and I felt his chest heave then stiffen. To get his attention, I muttered compliments to him about his body using my most soothing tone. That made no difference. Since I noted no difference I continued to just watch him. No curiosity. No judgement. We just lay there together trapped by distance. Strangers. As humidity seeped through the open window and stuck in mid-air, he wasn't really there. And I wasn't either.

Soon, I remembered my roommate and her boyfriend behind the glass doors. Since I hadn't seen them leave, I assured myself they were sleeping and, wanting to avoid embarrassment and awkwardness, suggested, "Let's go outside." I don't remember if he threw my arm off his chest. I do remember it seemed something slammed shut inside me.

He nodded slightly and muttered, "Yeah, okay." But we didn't move. "Just remember, I need money. Do ya have any?" I wondered if he was irritated or if it was just the heat that made me think so.

I sighed, disappointed that he wouldn't even make small talk and said wistfully, "Oh, okay, how much?"

"Thirty-five. In cash."

"I only have my checkbook," I apologized.

"Then, can you write me a check?" Now, he did sound irritated for sure, and I wondered about that. Only wondered. No caution, no concern. I didn't know any better.

"Yeah," I assured him, as he yawned, crossed his arms and leaned against the faded wallpaper. I returned to my bedroom to get the checkbook.

Finally we went outside. I noticed the steps were more creaky than usual as they complained by swelling in the response to the humidity. He said nothing. I confessed feeling embarrassed I only had forty dollars left in the checking account.

"Thirty-five is fine," he directed. I sat on the step and carefully wrote the check. It seemed like he grabbed it rudely. But I decided to forgive him because he was desperate for money to get the bus to get home because his brother had shot himself in the head and his parents needed him. He took in a noisy breath and announced, "I have to cash this." His tone changed to a demand, "Where can I get it cashed?"

"Oh," I chirped, "My bank. You can cash the check at my bank. I'll take you there right now. It's close to the bus station." Nothing in me protested any of this.

We climbed into my forest green Volkswagen Bug and drove to the bank. Even though it was only about 9 a.m. by now, there were no parking places since it was the opening day for the Nebraska Cornhusker's football team. He leaped out and sauntered toward the bank door.

I hollered, "I'm gonna drive around the block. I'll be right back." Then, at the stoplight, I started to sweat and remembered it was Saturday. The bank would be closed on Saturday. I froze and moaned aloud, "Oh no! I have no way to get any money for him 'til Monday. Now what? How will he get home?" Worry danced with guilt, I swallowed a sob of sympathy and drove around the block. Slowly.

The car behind me gave a friendly but piercing honk that shattered my pensive worry on behalf of the stranger I'd been lounging with all morning. Shocked by the sound, I resumed and, pulling forward, stopped where the Marlboro® man had gotten out. He wasn't waiting there. He wasn't. He just wasn't. I parked illegally and got out of the car to search on foot—for a while. There was no him.

He was gone. Poor man.

It wasn't until years later when reviewing my some-times romantic, sometimes comedic, and sometimes tragic relationships with men, I realized that on that scorching humid August Saturday in Lincoln, I'd been had. I'd been conned. By an aimless lollygag and my hunger for skin.

# The Memory Keeper

## Colleen Haggerty

I feel like I'm losing them both. I *am* losing them both. I have an aging mother whose brain is turning to mush due to dementia and a teenage son whose brain is still under construction. Juggling my relationships with each of them, though their lives are vastly different from each other's, is very similar.

Him
Seventeen years old. Charming. Handsome. Talented. He's diving deep into his passions and personality.

Her
Eighty years old. Addled. Weathered. Worn. She skims the surface of her personality like a pelagic bird gliding over the ocean.

Him
When I watch him sleep, I see the little boy I remember. When he touches me with his soft eyes, the recognition that we have known since his birth is reignited.

But who is this singer? Who is this actor? Who is this young man with confidence and flair?

It's not that I don't know him, it's that I can't see his future. Until now, his future has been in my hands. As parents, my husband and I decided where he'd live, where he'd go to school and, in the early years, what he would eat, what he would wear, who he would play with, if he would go to church. With each passing year, we've lost more and more control, had less and less influence.

Like daybreak, my son is slowly rising over the horizon of his life, emerging with blinding brilliance.

Her

When I first hear her voice on the phone, I hear the mom I remember. When she hugs me tight upon arrival, I feel the embrace I have known since I was born.

But who is this woman now? Where is my mother? Who is this confused woman who forgets where she lives?

It's not that I don't know her, it's just that the mom I know is losing herself. Gone are the intellectual conversations. Gone are some of the oft repeated one-liners. Gone, even, are the emotions.

Like day's end, my mother is slowly slipping over the horizon of her personality, waning, abating, fading.

Him

"How was your day, buddy?" I start to load the dishwasher to make it appear that I'm not too invested in this conversation.

"K." He opens the fridge. Sighs.

"Did you have your math quiz today?"

"Uh-uh."

"Do you have any homework?" I rinse the syrup from a few of the breakfast plates.

"Uh-uh." He reaches for the milk.

"What are you up to this afternoon?" I pull a glass from the cupboard and hand it to him.

"I-u-o," he says with the same rhythm of "I don't know," but without a single consonant.

"Luke, seriously, you need to actually move your mouth when you talk. Grunting simply isn't enough." I think I'm funny. I smile. I let out a little chuckle.

"Gawd, Mom. I AM!" Milk splatters as he pours it into the glass. He grabs the glass with his increasingly large, clumsy hand, storms from the kitchen, into his bedroom and slams the door.

I stand there. The clock ticks. I take a deep breath and wipe up the splattered milk from the counter. I have recently attended a workshop about how the teenage brain works and remember that he was responding from his amygdala, the region that guides instinctual reactions, but that is no excuse. He can't talk to me like that.

I walk to his room and knock on the door. No answer.

I open the door and am assaulted by the smell of sour milk, overly sweet Wrigley's gum, and deep brown earth.

"Luke, it's not okay to talk to me that way. I didn't mean to make fun of you. I'm sorry, but that doesn't give you the right to yell and walk off like that." The dirty jeans, socks, boxer shorts, and t-shirts littering the floor make my skin crawl. I resist the urge to pick it all up and throw it in the hamper. He is lying on his bed, his back to me.

"Luke." The trees outside his window whoosh in the wind. "Luke!" I yell.

He rolls over as he takes out his earbuds. "WHAT?" I hate it when we verbally spar like this. I repeat my initial admonishment.

"K. Sorry." He rolls back over and puts his earbuds back in.

Her

"How was your day, Mom?" The phone is scrunched between my ear and my shoulder as I cut onions for soup. I wear my cheater glasses not just to read the recipe, but to act as a barrier against the onion juice.

"Oh, we had a great day." She sounds so happy.

"Yeah? What did you do?" I reach into the crisper bin for the celery.

"Um. What did we do? Um. I don't remember, but it was a great day." She chuckles, nervously. I may not know who my mother is becoming, but I know who she was. I know that nervous chuckle. I decide to change the subject.

"Guess what? Tessa got an award." As I cut the celery I continue to tell Mom about the honor my daughter, younger than Luke by three years, received at school. Then, not sure she's following me, I change the subject again. "Are you free next Tuesday? I'd love to come see you."

"Uuummmm. Tuesday. I think so." The little old lady shake that is creeping into her voice unnerves me.

"Take a look at your calendar. Do you have anything written down on Tuesday?"

"What's the date? The 15th?"

"No, the date next Tuesday is the 22nd." As gently as I can.

"We're free!" She sounds like a young girl.

"Awesome. Write me down. I'm coming!" I wait and listen as she mumbles under her breath and writes my name. I hope she's writing it in the correct box.

The doctor at the memory clinic diagnosed Mom with vascular dementia. Along with losing her short-term memory, her frontal lobe is damaged, which has impaired her executive functioning, her ability to plan, sequence, and organize. Her memory would drastically improve, as would her executive functioning, if she stopped drinking and started exercising. She tried to quit drinking her nightly wine, but I think she forgot that she was quitting. If she couldn't quit drinking with all her faculties, I imagine it's even harder to do with them compromised.

"Okay, you're down for the 22nd! What time will you be here?" She sounds so excited.

"I'll be there in time for lunch – about 11:30. Say, have you heard from Aunt Marilyn lately?" Mom's sister in California is suffering from dementia herself.

I sauté the onions and celery in olive oil.

"No, I don't think so. . ." she wanders off. I imagine her meandering through her mind, trying to grasp a memory of a conversation with her sister and finding nothing. "Say, when are you coming down?" This catches me off guard, though it shouldn't by now.

"I'll see you Tuesday, about 11:30. I'll have lunch with you." I brush away the tears streaming down my cheeks.

Him

Rushing into the house after spending the afternoon skateboarding with his buddies, he smells of warm concrete, fresh mown grass and sweat. Luke brushes his hand through his already tousled hair, gulps a glass of water and pounds the cup on the counter. "Mom, the guys and I are going to shoot baskets at school." He is so sure of himself that he forgot that I have the final word.

"You mean, may I shoot baskets?" Gazing at him from the corner of my eye, my brows raised, I know I look just like my Mom.

"Oh, right." Quick breaths. "Sorry. So, can I?" His words are clipped, rushed. As if whether or not he gets to go is all that matters. As if shooting baskets, above all, is where he needs to be at that moment.

"What time will you be back?" I want a few more minutes with him, even if just to talk about logistics.

He knows the drill. His eyes soften, his shoulders relax, his breath slows down. "When do you want me back?"

"Be home at 5:30. No later. Are you hungry?" I want to be helpful, to be a mom in the way I am used to being a mom. He doesn't need me the way he used to. I'm not sure how much he needs me at all anymore.

"Uh-uh. Mom, did you buy me another math notebook?"

I shake my head as I remember he asked me about a new notebook this morning. "Oh, I'm sorry, I forgot. It was a busy day." I feel guilty that I didn't even think about him while I was at work. Here's one thing I can do to keep him in my mother's web, and I blew it.

He sighs heavily while he shakes his downcast head. He looks up at me. "Well, do you think you can get it tonight? My other one is full." I am reminded of the admonishing tone I heard from my father countless times when I was young.

"Sure, buddy." Why do I feel so small?

"Bye." He is out the door as quickly as he came in. The thump, thump, thump of the basketball leads him down the driveway.

Her

I look behind me and she is lagging, peering into window displays at things she doesn't need, things she doesn't have a place for since she sold her home of 50 years a year ago. I turn around and walk back to her, "How are you doing, Mom?"

"Oh, my knee hurts a little." Her nose crinkles as she reaches down and rubs her knee to punctuate the point.

"I'm sorry. I don't mean to rush. We can walk slower."

We are an eddy in the flowing stream of Christmas shoppers at the mall.

"Where are we going?" Her eyes hold the curiosity of a toddler.

"We're looking for a nice pen for Larry for you to give him as a Christmas gift."

I slow my pace and walk near her in case she needs to reach out for support.

"That's a good idea. Did I think of it?" Her chest puffs up.

"Actually, Larry told me he'd love to get a fancy pen. Once a writer, always a writer." I scan the stores in front of us, making a mental note of who might carry a pen.

"Where are we going?" She starts to limp.

"We're looking for a pen for you to give Larry for Christmas. Just a few more stores, okay? If we don't find one, we can order one online."

"I don't know how to do that," she says, as if it is something dirty.

"Don't worry, I can help. It's pretty easy, actually. Here, let's go in here." I take her elbow and guide her into a store. I just want to be useful, to be a good daughter, the way I am used to being a daughter. And I want her to be the mom I know. I want her to take me to lunch and buy me something I don't need or want. Not because I like that, but because that's been our dance for so long. But she changed the steps. I don't know this dance yet.

Him

His life is exploding before our eyes, like a race-horse blasting out of the gate. When he started high school, his choir teacher heard his voice and invited him to sing in the small, audition-only jazz choir, Show-stoppers. Little did we know that this would be the beginning of his future. Little did we know that when he donned the Showstoppers uniform—black pants, black shirt, red bow tie and red suspenders—he was finishing his transformation into a young man.

Potential sparkles in his eyes. Gone is the heavy, sickly sweet, rank scent of pre-adolescence. Now he smells like fresh possibility.

In between vocal lessons, play rehearsals, choir, and seeing his girlfriend, Luke sweeps through the house like a tornado. There are days when I say goodbye at 6:30 a.m. and hello at 10:30 p.m.

He is being lauded for his deep, resonate singing voice. His vocal coach, a former opera singer, is suggesting summer camp in Salzburg, then college in Indiana. Luke wants to apply to Julliard. Opera? Summer camp in Europe? College across the country? I didn't expect this path. I am dependent on the experts to help us navigate the twists and turns, to guide us as we steer our son into his future.

Her

Her life is imploding before our eyes. She's giving up. Is it fear, self-preservation, a natural occurrence? It's like she's bundling herself up into a chrysalis so she can morph into the next stage of life.

When she moved out of her home of 50 years, she forgot to pack her memories, she left a piece of her personality at the house. The transition from home to facility cemented her into old age. Her eyes are flat with the staleness of her life.

Her day is punctuated by meals: breakfast at 8:00, lunch at noon, dinner at 5:00. If I don't arrive at her apartment by 11:45 a.m., she starts to panic, fearful that she'll miss lunch—which is served until 1:00.

She plays bridge every Wednesday in the living room at the assisted living facility, but she stopped going to the Monday games at church.

The "Gardens," as we call it, has daily activities, some of which interest Mom and her husband. They especially love the happy hours or special parties in the living room.

Mom doesn't shop anymore, she doesn't volunteer anymore, she doesn't knit anymore, she doesn't read much anymore, she hardly goes out to eat anymore. I really don't know what fills her time except for going downstairs and chitchatting with the other residents and staff.

I try to do something special with them whenever I visit. Recently my brother gave a lecture at the university, and I offered to drive Mom and Larry so they could attend with me. On the half hour drive into Seattle, Mom asks, "Where are we going?"

"We're going to see Kevin's lecture at the university." Light, casual.

"What's he talking about?"

I explain the topic—marijuana use in a state where it's legal—and, for good measure, I remind her how long the talk would be. "But they are serving some appetizers before the lecture begins."

"Oh, that's good. I'm hungry." Larry and I talk about the best route to take so we can avoid traffic.

"Where are we going?" I hear the tense strain of confusion behind the words.

"We're going to see Kevin give a lecture about marijuana use now that it's legalized." Casual, not forced.

Larry and I talk about the new pope as we drive across the bridge into the city. Mom is incapable of joining in such conversations anymore. She sits silently while we talk.

"Say, where are we going?" As I try to hide the panic I feel at having to answer this question over and over, I hear her trying to hide her panic at having to ask it repeatedly.

"Mom, we're going to go hear Kevin give his lecture. We're almost there. He's really glad you're both able to come." Not forced. Compassionate.

"Oh, that's right." As if, *Aren't I silly for my brain fart.*

On the drive home Larry sits in the front with me; Mom sits in the back. We are talking about how eloquent and impressive my brother's speech was when Mom's hand suddenly flies to Larry's shoulder. She taps it repeatedly. "Larry, where do we live?" Panic. Fear.

It's clear he's used to these questions. Without skipping a beat, Larry calmly responds. "Well, we live at the Gardens now, Sharon, in our little apartment."

Mom relaxes into her seat again. "Oh." I can tell she isn't satisfied. I can tell that a mental image of her apartment is not in her brain. I can tell she doesn't know where the hell she lives, but she heard her husband's voice calling her home. That calms her.

I clutch onto memories as if they are the key to Heaven. His long-term memories: How old was I when I broke my leg, Mom? Her short-term memories: What time are you coming for lunch, Colleen?

More time with them both is what I want. My chest constricts with panic when I realize that Luke will be gone in 18 months. My breathing becomes shallow every time I leave my mom. She probably won't die for another ten years, but how much longer will she be here?

As I try to harness time to my heart, I feel it falling from the frame of my days. Days melt into each other and, as if in a dream, I am reaching for the unreachable, trying to grasp what turns out to be a puff of smoke.

And, as with anything, the harder we hold something, the more likely we are to break it. My grasp on my own memories is failing. Is this a natural progression of aging or is my brain failing me? What will I be asking Luke to remember for me in thirty years?

Memories or no, I can only impact the present moment. I might remember it.

Or not.

# Dr. Boser's Question

## Anneliese Kamola

I walk slowly down the Dachau Art Museum's exhibit hall, looking at the iconic European landscape scenes painted in the late 1800s and early 1900s. Inside gild frames, vivid green hills roll in their evening dusk, ethereal mists cling low over swamp reeds at sunrise, and the Alps reach up to cradle pink clouds. Until the early 1800s, painters focused their images on people or activity. But around the turn of the 19th century, 'open air' painting came into fashion for the first time, and the land itself became both character and action. My great-grandfather, Tony Binder, was part of this movement—first in Egypt, and later in Dachau, Germany, where he lived from 1922 to 1944. I've traveled to Dachau to walk amidst my family's history, to learn through my own footsteps and experiences who they were, and, therefore, who I am.

Pausing, I lean forward to read the placard on the wall written in German and translated into English: *Trains made traveling more pleasant, particularly for the influential bourgeoisie. One went on summer holiday 'into nature,' which was considered the area of relaxation for working people. In this atmosphere of new horizons, 'nature' was linked to a feeling of freedom.* Dachau had already turned from a wild moor into a town by the time my great-grandparents, grandmother, and her siblings moved here. And in the 89 years since, Dachau has practically become a suburb of Munich. The train ride this morning from the center of the bustling city to Dachau's quiet *Bahnhof*, or train station, was short, with neighborhoods and community gardens lining the tracks the entire way.

*Today, the museum's purpose is to preserve the artistic heritage of the Artist's Colony in Dachau.* I stand back from the painting as a realization dawns on me—of course, the artistic heritage of this town must be actively preserved. Most foreigners today know Dachau, Germany for its history of Nazi-forced brutality; to me—because of my family's story—Dachau has always been an artist town first, a concentration camp second. Without any preservation, this life-supporting piece of the town's history would likely be lost to the outside world.

"Anneliese. Here you are." I turn to see Dr. Elisabeth Boser, a stately middle-aged woman wearing an elegant suit with low black heeled pumps. Large golden earrings swing from the lobes of her ears. She walks straight across the light wooden floor towards me. The click of her heels echo off the white walls, loud in the museum's stillness.

"*Hallo*, Dr. Boser!" I greet her with a big smile, extending my hand to shake hers. "Thank you for taking the time to see me this afternoon."

"*Ja*. You have come all this way, of course you should see your great-grandfather's works in the archives." We shake hands. "You like these paintings?" she asks, indicating the landscapes of Adolf Hölzel in front of us. I nod. "Good. Follow me."

We exchange further pleasantries—how long am I traveling, am I on holiday, do I still have family in Germany—as I follow her down the hallway, past the docent desk, down a grand granite staircase, across the main foyer, and through another long, white hallway. Finally, she unlocks a door labeled *Archiv*—Archives— and pushes it open. Motion-detecting lights glow on, revealing a large room set down into the earth about four feet below the landing on which we stand. A short set of cement stairs descends into a collection of thousands of framed paintings, leaning together on long, low shelves, like a library. I can smell the musty scent of old paper, canvases, oils, and watercolors.

"Please, place your rucksack here, so you do not knock over any paintings," she requests. I oblige, leaving my pack at the door, and walk down the seven stairs to the archive floor. The air becomes cooler on my bare arms.

I follow Dr. Boser through the labyrinth until we stop at a long table where five paintings, each about fifteen inches by eight inches, lie out, ready for me. My great-grandfather's characteristic accuracy and tiny brush strokes seem to greet me. Seeing his work here, half-way around the world, feels half confirming, half surreal: yes, my great-grandfather was, in fact, a man beyond the stories of my family home, and, yes, he truly was a museum-worthy painter.

"These are the only paintings we have of your great-grandfather's," she says. Five? This is it? Where are the rest? As if reading my mind, she continues, "Of course, there are many more out there in the world. We just don't have them."

The first, second, and third paintings are gentle landscapes—one in watercolor and two in oils. Lush green countryside, mist hovering over a pond reflecting winter sun, people meandering through a park under enormous trees. The fourth painting is of a young woman I recognize immediately—his daughter, Stephanie; my grandmother, *Meine Oma*. I smile, amazed to see the face, albeit young, of someone I know so well, looking back at me. In the painting, Oma sits on a low bench and wears beautiful Egyptian clothing and bangles, certainly an outfit of her mother's from when they lived in Alexandria before WWI. In the fifth painting reclines an unknown woman, fully nude, against rich brown cloth. She makes direct, coy eye contact with the viewer.

"Shocking, yes?" Dr. Boser asks. I look up at her and she raises her eyebrows briefly. "He was a man, after all."

I smile, a bit embarrassed, but not too much. Of the dozens of Tony Binder paintings I have seen, this is the first of an unclothed woman. I bend down to look at it again. Who was she? She's definitely not my great-grandmother; Marie's hair was not blonde.

The paintings don't sweep me off my feet as I had hoped. In fact, the paintings in my parents', aunt's, half-uncle's, and grandparents' houses are much better examples of Binder's skill, artistry, and transportive beauty. Instead, I feel a surprising warmth spreading across my chest: pride. How lucky I am to have grown up with better-than-museum quality art hanging on the walls of my home! And how privileged, and grateful, I am to have such a direct link of great magnitude to an ancestor, and to know the details of his story. For all that I wish these five paintings hung on the walls in the museum gallery upstairs, instead of living in the stacks down here, I also feel relieved somehow to know that better quality pieces live and are seen every day in the homes of people I love.

I glance at Dr. Boser. I don't want to tell her this isn't as special as I anticipated—saying that would feel disrespectful. "These are lovely!" I say instead. "I'm pretty sure this is my grandmother," I comment, bending over to look at my Oma.

"Ja. We know. That is his youngest daughter."

"And do you know who this woman is?" I ask, pivoting a bit to look more closely at the nude. Dr. Boser shakes her head, no. "Isn't it interesting," I ask her, straightening up, "how there are people all over the world living just ordinary lives?" I am momentarily struck with a sense of simplicity, like there is nothing, really, that I need to figure out. "All of the people in these paintings were alive once, too, living and working."

"What do you do professionally?" Dr. Boser asks me.

Professionally? I feel a surprising pang of shame at her abrupt and personal question. I'm only twenty-two. I have only worked an assortment of odd-jobs to pay the bills, but nothing professional. I am tempted to ask her, *Do twenty-two-year-olds in Germany already hold a place in the professional world?* but instead I answer, "Graphic design." It's sort of truthful—I designed posters for my high school's drama club for many years, even after graduation, and have made half a dozen different wedding invitations for friends and family.

"Makes sense," she says. "The arts must run in your family."

Her observation startles me. Is it true? I always thought of us as a family of academics, or business people, or teachers. Artists?

But before I can ponder this more, she asks, "Why do you travel here in Germany?"

Out of habit, I rattle off my family's story, briefly, about how my German grandmother, the one in Tony Binder's painting, owned a small weaving factory in town, and how my Polish grandfather—a political prisoner of war in the Dachau camp—was forced labor in her factory.

"She helped him escape from the camp in the last days of the war," I say. "A few days later they married, and over the next five years built up the factory. They had my father and, later, my aunt here in Dachau before selling the factory and moving to California."

"Yes, yes. But why are *you* here?"

Her question makes me stop in my tracks. Why is this stranger seeing me in a way no one else has seen me before? Not my parents, not my friends. When asked, I have always told about my grandparents as my reason to travel, and the magic of their story has always been enough. But Dr. Boser's laser focus on me and my intention is exposing and, at the same time, a relief. A relief to be seen for myself. And, through her attention, I feel a clarity forming within my body that I have never been able to articulate before.

"I. Um. I think I'm trying to find my place within my family's story," I say, looking at the painting of Oma.

"*Ja.* That is an important thing to do."

"I think I want to learn the truths behind the stories I have heard so often."

"Mmmm." She nods, continuing to look at me. "But what is truth? One person's perspective is not another's. Is truth caught in the details, like these strokes of the paintbrush? Or is it something larger, intangible," she waves her hand to sweep across the room, "like whatever similarity holds all of these paintings together? And, ultimately, does it matter?"

"Well," I say, pausing to take in her meaning. "I suppose I'm also coming to find my place within my own story. You know? To learn my own version, I guess, as it's the only one I really have any authority in."

"Very good," she answers, as if I have passed some sort of test. "That is good to be clear about." I nod, still taking in my own answer as new information. "Is your father interested in coming back to Germany?" she asks.

Her question surprises me. I have never heard him speak about revisiting Germany, let alone Dachau. "I don't know. I don't believe so," I say. "Should he?"

"When you go home, ask him why. It will be interesting what he responds." There is a sense in her tone that she already knows his reason.

Why would anyone come back to Dachau? People left Germany in order to escape their histories and connections to the atrocities of World War II. I suspect my grandmother left because she could not live in Dachau any more, surrounded by an internal guilt and confusion around her role as a German civilian and a

Nazi sympathizer. I don't remember my grandfather saying anything directly, but surely he did not mind having more distance between himself and the reminders of his five years of starvation, brutality, and loss in the camp.

But even though they left Dachau, there is no question they brought their traumas with them across the Atlantic Ocean, inside their bodies, inside their minds. And when the second generation—my father, aunt, and half-uncle—moved with them to make a full life in America, they had to endure the physical and emotional effects of their parents' repressed traumas.

For me, the third generation, I still experience my grandparents' traumas through navigating my own responses to my father's illogical outbursts. When I was a child, I didn't understand his eruptions towards me—where did they come from? As confused as I was, I always sensed they were fueled by something outside of my picture. Though now, after twenty-two years, I know his emotional floods are just his nervous system's built-in defense responses to his own parents' outbursts, stony silences, and harsh judgments. As I grew older, my own explosions developed. In my own way, I honed my ability to fight back as a way to stay close to him, to feel his presence no matter what, while, at the same time, building a wall of protection between us. And even though I burst out at him sometimes, I know that, in truth, my emotional conflagrations are really in response to my grandparents' actions and not him. I have built the capacity to emotionally remove myself enough to be fascinated by—inexplicably drawn towards—the brutality at the center of my family's history. I want to know intimately, and differentiate from, the source of my own repressed rage, shame, guilt, confusion, and terror.

And maybe this is why I am here. This trip to Europe, a post-college pilgrimage into my family's history, is much more than a genealogical road trip. Perhaps I am here so I can find—and claim—the parts of my history that are inherently wise and vital; things I also sense within my body. Perhaps I'm seeking something not often focused on in my family's story—the resiliency of beauty.

I stand and watch Dr. Boser return Tony Binder's paintings to their places on the shelves. As she does so, I take an opportunity to really look at her. I take in the slight tension around her mouth, the tightness she carries in her shoulders, the rigidity in her back. I can't help but feel instinctively that she has been left behind somehow, or is staying behind of her own choice, despite the challenges to *her* body of living in this place with such a hard history. She preserves parts of the German story that run contrary to the common narrative. The parts that must not be forgotten in order to retain a connection to humanity. She is an historian—not just of art, but of the parts of the German identity that never stopped believing in life and love.

"Dr. Boser?" I ask. "Have you been to the Tony Binder Haus?"

She nods. "Yes. Why?"

I shrug. "Just curious."

"I was in there a few years ago, to retrieve some paintings. And a few times since. It's not the same now as it was the first time I was there, years ago."

"How so?"

"It's cold."

"What do you mean, cold?"

Dr. Boser pauses, and exhales a short sigh. "It's lost your great-grandfather's...smell."

"His smell?"

She purses her lips. "Are you going to get to go inside?"

"Yes," I say. "The doctor who owns it now has promised me a tour."

"Then I think you will know what I mean. I can't find the right English word." She looks around the room and then back at me. "Finished here?"

"Yes. Thank you so much, Dr. Boser, for sharing these with me."

"You have come a long way and now you have seen them. But perhaps they do not surprise you?" She must have noted my lack of oohing and aaahing.

I smile and nod. "I've seen a few others in my life. But these are quite lovely," I say, diplomatically.

"*Ja.* Of course, you have seen more."

"I'm glad I saw them, though," I say, as we make our way through the rows of paintings and back up the stairs to my backpack and the heavy door. "It completes something. Makes the stories real, somehow."

I adjust my pack as we walk down the hallway towards the museum's main door. Looking up from clipping my waist belt, I can't help but notice that Dr. Boser seems slightly distant. What has our conversation brought up in her? What is it like for her to work with this place's history all the time? What happened in her family? To her parents? Is it possible for her, as a German civilian of the town of Dachau, to live fully in the present with access to joy? Or does she get stuck looking to the past? Does she hold guilt or feel complicit, like my grandmother? Or has she somehow found a way to let it go? I want to ask her these questions, but I know they are too personal, too vulnerable. And we have run out of time.

We stop at the large glass entry to the museum; the building is already closed for the evening. She unlocks the door for me. "Thank you for coming," she says, shaking my hand again. "It was a pleasure to meet you, the next generation."

"Thank *you*, Dr. Boser, for your time. And for all you do here."

"And be sure to ask your father why he does not return to Germany. I think you will find a story there." I nod and cross the threshold onto the cobblestone street. Looking back, I watch as she locks the door behind me, then turns and walks down the hallway, disappearing around the corner.

I turn, too, and walk through the early evening light, down the hill through the old town between cream, white, and rose-colored historic buildings, towards the house of my ancestors. And as I walk, I wonder, if I am here to claim my own story, then is it possible as well to let go of the pieces that I don't want? To disentangle from the generations of struggle, rage, confusion, shame? Might it just be possible to choose to live my own life in my own way, a life of creativity and beauty, a life of connection and peace?

# Puppies and Babies

## Nicki Lang

Two months after the birth of my second son, Leo, I found myself driving our car, praying very fervently that I would get rear-ended. I had just dropped off our boys, baby Leo and 22-month old Jude, with my mother-in-law, so that I could accompany Kevin to get a vasectomy. If I got into a car accident, surely, he could not get a vasectomy that day. This was the reasoning of a slightly hormonal woman, seeing all of her future children dissolve right before her eyes.

We had made the decision "together" months earlier when I was uncomfortably pregnant and caring for our one-year-old. It seemed like a no-brainer that more babies than parents would be a terrible idea for us. But now that I was facing the reality of never bearing another child, I was devastated. And mad at Kevin for not understanding.

"We could just wait a few more months," I said as we drove to the appointment. "Just to be sure."

"Nicki, you hate being pregnant," Kevin said.

"So?" This was true, but I refused to consider it a valid point.

I hated the restrictions that pregnancy put on my body. Kevin would leave to go climbing or mountain biking, activities we used to share, and I was stuck doing pre-natal yoga with my huge belly as a companion. I was also constantly afraid that something would go terribly wrong, either with the births or that my babies would have some kind of major health challenge to deal with.

"It's not quantity but quality that counts," Kevin argued. "We have two healthy boys who we can spend the rest of our lives loving. Isn't that enough?"

"But what if something happens to one of them?" I had lost my only sister to leukemia when we were both teenagers. I knew that not everyone lived to adulthood and I needed to buffer the worst case scenario.

"Nic, nothing is going to happen. We are going to be fine. This is the right decision." Kevin sounded so sure.

The real, hard, truth was this: he was taking away my last chance at creating more family. Not just my sister, but all of my immediate family was dead. My mom had died a slow death to MS and my dad had basically sacrificed his life taking care of her and died of cancer. Kevin still had his parents and his three siblings—his original family unit was intact. Mine had been obliterated. Those two, precious (screaming, pooping, peeing, puking) insomniacs were my closest blood. My people. I had family again. And everything in me wanted more.

"Nic, we can't just go on having babies indefinitely."

"Why not? Look at the Russians! Women get a medal of honor for having lots of children!" I was grasping for any argument now.

"It's the Mother Heroine," Kevin said.

"What?" I snapped.

"The award Russians get. It's called the Mother Heroine." Kevin had studied Russian things during his time in the Army. "And I know you don't want to keep having babies indefinitely."

"No, but I need to know I could if I wanted to."

So, sitting in the waiting room, waiting for Kevin to get snipped, I said a prayer that if God wanted me to have more babies, somehow I would. And then I cried.

Is it wrong to wish that vasectomies hurt more? Kevin said he was chatting with the doctor about rock climbing while the odor of burning vas deferens filled the air. I mean, relative to pregnancy and birth, it's really like stubbing your toe. He was back in the waiting room before I could get up the nerve to run in screaming for them to stop the procedure.

"The worst part was the shot in the scrotum," Kevin began the report. "That really hurt. The rest was fine."

"Umm hmmm." My sympathy dial was switched off for the day.

"They did say my testicles might swell to the size of grapefruits."

"Well, that will be exciting," I mumbled, thinking about how far my belly had expanded to grow each of those babies and how the stretch-mark laden folds of skin still rested across my mid-section.

In silence, we drove to Kevin's parent's house to retrieve our boys. Kevin's mom met us, exasperated, at the front door. "Leo cried the entire time!" she said, passing me my wailing child. Jude came running toward us, trucks in both hands.

I grimaced and sat down in a recliner to feed Leo. He immediately stopped crying and suckled fiercely like a starving puppy. Jude crawled up beside me and snuggled in. Oh, these boys. These precious, precious boys.

I'm not sure I ever completely forgave Kevin for going through with the vasectomy. Even years later, every time an announcement was made that someone else in the family was having another baby, I would fight back tears and sulk for the rest of the day. My sister-in-law, Carmen, noticed this once and offered me her husband's sperm if I really wanted to have another baby.

"The genetics would be pretty close," she said, sounding almost like she was serious.

"Thanks. I'll keep that in mind." I forced a smile. I had no interest in being consoled.

That was the strange part about it: *I* could still technically have babies. My body hadn't changed, and neither had my biological urges telling me I needed more creatures to take care of.

Which is why I started to look for a puppy.

Once the boys had survived toddlerhood and were sleeping though the night, I began a full-fledged search for a new furry family member. My resentment gave me a large amount of very manipulative ammunition in this battle.

"Kevin, we are not having any more babies, thanks to you, so the least you can do is let me get a puppy."

"But we *have* a dog!" Kevin would say. Again, not a valid point. Zion, a beautiful red-merle Border collie mix, had been my most trusted companion for over a decade. When Kevin married me, he got Zion as part of the deal. Zion had made dozens of trips back and forth to BC during and after my parents decline and eventual deaths. He was my soulmate, my co-pilot. But he was getting old. And I knew that when he finally went to the big fire hydrant in the sky, I would be devastated. I would be losing another member of my family.

"Plus, Zion needs a friend," I replied, attacking from all angles. "He loves puppies. He'll help train her. He deserves to be happy in his final years!" For the record, I did think this was true. I thought a companion for Zion would be a great idea.

"But think of all of Zion's hair you already have to clean up. There will be twice as much with another dog!"

This was (finally) a valid point. We would go on vacation without Zion and still find his hair in our hotel room.

"Ok, we'll get a dog that doesn't shed," I reasoned. "You could train it and use it as a therapy dog at school!" Kevin was a middle school counselor and part of the disaster response team that went out to console kids and teachers if there was a death or other tragedy connected to a school. He had just been telling me about another counselor who brought a dog to their last call and how effective it was. "We'll train her together! It will be a project for us!"

He paused to think about this. Oooh. I could see the wheels turning, and then his face changed. BOOM. I had him.

"Well. okay."

"Okay?!?" I couldn't believe he had caved. Actually, I could. I had been pushing pretty hard, and he was tired of the hours I was spending looking on Craigslist® and Petfinder® and every breeder site this side of the Mississippi.

"You won't be sorry, Kevin! It's going to be great. And the boys will be so excited!" I was ecstatic. I forgave Kevin, just a little, for the vasectomy.

Zion was born on the fourth of July, which was a cruel twist of fate because he was deathly afraid of fireworks. On his birthday and the days before and after, he could usually be found cowering in the bathtub, which must have seemed like the safest place. So, when a litter of Aussie-poodle mix puppies was born on the fourth of July not far from where we lived, I took it as a sign. Fuzzy, little, Lupinella joined our pack (named for the flower, Lupine, and for the famed Seattle baseball manager, Lou Pinella).

We picked her out of the litter for several reasons. One, I wanted another girl in the house, even if it was just of the canine variety. Two, she was spotted like Zion, so they looked a little like a matched set. Also, when we went to visit the puppies, she seemed to have a feisty personality, and the rest of the puppies acted like lethargic guinea pigs.

"Are you sure?" the breeder asked. "They are all going to perk up in a couple of weeks, I can guarantee it. If I was going to pick a therapy dog, she wouldn't be my first choice."

But I was smitten. She seemed destined to be ours.

The boys accompanied me to the farm to pick her up. The breeder led us to a back room in the basement of her house.

"She's a little shaken up from her first bath and blow dry," she warned, opening the door.

Blow dry? I thought. What kind of maintenance was this dog going to require? We walked in, and there in the corner was a quivering, whimpering, little spotted puff-ball of a creature. The whole room smelled like perfume. As I picked her up, I realized the smell was coming from her fur. This will probably be the cleanest she would ever be, I thought.

From the moment Lupine recovered from her traumatic beauty treatments, she was a spitfire. Her needle-like teeth were constantly nipping at everything and everyone. Leo, who was five at the time, must have seemed to her like another puppy (or maybe a sheep) as she was constantly chasing him and biting him to get attention. Jude, now seven years old, could fend her off a little better, but got his fair share of teeth marks. She gnawed on everything in sight: shoes, clothes, the corners of the cupboards, the carpet, the kids' toys, sticks of butter, shrubs in the yard, Zion's face—she was an adorable ball of terror and destruction.

"I want to return Lupine!" Leo would declare on a daily basis. He had, after all, wanted the black puppy and not the spotted one. He was sure the black puppy would have been a nicer dog. I wasn't sure he was wrong.

We were exhausted. Lupine couldn't be let out alone because she would dart into other people's houses and eat all of their cat food or run madly around the neighborhood trampling flowers and chasing chickens. And, to make matters worse, she was far larger than we had anticipated. When on her hind legs, she was tall enough to reach her head all the way to the back of the counters and into the kitchen sink. This meant anything left out was fair game, and she took advantage of her advantage often.

I began to deeply regret the decision to get a puppy, but told myself she would grow out of this phase. We would train her, and everything would be fine. I wanted her to be more like Zion. I thought Zion would take her under his paw and teach her how to be a *real* dog, but Zion had no patience for this little demon.

Kevin took ample opportunity to remind me, "This was your idea."

"See, we should have just had another baby!" was my repeated response.

When Lupine was about a year old, my friend KC was visiting from out of town on a summer weekend. Our friends a few houses down, Chris and Gretchen, invited us over for happy hour. They were hosting a dinner party later that evening with friends they had in common with Kevin. Nice enough folks, people I really wanted to get to know as we built community for ourselves and our kids, but I had my own friend in town. So after one friendly drink I excused myself and KC and I went back home to start dinner.

Not long after, Kevin came back to our house. "I'm going to take Lupine over. There's another dog and they can romp around."

"Are you sure?" I asked. "You know, you really need to watch her." Kevin had a tendency to get lost in conversation and forget all other responsibility.

"It's fine, Nicki. She'll be fine. The boys are out there, too." And off he went to the neighbor's, Lupine bounding ahead.

KC and I chatted while I puttered around the kitchen making pasta for our dinner. Ours was an unlikely friendship, as he was old enough to be my dad—though perhaps could not be more different. Where my dad was all about the rules, KC had broken them all. He was the kind of person my dad would have advised me to avoid. No matter how brash or offensive, he always spoke his mind. There was something refreshing and repulsive about him all at once, like a well you keep going back to even though you know the water is tainted because there's something strangely comforting about the taste.

I was draining the pasta into the sink when I saw Jude running up the trail to our house. I turned to greet him as he burst through the door.

"Perfect timing—" I started to say.

"Lupine bit Leo! He's crying," Jude said. "You better go over there."

I sighed, put the pasta back in the pot, and covered it to keep warm. "I'll go check on him."

Before I could reach the door, I saw Kevin coming up the trail, Leo on one hand, looking just fine, Lupine in the other hand by the collar. I went out and met them on the trail.

"Leo, honey, are you okay?" I didn't see any visible damage.

Without an answer, he smiled and pushed past me into the house. I looked at Kevin, puzzled.

Kevin took a deep breath and with a very calm voice said, "Lupine just ate fourteen chicken breasts off of the counter."

This was not the news I was anticipating. I stared at Kevin for a second before I laid into him with a lot of unkind words I immediately regretted, the summary of which was: "ARE YOU A COMPLETE IDIOT? HOW COULD YOU LET THAT HAPPEN?"

My words hung in the air for a moment before Kevin dared respond. "Everyone was outside, and someone left the door open, and the dogs just got in..." Kevin explained as he watched the blood drain from my face.

The boys and KC stood awkwardly frozen, waiting to see what was going to happen next. They had never heard me use the kind of language that had just erupted from my gut.

I had never felt so utterly mortified in my life. My dog had completely ruined a dinner party for a bunch of people I had just met and would like to have made a good impression upon.

I tried to think quickly about what to do to fix this. "You need to go to the store and get some chicken," I fumed. "NOW!"

"Gretchen said she was taking care of it." Kevin put his arms up as if the situation was out of his hands.

I called Gretchen's cell immediately.

"Hiiii!" she answered with a laugh.

"Gretchen, oh my gosh, I am so embarrassed! Let me go pick up some chicken."

"I'm at the store right now. Don't even worry about it!" She seemed far less bothered by the whole ordeal than I was.

I hung up the phone, still seething at Kevin's carelessness. I did not want to be known as the owners of the poorly behaved dog.

KC, who had been silently watching the whole disaster unfold, including bearing witness to all of the choice words I used to disparage my husband, finally spoke up.

"You know," he said with a bit of a twinkle in his eye, "this reminds me of that scene in the movie, *A Christmas Story*. You know, the one where the dogs run through the house and eat the whole Christmas dinner off of the table and then the family has to go out for Chinese food! For Christmas dinner!" he was laughing.

I was not ready to laugh about this.

I needed a way to redeem my family's reputation.

"I just bought a bottle of good gin. I'll bring that over as a peace offering." I was determined to fix the situation, but I was not ready to face all of those strangers whose party I had ruined. "Kevin, you're taking it over. This was *your* doing."

I handed him the bottle. He conceded and headed back to the neighbors. I got dinner on the table and the rest of us sat down and waited for Kevin to return. The boys, usually chatty or bothering each other, sat silently glancing at one another. Minutes later, Kevin returned, bottle still in hand.

"Why didn't you leave it?!" I bellowed.

"Chris said it wasn't necessary," Kevin shrugged. In his mind, the situation had been resolved.

I closed my eyes and shook my head. "Let's eat. I'll bring it over after dinner."

We ate in silence. Lupine sat in the corner licking her lips. KC snickered at regular intervals. I heard a text message come in on my phone. I checked it so see if maybe Chris had changed his mind about the gin.

It was, indeed, from Chris: "It wasn't Lupine after all! Our security camera caught the whole thing on video!" Attached was a video clip.

I pushed play. It was the clip from the movie *A Christmas Story* KC had referenced earlier.

I tipped my head back and let out a huge belly laugh.

"What is it?" everyone asked. We all watched the clip, and with great relief, we had a good laugh together.

I turned to Kevin, tears of laughter welling in the corners of my eyes, "I'm so sorry for all the things I said." I turned to the boys, "And never repeat those words!" I looked Kevin right in the eye. "Will you forgive me?"

"Yeah, I'm sorry, too," he smiled sheepishly. "I probably should have kept a better eye on Lupine."

Not ready to let him off the hook completely, I added, "You're lucky we have the best neighbors on the planet."

He agreed. We settled in for the rest of the evening, into our home that provided such rich amounts of love and connection—even without more babies.

# All I Want Is Chocolate Milk

## Emerson Lee

STRAWBERRY SORBET
Recipe from *ZOOM*
Season 3, Episode 32, Aired: 2001

Here's what you will need to make it:
- 24 ounces of frozen strawberries, slightly thawed
- 3/4 cup of sugar
- blender
- 9 x 13-inch baking pan
- spatula
- large spoon
- bowls and spoons for eating sorbet

Here's what you have to do:
1. Check with a grown-up before you start this.
2. Put about half the frozen strawberries and 3/4 cups of sugar into a blender and blend until smooth. Sometimes you need to stop the blender and pack the strawberries down with a wooden spoon so they're easier to blend. Make sure the blender is completely stopped before you take the lid off.
3. Now add the rest of the strawberries. Put the lid back on and continue blending.
4. Then, pour the mixture into a 9 x 13 pan and freeze it until it's hard, about 2 hours.
5. When it's ready, let is soften a little bit by leaving it out at room temperature. Then, break it up using a wooden spoon.

6. Pour it back in the blender and blend it again until it is smooth.
7. Then spoon it into dessert dishes and freeze it again for about 20 minutes before serving. Bon Appetit!

I did not check with a grown-up.


## CHOCOLATE MILK

All I want is chocolate milk.

I let out a big breath and drop my backpack onto the hardwood floor, kicking off my strappy leather sandals. It was a fun school day and a short bus ride, but I am always so glad to come home. I like second grade but I'd still rather watch TV.

I step into the sunroom where it is warm from the light that falls through the skylights. I can see the dust in the air. My brother is at baseball practice. Dad is at work, and Mom is doing laundry, like usual, which she always complains about. I find the remote, stuffed into the sides of the gray corduroy recliner I'm about to sit in, and I point it at the dusty black screen. I press the big red button, and I hear the satisfying buzz that comes right before the screen flashes to life. This is my favorite time of day—the hour between when I get home from school at four o'clock and my brother and dad get home around five—the only time I get to be in charge of the TV.

I flip the channel from ESPN—my brother's favorite—to PBS on Channel 9. It is time for *ZOOM*, my favorite after-school show.

It is also time for chocolate milk.

I have to crawl onto the counter to reach the cupboard with the tall blue glasses. I crawl back down and pull a spoon from the silverware drawer. I get the tub of chocolatey powder from the pantry. I come back to the counter, pour a big scoop of powder into the tall glass, some milk from the fridge, and I stir, stir, stir. I feel like a chef, whipping things up in the kitchen. I finish my creation and slurp it with the spoon, like soup. Just for fun, I plunk a bright green silly straw in the glass. It has loops like a roller coaster and I like to watch the milk swoop around before making it to my mouth.

I carry my chocolate milk with both hands and settle into the recliner in the sunlit room, my favorite room in the whole house besides the play room and my room. I have a lot of favorite rooms, I guess. This one is a big room with a ceiling with four big skylights. When it rains, I watch drops dance and slide across it. When it's cloudy, it feels like a gray blanket. When the sun shines through it, it's warm and bright, like now.

There is a plant in the corner, with arching leaves like a palm tree. It is like a little paradise in here. If I step outside, there is a big back yard that I can play in. My dad has a big veggie garden back there. He also takes care of our apple orchard that has nine trees and a big, bright patch of dahlias. Raspberries and blueberries and strawberries, too!

This is my home, and I love it.

I am happy here, today, in this recliner and in my home.

Once I'm settled back to the recliner, the *ZOOM* opening song is done and the show has begun. *ZOOM* is showing a recipe for something that just has strawberries and sugar in it. My mouth waters.

I'm so excited because we have both of those things!

I want to make it!

I *love* strawberries, especially when I pick them from the garden and they're still covered in dirt, just like my hands. Sometimes, I forget to wash them: the strawberries and my hands.

I run over to my mom's recipe drawer, hoping that I won't miss the first steps. Her drawer is full of note-cards and sheets with lots of different peoples' hand-writing. There are so many recipe cards from so many church potlucks. These are our comfort foods—the Jello® dishes, the ham-and-Swiss loaf, the casseroles that I usually don't like.

"Strawberries," the voice on the TV says. "Three fourths cup of sugar."

As fast as I can, I scrawl on an empty neon pink notecard.

Pink like strawberries, pink like lemonade.

I'm excited. I don't want to miss an ingredient, so I'm listening carefully for the voice on the TV.

I don't hear Mom come into the kitchen.

Now she's standing over me, hands on her hips.

She sees the notecard that I'm writing on.

I know before she says a word.

She is *not* happy.

One look and I know that I have done something Bad.

"What are you doing?" she asks with tightness in her teeth.

It is a tightness I can translate, like I'm fluent in this a second language. I know when she is tight like a rubber band about to snap. I know I have to do something to unwind the rubber band, to loosen it, to stop it from slapping my skin with a sting that will hurt too much.

The snapping makes me cry every time.

I don't want to cry today.

I just want to drink chocolate milk. And write down ingredients

"I'm...," I point to *ZOOM* in the other room and hold up the notecard. "I'm writing down a recipe." I say it cheerfully like she will realize it is a brilliant idea, and I should just carry on. Her face is unmoved so I add, "It has strawberries!"

She does not think it is a brilliant idea.

"You know that's my recipe drawer." Her face flushes. "You can't just go and take whatever you want. Those are my notecards. I bought them especially for a project and now I won't be able to do it because you took one of the cards. You didn't think about that, did you?"

I didn't think of it. But I don't understand how one note card can ruin her project.

"You don't think about anyone but yourself and whatever you want to do. Little princess, hogging everything."

This isn't true. I don't hog everything. I share my things all the time. But I don't remind her of this.

"But I'm the queen of this castle, and I won't let you take things that don't belong to you. Give the card to me!" She grabs the pink notecard I've been clutching in my now shaking hands. She reads it, rolls her eyes with disgust, and rips it up.

I step back, startled, but I nod and let her. I just have to nod and agree and not fight back.

I don't want the rubber band to snap.

"Okay, I'm sorry, I didn't mean to," I say. I'm backpedaling. I'm trying to get back to where I was, with chocolate milk and *ZOOM* and strawberries that didn't make me want to cry.

"Oh, you're *sorry*? You should have known better. You're always taking my things. Getting your dirty little hands into all of my stuff and doing whatever you want with them. Selfish! And you don't learn to stay out of my things no matter how many times I tell you, do you? What do I need to do, lock you up and throw away the key? Would you learn then?"

I'm scared now. I don't know what she plans to do. I don't want her to lock me anywhere.

"I'm sick of this. No one appreciates everything I do for all of you. Just for once, I want someone to appreciate me. Is that so hard?"

I watch her carefully, not knowing what to do. I'm not sure she sees me anymore.

She slams a cupboard shut. She's breathing heavily and shuffling around the kitchen. She slams the still-open recipe drawer. She opens another cupboard and grabs dinner plates from the shelf. Dad will be home soon, and she has to get dinner ready. I'm afraid that she'll break them. I'm afraid she'll throw them on the ground so they shatter. Her anger is the kind that shatters things.

I step back further.

She doesn't say anything else. Just looks so angry that even though I want to hide, I decide to say something to try to smooth things over.

"I appreciate you," I whisper.

I think this will make her calm, to know I care about everything she does for us, but it has the entirely opposite effect. I don't know why, but this is when the rubber band snaps.

"You appreciate me? No, you don't! If you did, you wouldn't take my things and make so many messes and cause so many problems! You will be the death of me." She says this sometimes. I don't know what it means. "If I have to deal with this... this *shit* for one more day, I'm going to go crazy! *You* are driving me crazy." Then, something new, "I just can't do it anymore. I'm done. So, you know what? I'm just going to go. I can't deal with this right now. I can't deal with *you* right now. I'm leaving. You can find yourself another mom."

Her words punch me in the stomach and I can't breathe.

What does she mean, she's leaving? I don't understand. I can't understand. What did I do? I'd better figure out a way to replace her notecard. If I buy her new cards, everything should be fine. It'll be fine. I want to tell her this but I'm afraid to speak.

I stand very still, and I see the look in her eyes and I know. She means it. She's going to leave us. Every alarm goes off in my brain. Every bit of my body is on fire.

I hear *ZOOM* in the background.

I wanted chocolate milk and my favorite TV show, but now I have life or death.

She storms out of the kitchen and goes to the mud room, still yelling something, I'm not sure what, still mad. Mad at me, mad at the notecard, mad at *ZOOM*

I call after her, trying to make it better, "Mom, I'll be better. I promise." I'm telling her I'm sorry, saying that I won't do it again, not ever.

She doesn't turn around.

She gets her heavy purse, always full of any little thing that I could ever need. *Band-Aid®s*, tissues, quarters to play arcade games at Red Robin.

I see her and her purse and the open door to the garage. Her keys are in her hands, and it strikes me like lightning.

No, no, no, no, no, no, no.

The garage door heaves open.

I run up behind her and I slam the button that opens the garage door.

It stops.

*Ha*! I think. She has to stay.

She comes back to the button on the wall, pushes me aside, and presses it again so that the garage door creaks all the way to the top.

I follow her down the two steps from the button to the cold garage floor. I'm barefoot, and I want to go inside. Want both of us to go back inside.

I grab her arm and pull on her purse. She's wearing a blue polar fleece jacket. Sometimes, when I'm cold, I put it on even though it falls to my ankles like a nightgown.

Her hands are freezing.

She pushes me off.

She gets to the car and continues to push me away so she can close the door. I want her to stay, but I don't want to get my fingers slammed in the door so I jump back but I keep begging.

"Mom, please, I'm sorry, don't go. I'm so sorry!!!"

She just looks ahead and turns the key.

The engine starts.

The car moves backward.

She is going.

She is going.

She is actually going.

She is... gone.

My world goes dark.

An abyss opens before me.

In one gulp, it swallows me whole.

I do not know when I come back into the light. When I do, all I know are big sobs and fast, fast breaths and pain in my chest and shaky hands and panic. I do not know what happened while I was gone.

I think I screamed.

I think I yelled, "Mom!!!" to the van as it disappeared.

I think I ran into the house and picked up the phone.

I think I didn't know who to call.

I think I wanted to call 911, but I couldn't do that, could I?

This isn't an emergency but... but... this *is* an emergency!

I think I ran around the house, looking for... her? Looking for anything, looking for something to hold onto.

I think I didn't find anything. Or anyone.

I think I couldn't catch my fast breaths going in and out and in and out and in until I was dizzy.

When I come back to myself, I'm standing in the sunroom again, sobbing. I reach out and touch the wall so I don't fall.

I sink to my knees and I sit on the ground.

The carpet is short and almost-but-not-quite scratchy, speckled with brown and white and gray and orange flecks.

I put my hands on it.

I stare at it.

It's like a kaleidoscope, but I don't like the colors.

My breath is getting slower.

I'm still dizzy.

The world is still dark.

She is still gone.

I hear the garage door grind open and I fly to the door.

She's back!

"Mom?"

But... no.

She's not.

She's not back.

I breathe fast again.

In and out and in and out and in.

That's Dad's car.

Dad is home.

The fast breath doesn't stop because he isn't Mom, but now, there is someone here I can reach out to, hold onto. He looks confused by his crying kid, but as he gets out of the car with his lunch box and jacket, I tell him. I tell him about chocolate milk and *ZOOM* and strawberries and the notecard and Mom and how she drove away even when I begged her not to.

"Let's go inside, kiddo," he says, softly, like a blanket wrapping around me.

We walk inside and he puts his lunch box and jacket on the counter.

He walks into the dining room and sits down in his spot at the far side of the table. Behind his spot, there is a big window. The window looks out on a big purple butterfly bush. When springtime comes, the butterflies come to it, and Mom always calls me over when she sees one. Then I run to the window and we watch them together.

There are no butterflies today.

I crawl onto his lap like I'm still little. He brushes the tears from my cheeks with the pads of his thumbs. These are the thumbs that take care of the garden and the orchard and the dahlias. They're calloused because he works so hard. He's good at taking care of everything. He likes to grow things, and I like to help him. He says I have a green thumb but I've checked and my thumb is just small and sort of pink. In the summer, when the vegetables are big and ready, we put them in a wheelbarrow and bring them to the neighbors.

There are no vegetables right now.

"Is she... is she... is she... ever... ever... coming... b-back?"

I cannot catch my breath, and I cannot catch my mother, and I cannot catch the earth that has fallen underneath me.

I'm just falling and falling and falling and falling.

"She has to," he says into the darkness.

His words catch me.

Because now I'm curious.

"Why?"

"Well! Because she didn't bring any underwear with her."

He smirks his silly Dad smirk as if he has solved a riddle.

He's right.

He did solve the riddle.

This makes sense.

She has to come home.

She didn't bring any underwear.

She does come home.

I don't think it's because she didn't have any underwear. I think it's just that she didn't have anywhere else to go. She says she went to get a treat at Dairy

Queen, then she came home. Just a little outing to get a late afternoon snack, she says.

I wish she would have taken me with her.

But she made it very clear she needed to get away from me.

We pretend it never happened.

We pretend it was just an afternoon trip to get a snack.

We pretend it wasn't the end of the world.

A week passes. Or two?

It might only be a few days.

Then, she gets Big Mad again.

This time, it is about a wooden spoon.

Dad put it in the wrong drawer.

From my room, I hear slammed cupboards and raised voices.

I can hear her say she's going to leave.

Now I am the one who feels as tight as a rubber band that's been wound tight, tight, tighter.

I listen and wait and hope and pray.

They keep fighting.

Then, their voices get quieter.

Then, they talk.

Dad is good at loosening her rubber band, too.

I like when he does it so I don't have to.

She decides to stay.

For now.

But a few days later, she is yelling about something again, and I hear the garage door open, so I run to the window.

It's just my brother going out to shoot hoops.

We spend days and days and days like this. Her getting mad, me watching out the window for her car to leave the garage. I try to stay out of her way, but I watch and listen and wait.

I don't keep track.

I can't keep track.

I just know that it is constant.

I do not get a break.

I do not sleep.

I follow her like a shadow.

I listen for loud words.

I choke back my fast breaths and I hold back my tears.

I pretend it isn't always the end of the world in our house.

Days and days and days like this, living at the end of the world, on the edge of the abyss, in my dark closet, alone.

Twenty years later, I come home from a long day and drop my keys into the clay bowl by the door. I set my shoes on the shoe rack, and I hang my rain jacket on the hook. The dogs eagerly greet me, and I take time to say hello to both of them. We do this cute thing where they each like to jump up for a hug. It goes like this:

They run to the door. I say, "Hello, hello, I love you too, I missed you so much!" They wag their little tails and exercise serious restraint to not jump up on me. They know that they need to sit so they put their wiggling butts on the floor. Then, I say, "Okay, can I have a hug?" I pat my stomach and the bigger one jumps up to put her paws where I was just patting, and I wrap my arms around her. "Okay, off," I say—their command to get down. Then, it's the little one's turn. I bend my knees because he is so small and he puts his paws on my knees. I give him a little hug, too.

We do this, every day, whenever I come home.

This is all I've ever wanted.

Because here?

Here, I am safe.

Here, I am calm.

Here, I am happy.

It is so nice to come home.

I don't have plans for the evening so I ask myself what I want to do.

"We can do whatever you want, babe," I say to myself. I feel excited by the prospect, the freedom, the gentleness, the love.

"I want to lie on the bed watching a comedy special, sipping chocolate milk, and petting my dogs," I say back to myself.

That sounds about right. I am a big fan of my bed, stand-up comedy, chocolate milk, and popcorn.

It will be a perfect night.

I walk into my small kitchen. My bare feet step on the cushioned mats I bought for when I'm standing by the stove or washing the dishes. I stand on my tip-toes to reach the highest shelf, taking down a purple Mason jar. I also grab a lid.

I take almond milk from the top shelf and Hershey's chocolate syrup from the door of the fridge. I lazily pour a shameful amount of it into the jar. Then, I put the lid on and I shake it. That's it. The easiest thing I could make in the kitchen, but I still feel like a chef.

Then, with my jar of chocolate milk, I hop onto my lofted bed. I invite the dogs to jump onto it with me and they curl into the pillows beside me. I open my laptop and find the latest unwatched comedy special, my favorite entertainment at the end of a long day. I press play, leaning back into the pillows, and I am immediately enraptured by the laughter, craft, stories, and humanity.

I take a sip of my chocolate milk.

"This is good," I say to the dogs.

Then the voice within me adds, "Actually, no, this is *perfect*."

# Halo Halo Means Mix Mix—
# A Short Story with Recipes

## Rebecca Mabanglo-Mayor

Sometimes, when the night is hot and sticky, the air still and thick, I spill out of bed, my feet seeking the coolest spots on the hardwood floors as I pad to the kitchen. The light from the overhead fan leaves blurred shadows on the cabinets as I stand by the stove and reach for a binder between the toaster and the crock of kitchen tools. The blue canvas cover bears the tattoos of late night doodling and grease stains; its corners tattered and grey. As I thumb through the recipes, I tell myself I'm searching for something cool to drink, but I already know what I'm going to make. This is just the ritual I've formed over the past months, when the nights turn long and empty. Empty except for Jerry's gentle snoring and the sound of pages turning in a book that is my only permanent possession in his apartment.

## Chicken Adobo - (Dad's recipe)

> 1 chicken, separated
> 1 cup soy sauce
> 1 cup vinegar
> 1 head garlic, mashed
> 1/2 cup lemon juice or wine
> pepper and paprika

Sauté chicken pieces to brown. Add soy, vinegar, garlic and wine. Season. Bring to a boil, then simmer at least one hour or until meat falls off the bone. Serve with rice. Always serve Filipino food with rice. Rice is the center of the Philippines. Barangays have thrived or failed because of rice. Never waste rice. Make it into fried rice with eggs and bacon and maybe some frozen vegetable, but never throw it out. Eat it and remember that there are children still starving back home.

When I was growing up, I had a game I used to play with people who got too nosy.

"Where are you from?" they'd ask, looking at my straight black hair and milk chocolate skin.

And I'd say, "Queen Anne." And they would laugh uncomfortably. "No, I mean, you know, what nationality are you?"

"Guess," I'd say.

"Chinese? Japanese? Hawaiian? Indian?" They would shrug.

"East or Native?" I'd ask and they would shift their feet and smile. "My name's Ellen." I'd say, "Ellen Christine Zamora. It's nice to meet you."

But in my head there'd be the litany of names we call ourselves: Pinay, Pilipina, Filipina, Pilipino, Filipino. And the names they called us before: Brown brother, Flip. And the politically correct ones: Filipino American, Pinoy, Fil-Am.

I prefer American, but my family still calls me Baby.

## Pancit - (Mom's Recipe)

Pancit is easy. You just cook your onion and your garlic nice then add your meat, chicken is good and cheap too, all chopped up, and you cook it good so there's no blood. Then you put in your vegetables. You know, celery, carrots, bean sprouts, things you like, and add a can of chicken stock to the pot. Let it boil then put your noodles in but keep stirring them around and around to keep them from sticking. You don't want anything sticky. When that's done, you put in your little shrimp, the cooked kind, just at the end so they don't fall apart. Then you put it on a nice platter with lemon. It should be limes, you know, calamansit, but they don't have that here in the States, not even at the commissary. So you have to make do with the lemons. They're too tart but okay. You have to learn how to make do—especially when you get married. Things don't always happen the way you want them to, but when you marry it's too late to change things, so you'd better be sure. You don't want to be like those other girls who leave their husbands. Except maybe if he beats you. Then I guess it would be okay to go. But you wouldn't marry anybody like that, would you?

Jerry was a Junior and I was a Sophomore the year we met. Marisol had convinced us both that it was a solemn obligation for us to help her with Filipino Heritage month activities. We both managed to dodge the dance festival and the parade around campus, but there was no getting around her about fixing food. In the gathering space of St. Philomena's Church, I tried not to laugh out loud as I watched Jerry try to roll the thin lumpia wrapper around the filling he had generously slopped on its surface. Tongue poked between his full lips, he resembled a third grader trying to master the curls of cursive writing. His unpracticed fingers tore the fragile wrapper in three places, spilling ground meat and vegetables all over his lap as he tried to fold the edge underneath.

"Next time try it with less filling," I said, handing him a paper towel.

"Thanks," he murmured. "My aunties usually took care of this stuff. I just like eating them."

"Me too." I said and deftly turned the edge of my rolled lumpia over and placed it on a waiting tray. "Only three or four hundred left to go!"

"Why did we volunteer to help with Fil-Am fiesta again?" he asked as he gamely grabbed another wrapper with a smile.

My eyes never left the smoothness of his narrow hands.

Mom said she went shopping with Auntie Fe today to find a dress for the wedding. She didn't sound very happy about the trip. I can just imagine...

"So Lena's finally coming home? For Baby's wedding!" says Fe, sliding another dress down the rack. She hears her sister sigh in agreement beside her. "Ooo, now this one would look nice for the wedding." She holds up a mint green chiffon dress accented with silver beads for Mom to see.

Mom reaches into the collar and pulls out the price tag. "Too much!"

Fe nudges her with her elbow. "Too much! How can you say? Not too much for your daughter, hmmm? Bad luck to put a price on such a happy day." She slides the dress back on the rack and begins thumbing through the next set of size 10's.

"It should be Lena getting married, not Baby," says Mom turning away. "Too young!"

"Jerry will take care of her," says Fe looking over a blue dress with green trim. Nah, too much like a navy uniform, she thinks putting it back. "He's got a good job with a future. She'll have enough money to take care of you when you're old. And most of all he's one of us and that's what's important."

I first met Juan Tamad when I went to Pike's Place Market to talk with Lola Mimi about the wedding flowers. He lounged behind the mounds of lilies, carnations, and statice that Mimi and her daughter were painstakingly winding into stunning bouquets. FOB, I thought, he's Fresh Off the Boat. Looking a few years younger than Dad, Juan had that unmistakable Filipino posture, one foot on a bench, body leaning forward propped up by an elbow on his knee. His dark skin shone with sweat and a towel was draped over one shoulder. His black hair was slicked back in a duck-tail hairstyle and he wore faded blue jeans and a white t-shirt. He jutted his chin at me in greeting and smiled. I wondered if he knew how to speak English at all and hoped I'd be able to get my order done before he decided to start talking to me.

## Lumpia - (*Lola* Mimi's Recipe)

Lumpia is one of those "left over" foods. The kind of food you make when there's nothing special to eat, but there's all this stuff in the fridge that needs to be eaten. Back home, of course, there weren't any refrigerators, but I bet it's like the Chinese fried rice, you know, throw it all together and cook it good in oil. Makes a nice meal when you don't have much to share with compadres that come for a visit. But it takes a long time, yah? To cook it and roll them up. It's better to have a whole bunch of aunties over to talk while you roll them. Then you can get all the good gossip from the family you only see on the holidays. You hear about the babies coming or how well someone is doing at school. Or maybe you finally find out about how come Boy doesn't come around anymore. Or what happened with Glory's doctor's appointment. All of you around the table, the windows steamy, and the stories even more so. Yah, it's good to make lumpia once in a while.

Juan told me a story the other day when he asked me to take him shopping for shoes. He said that before the Spanish came, Pinays were strong women, not the weakling flowers you see in the tin-types. They were strong warrior women who fought next to their brothers in heroic battles, who remembered the stories of their ancestors and would recite them after a hunt, who had magic to turn skirts into trousers and daggers into spears. Women who would fight for their tribe, then marry the leader of the opposing tribe to assure peace. Women who knew that power came from honor and honor came from action.

He asked me if I was a warrior woman or a Spanish sampuagita and I could not say for sure.

## Lechon - (Juan Tamad)

First you have to catch the pig. Make sure he's a nice, big fat one, so everybody in the village can come to eat. Run him around the house to make him feel like he might just get away. But when you catch him, kill him quick. No need to let him suffer. Keep the blood in a pan for dinuguan later. Let the men remove the entrails and singe the hair off the pig. Dig a pit. A big pit. And line it with banana leaves and hot rocks. Put the pig inside and cover him with more banana leaves and hot rocks. Bury him all day. If he's really big, let him cook all night. Doesn't matter. The longer he cooks, the more tender he'll be. Make a big show of taking him out of the ground. A miracle! Food from the earth! The smell will carry for miles so everybody will know it's time to eat. So good! So crispy! So juicy! Make a big pot of sauce out of the liver. Make sure you put garlic in it. Lots of garlic. And vinegar so it will keep. Oh, I'm so hungry! Make sure you save the head for the mayor. He never comes to village except when there's lechon. Let him make speeches. Let him make promises. The rest of us will eat. Just be sure you leave me the ears. I love the ears. So crunchy and when I eat them I learn the secrets only pigs hear. People will tell them anything.

*Lola* Mimi and Auntie Fe stopped winding the bouquets of flowers they held in their hands and looked at each other, lips pressed tight. We were finishing up the last of the bridesmaid bouquets and I mentioned that I had taken Juan Tamad to buy shoes for the wedding.

"You shouldn't take him around places alone, Baby," my mother said, snipping rose stems. "Next time be sure Jerry goes with you."

"Why?" I said, looking at each woman in turn. "He's harmless."

"He's up to no good," said Auntie Fe, clicking her tongue. "Always stirring up trouble back home in the province. Our grandpa almost took a machete to him when he stole our carabao during wartime."

"He brought it back," my mother said smiling. "And even bought us kids milk candy on market day."

Auntie Fe looked at my mom sidelong and snorted.

"Wartime?" I asked confused. "He doesn't look that old."

"Juan's old," said Mimi, taking up a handful of statice. "Old and wily like a morning glory vine. You think you pull that weed up and it just tunnels underground to come up another place."

The other women nodded, stifling more talk of Juan in the rustle of fresh cut roses and crisp ribbon.

## Lumpia - (Auntie Fe's recipe)

1 package lumpia wrappers
1 pound ground beef
1 package green beans, the big kind, sliced thin
4 cloves garlic mashed
4 potatoes cooked and cubed
1 can garbanzo beans or 1 package bean sprouts (tastes better)

Brown the meat and garlic, drain. Then add beans and potatoes until cooked. Add seasoning. Drain. Fill lumpia wrappers and fry in oil. Serve hot to your compadres with a mixture of soy sauce, vinegar, pepper and garlic. Bite the end of the lumpia and blow gently between your teeth to help it cool. Spoon the suka sauce into the open end letting the garlic and soy stain your fingers with its taste and smell. Laugh at yourself for trying to be different when it's really not so bad to be the same.

If you asked me when I fell out of love with Jerry, I couldn't tell you. Maybe it's when we got our apartments in Seattle, separate, of course, since we weren't technically married. Yet he always expected me to stay over at his place and he hardly visited mine. Maybe it's when I told him I wanted to wait to have kids and he gave me that "look" that reminded me of Dad, eyes wide with disbelief and dark eyebrows arching. Maybe it's his certainty that everything will be perfect once I'm Mrs. Jerry Aguinaldo. His wife. Mother of his kids. Hostess of his office parties. His stand-in at church events.

"Baby," he'd say. "I'll take good care of you."

Couldn't tell you when I fell out of love. But I know it's true.

## Dinuguan - (Auntie Fe's Recipe)

1/2 pound pork intestine
1/2 pound pork heart
1/2 pound pork liver
1/2 pound pork meat
1 1/2 cups pork blood
1/2 cup vinegar
1 onion, some peppers, and seasonings

Boil meat until tender. Keep 3 cups of the broth. Cut up the meat into nice pieces then sauté the onion with some garlic until it's browned. Add the meat back in and pour in the blood and vinegar. Let it cook a while, until it's done then add the peppers and seasonings. You can substitute chicken if you'd like. You know, you used to call it chocolate meat when you were little. You hated the stuff. But now, you see, bring it all together, all the things that mean the most in life, and cook it with sweet blood and tangy vinegar. Add little onion and garlic; they're the spicing of our souls. Then you see that sacrifice is a good thing to feed your family. They can thrive on that.

Jerry and I had coffee downtown the other day to finalize our honeymoon plans. I tried to pick a fight with him about it; I still wanted to go to Alaska instead of Hawaii. But he didn't take the bait, saying he knew I was under a lot of pressure and not to worry, he'd take care of everything, as usual. I looked down at my coffee cup and noticed the figure of a man painted on our table.

"Coffee gods," I whispered.

"What?" said Jerry not looking up from his day-planner.

"Juan Tamad said these guys on the table were coffee gods. Old friends from back home. He laughed and said he couldn't believe they'd become famous over here. Something about them being big mouthed, big shots, who talked until dawn and didn't share their whiskey with him."

"That old guy is weird, Elly. Don't listen to him."

Jerry was probably right, but I couldn't help but notice the generous smiles of the painted gods. Smiles like I had never seen curve Jerry's lips.

Jerry first met Juan at Lola Mimi's summer party at Gasworks Park. Juan was running around the park with the kids trying to get this paper sack kite he'd made into the air. The kite didn't even have a tail and the string was too short, but that didn't seem to matter to Juan. He zigzagged the field, jumping up and down once in a while to give the kite a lift. On one of his passes, he nearly ran into Jerry and me as we made our way to the picnic tables.

"Whoa! Watch it!" said Jerry trying to keep my bowl of salad from spilling on the ground. Juan stopped abruptly in front of Jerry and smiled broadly, a gaggle of children pooling at his hips. When Juan met Jerry's eyes though, his own narrowed and his smile became stiff.

"You cannot erase your family and remake yourself with wealth," said Juan as he fingered the kite string. Turning to me, he placed the string in my hands. "Becoming his jewel will only diminish your worth."

I wonder what Jerry could be dreaming now, with the deepness of the night still to come. There was a time when I knew our dreams were the same, that I could count on him to know my thoughts so well he would have a problem solved for me by morning. He's good at giving answers, especially to his bride-to-be, but tonight I doubted that he would even comprehend the question I wrote on the inside front cover of my recipe binder.

Do you know who truly I am?

## Halo Halo - (Ellie's Special Recipe)

Shave the ice carefully, letting the soft curls gather in a basin near the block of ice. Don't use crushed ice, it's not the same and the Halo Halo will not taste right. Gather the ice with your hands and let it slide into your tall glass. Watch the air condense on the outside of the glass, concealing the special drink you are creating. Spoon the coconut sport and sweet bean mixture from the bottle you've found in the back of the refrigerator, a forgotten remnant of a dinner you'd planned weeks ago for your fiancé. Open a can of creamed corn and while you spoon the yellow lumps into the glass, remember how your fiancé thinks vegetables don't belong in cocktails. Recall that he'd never asked why you liked corn in your Halo Halo. Remember that there should be the coconut liqueur called Inebra in this drink. You could have gotten a bottle on that the trip to the Philippines you cancelled after he asked you to marry him. Instead, pour chilled evaporated milk over the layers of ice and fruit. Let its thick whiteness cover it all. Take a long-handled spoon, twirl it slowly into the depths of the glass. Watch the reds, yellows, and creams mix themselves into a salty sweet salve to ease the deepness of the night.

# Anam Cara

## Linda Morrow

*Love allows understanding to dawn, and understanding is precious. Where you are understood, you are at home. Understanding nourishes belonging. When you really feel understood, you feel free to release yourself into the trust and shelter of the other person's soul.*

*Anam Cara: A Book of Celtic Wisdom*
—John O'Donohue

Stories. All families have them. Tales birthed in innocence, which over time develop muscle and power with each retelling until they gain the status of LEGEND. All you need to know about the one I'm about to share is the seed was planted long ago on a mid-summer day, sprouted and grew deep roots, and then blossomed decades later tended by a girl and a boy representing the third generation of two tightly entwined families.

The maternal grandmothers met on an August afternoon in 1941 in a Massachusetts town while pushing their first-born progeny, both girls, in their respective baby buggies. As the mothers' friendship flourished, so did the connection between the little girls. Jane and I played together in sandboxes, attended each other's birthday parties, shared giggles and secrets. We were as much at home in each other's houses as we were in our own. We graduated high school in 1958 and college in 1962. The ink on Jane's diploma from Skidmore College had barely dried when she married Kevin Murphy, her sweetheart since junior high. By the time my wedding to Roger Cohen occurred the following summer, Jane and Kevin's daughter, Jamie, was several weeks old.

Fast forward to the fall of 1966 when our first child, Steve was born. By now Jane had three "ankle biters." Jamie, Heather, and Sean Murphy formed a toddler trio when they first laid eyes on him. Steve's siblings followed; Michael in 1967, Josh in 1970. By this time, I knew my friendship with Jane was special, although I had no words to describe our bond. But I never suspected a similar relationship would develop between two of our children. Both families owned homes in Marshfield, Massachusetts, a seaside town thirty miles south of Boston. Our six kiddos were a tight pack moving freely between each other's houses, as Jane and I had once done. But within the group the connection between Heather and Steve ran especially deep.

Long before she could have had any understanding that Steve had been born with Down syndrome, Heather somehow sensed Steve's uniqueness. She turned toward him with unwavering devotion and commitment. As a three-year-old she stood beside Steve's crib singing songs to him. She cheered him on when he took his first shaky steps shortly after he turned two. During summers at the town beach, Heather built sandcastles with Steve, and sat beside him at the water's edge as waves tickled their toes. In winter, when storm-driven snow piled up outside, she read stories to her buddy while logs snapped and popped in our fireplace. But when I think back on their shared childhoods, one memory stands out.

In 1976, as the calendar flipped from August to September, Steve began thinking and talking about his 10th birthday.

"Heather come my party," he announced to me one afternoon.

"I don't know, Steve," I answered. "Remember, we live far away from Heather now."

Five years ago, our families had been rent asunder when my husband Roger accepted an assistant professorship at the State University of New York's Stony Brook campus on Long Island. But the 150 miles separating the Cohen and the Murphy clans meant nothing to Steve. He simply wanted Heather beside him on his big day.

Steve's lower lip stuck out and he crossed his arms over his chest while repeating, "Heather come my party." He paused and then added, "Tank you."

I knew he meant, "Please" not "Thank you." Steve understood everything said to him, but his ability to speak his thoughts lagged far behind. He still mixed up certain words that were closely connected. You just had to know "Steve Speak."

"OK Steve, I'll try, but I can't promise anything."

Steve's transition from single to double digits represented a huge milestone and his fervent desire to include Heather in this celebration had sparked an idea in me; one which could turn Steve's wish into a learning opportunity for him.

When we'd moved to Long Island, I'd tried to enroll Steve in the town's local elementary school; the one Michael, and later Josh, attended. But my continued efforts had been repulsed at every turn by an established system which grouped "retarded children" in segregated classrooms in a centralized location. Thus, I looked for any opportunity to use our home and family to organically teach Steve many skills I felt he needed to learn. But before I could move forward with my current idea I needed to make certain Heather and the rest of the Murphy family would be able to attend Steve's party. That evening I made a long-distance call to Jane and pitched Steve's idea. Several days later, when she returned my call and guaranteed Heather's presence, I activated my "lesson plan."

The next afternoon I approached Steve. "If you want to invite Heather to your birthday party, you need to let her know. Why don't you find Michael and see if he will help you write a letter to Heather?"

Michael, a fourth grader with wavy auburn locks and a slight build, agreed. He'd adjusted well to his peculiar position in our family: a middle child, but the oldest developmentally. Most of the time he enjoyed being the "big" brother. Within minutes the boys gathered at the kitchen table. Steve clutched a tablet of drawing paper, Mike a pencil and tin of well-used crayons. I shot a warm smile and a quick nod in Michael's direction.

"OK, Steve, what do you want to say to Heather?" asked Michael.

"I say, 'Heather, come my party. I be ten. Peas.'"

Michael helped his brother separate a single sheet from the pad and used his pencil to lightly write Steve's message in large block print. As he reached for the container of worn waxed sticks, I pulled from behind my back a new, and highly coveted, set of fluorescent crayons purchased especially for this project. I handed them to Michael. I knew this surprise would engage Steve.

"Wow, these crayons are so neat," exclaimed Michael. "OK Steve, now you pick one and trace over my letters. What color do you want to use?"

A smile filled Steve's face as he grabbed the box from his brother and spilled the contents onto the table. "Pink! My favorite!" replied Steve, as he plucked Ultra Pink from the pile with the stubby fingers of his right hand. The bangs of his fine brown hair almost brushed the table's surface as he lowered his head and peered closely through slanted eyes at each letter. Warmth spread though me and I moved away to let "school" begin. Quiet ensued, broken only by Michael's murmured encouragement.

"Good job, Steve. Nice work. You stayed right on the lines."

Fifteen minutes passed before Steve's proclamation floated out of the kitchen and into the living room where Josh and I sat reading a story. "I done!"

"Mommy," called Michael. "We need a stamp."

Michael copied Heather's address on an envelope, checking with me to make certain he had the correct placement of the return information. Then Steve folded and folded and folded the paper, stuffed his letter into the envelope, and licked it shut. Michael pointed to the envelope's upper right corner as Steve's tongue wet the stamp before placing it down next to his brother's finger and gave it a couple of hard and determined pats with one hand.

The following afternoon Steve patiently waited for the mail truck to pull into our driveway and proudly handed his letter to the postman.

Days passed and Steve seemed to have forgotten about his invitation. Like most kids his age, out-of-sight, out-of-mind. But when the postman knocked on our door one day and announced he had mail for "Master Steven Cohen," Steve tore open the envelope and trembled with excitement while Michael read Heather's reply.

"Yes!" he squealed. "Heather come my party. I so happy!" I swallowed hard and wrapped my arms around my son.

But I soon grew weary of Steve's repetitive questioning. "Today? Today Heather come?"

For my own sanity as much as to teach Steve another lesson, I lined out a calendar, and Josh, a first grader, took on the countdown job. Every morning he and Steve huddled together and Josh supervised while Steve crossed out another box. Then Josh slowly counted out the remaining days while Steve repeated after him "1, 2, 3 ..."

Finally, on Friday evening, September 24, the Murphy's VW bug pulled into our driveway.
"Heather! Heather here," yelped Steve who'd been keeping watch at the front door for more than an hour.

The three brothers raced down the flagstone path and surrounded the car, jumping and waving their hands.

Jane barely had time to exit from the passenger side before Sean hit the lever which sprang the back of her seat forward. Three cramped and sweaty Murphy kids tumbled out. Discarded McDonald®'s wrappings littered the floor of the car and a telltale smudge of ketchup lingered at one corner of Sean's mouth. Roger handed Kevin a cold beer.

"That was one long and noisy drive," breathed Jane as we wrapped our arms around each other.

The following afternoon, the four adults gathered on the back deck where we'd been told we needed to remain until summoned. "We are planning a surprise," explained Jamie. "You can't leave the deck until we call you. NO PEEKING!"

Because I was trying to lose my "childbirth" pounds, I'd made a pitcher of iced tea and stayed away from the beer. Jane and I, still sporting our beach tans, filled our glasses and happily began catching each other up on our lives. But iced tea was decidedly neither Roger nor Kevin's beverage of choice. Instead the guys fought off the Indian summer heat by consuming can after can of the recently introduced Miller Lite. While we waited for the kids to reveal their surprise, Kevin's classic Irish face took on a ruddy glow, while the bushy Afro framing Roger's head gave him a wild-man appearance.

Finally, Michael opened the kitchen door and scurried out on onto the deck. His hair was wet and slicked down to the extent possible given his thick unruly locks. He wore dress pants and a dark colored shirt smartly set off by a fully buttoned white cardigan sweater. "Wow, you look really sharp!" said Jane. "What's the big occasion?"

"You'll see," he giggled. "Would you all please follow me?"

Michael led us through the kitchen, down the entry hall, and out the front door. Four of our dining room chairs sat in a row on the lawn facing the porch. "You need to sit there," he said, pointing to the chairs. "The show is about to begin," he added as he went back into the house. We could hear muffled voices and much laughter. I suppressed a giggle myself. What fun to be here together with Jane and Kevin and our children, who were all scheming to put on some kind of show for us.

The door opened and Michael and Sean emerged, walking side by side. Sean wore khaki trousers, a white shirt and tie, along with a plaid sports coat which strained to enclose his sturdy build. His curly hair was neatly parted to one side and he carried one of Roger's thick black textbooks in one hand. The two boys moved to one side of the porch.

The door parted a second time and there stood Jamie and Josh. Jamie looked stunning in a white dress, with short puffed sleeves, which fell just to her knees; her shoulder-length light-brown hair flowed from beneath a white hat with a wide floppy brim. In her hand she carried a bouquet of artfully arranged weeds enhanced by some pink and purple asters obviously harvested from the neighbor's yard. I hoped they wouldn't notice someone had borrowed a few flowers. Josh was outfitted in the "pretty clothes" he'd requested months ago for his sixth birthday: grey flannel pants, maroon and white checked shirt, maroon bow tie and a maroon plaid jacket. Jamie and Josh stood across from Sean and Michael. The four children stood stiffly and solemnly framing the doorway.

Jane and I looked at each other in amazement. The spectacle of such an elegantly coifed and dressed foursome was the last thing we expected to see from this rambunctious brood—especially the boys.

"Do you have any idea what is going on?" I asked.

Jane rolled her eyes and shrugged her shoulders. "Not a clue."

Roger and Kevin swayed slightly in their seats. I gave both guys a look: *Shape up and don't wreck this.*

At a signal from Jamie, who, as the only teenager was clearly in charge, the kids launched into a barely recognizable rendition of Mendelssohn's *The Wedding March.*

"DUM-DUM-DA-DUM, DUM-DUM-DA-DUM!!!"

The door opened for the final time and Heather and Steve stepped through arm-in-arm. Heather looked elegant in a floor length green satin gown with a matching shawl draped over her slim shoulders. What appeared to be a large cloth napkin secured with bobby pins, sat atop her golden red curls. Steve, ever the cool dude, wore matching light blue bell-bottomed pants and a collarless Beatles-style jacket. A blue dress shirt and navy bow tie completed his outfit. His mop-top haircut covered his ears. A limp sprig of goldenrod peeked out of the breast pocket of his jacket.

We—the audience—burst into applause.

"SH-H-H-H!" admonished Jamie.

Sean stepped down from the porch and faced the happy couple. Given the age and relative inexperience of the officiant, the ceremony was quite brief. "Dearly loved," intoned Sean. "We are gathered here to see the wedding of Heather and Steve." The minister paused, took a deep breath, and continued. "Heather put your hand on this book."

"BIBLE!" corrected Jamie in a loud stage whisper.

"Bible," muttered Sean. "Will you be Steven's wife, have and hold, 'til you're dead?"

"I do!" grinned Heather.

"Steve, put your hand on this book...uh, Bible. Will you be Heather's husband, have and hold, 'til you're dead?"

"I do!" replied Steve, before adding, "I not dead!"

We laughed out loud at this proclamation but quickly regained control of ourselves.

As Michael stepped off the porch and faced the bride and groom, Heather and Steve leaned toward each other as if to kiss. "NOT YET!" yelped the assistant minister, and Heather and Steve drew back. "I announce you wife and husband." Michael bowed slightly from his waist. "You are married. NOW you can kiss!" Heather bent down, Steve stood on tip-toes and the two exchanged cheek kisses. Then Michael turned around, faced the audience and announced with authority, "And now you can clap!"

And we did!

As the adults gathered to congratulate the happy couple and their attendants, Heather confided in me. "We planned this when our families were at Lake Winnipesaukee in June. Jamie and I came up with the idea one night. Then I told Sean and Mike and Josh that we'd do this the next time we were together. We didn't tell Steve though until about an hour ago. We all knew he couldn't keep the idea a secret for very long!"

"Wow, you are all great planners!" I gave her a quick hug. "I wondered how you knew to pack your fancy clothes!"

"Yeah," Heather replied. "Actually, Jamie and I packed Sean's stuff. He said he didn't have to dress up to be the minister. We just ignored him and once he saw your kids in their clothes he was glad we'd brought his things."

Prompted by Steve, everyone began heading inside. A wedding was nice, but after all it was his birthday! Ice cream, cake, and presents were waiting.

I lagged behind, struggling to compose myself. Within seconds a switch in my brain flipped. The sweetness of what I'd just witnessed dissipated, replaced by a weary sadness. I recalled our pediatrician's prognostication given shortly after Steve's birth. *Your son is unlikely to survive his teens.* But suppose Steve did beat those odds? The concept of him marrying was beyond belief. This might be his only wedding.

"Mom, come on," yelled Michael. "It's time for Steve to open presents. We all want cake and ice cream."

"OK, I'm coming." I replied and headed inside.

Later that evening, after our boys were asleep and the Murphy kids lay sprawled on the floor in their sleeping bags in front of the console TV in our family room, Roger and Kevin headed out to a nearby bar. Grateful for some quiet alone time, Jane and I meandered out to the back deck, wine glasses in hand. We sat in comfortable silence as fireflies flickered by and stars twinkled above. I released a deep sigh.

"What's that all about? asked Jane, always on my wave-length.

"Oh, I don't know. Nothing. Everything."

My friend reached over and rested one hand on my arm. "Tell me," she commanded. "I'm, guessing it has something to do with the 'wedding' this afternoon."

Tears filled my eyes. As she had done so many times since Steve's birth, Jane listened with compassion and presence as I shared my concerns about Steve's destiny. She reminded me we can never know the future: not for ourselves; not for our children. Her calmness grounded me. Her friendship sheltered me. My heaviness lifted.

The story of Heather and Steve's wedding continues to be told this day. It has become part of the fabric of our families' history and of the friendship between Jane and me which now spans over three-quarters of a century. Jane continues to live by the Atlantic Ocean, while I live in the Pacific Northwest. But the 3,000 miles between us seem small. Our souls unite us.

Heather and Steve grew into adulthood and shared many milestones together. They danced together at Steve's 21st birthday party. When Heather gave birth to her two daughters, Steve became "Uncle Steve." Steve had an opportunity to visit Heather's workplace in

Western Massachusetts. She gave him a tour of the elegant home she managed for years where "her ladies" with developmental delays lived. Established by a group of parents for their adult daughters, Heather enabled these women to live a rich and dignified life. In 2007 Steve proudly reciprocated with a tour of his newly purchased condo in Burlington, Vermont. At Heather's wedding to her wife many years later, Steve gave the toast and boogied with the brides.

But the memory I most closely relate to the long ago "wedding" in Long Island is Heather's tribute at Steve's celebration-of-life in November 2015 after he had passed away at age 49, too early but long beyond what the doctor had predicted. In her talk, Heather claimed Steve had been her Anam Cara, the Celtic term for soul friend. I'd never heard the term before, but as Heather explained the essence of Anam Cara I gained an important insight. Their friendship was a true blessing. No masks or pretentions existed between them. Each felt understood at a deep level. Each knew they belonged. Each could be who they truly were.

And now I finally have a name for the connection between Jane and myself. From the moment we met as babies, a light broke over us and we too became Anam Cara.

# Finding Avalon

## Cheryl Nelson

"Cheryl, Cheryl," my mom called from the kitchen window. "It's time to come in now. Time for your nap." I was outside in our fenced back yard, turning summersaults. The smell of the fresh, green grass and the warm sun felt great to my little, three-year-old body.

"Ok, Mommy! Coming."

I ran inside the back door and through the kitchen leaving the afternoon light for the coolness of the kitchen. I slowed down as I reached the hallway to my bedroom, my mom following close behind.

"My head hurts, Mommy." I'd felt the ache all morning.

Up I went onto my bed and under the blankets.

"Sweet dreams, Cheryl. Here, I'll tuck you in. Sleep well."

"Ok, Mom."

She gently closed the door as she left my room, and I fell asleep right away.

I woke up tossing and turning in the bed. My head hurt even more than it had before I'd started my nap, and I was hot, really hot. I pushed the blankets off and tried to get my legs out from under the covers so I could cool down. But I couldn't. They wouldn't move.

Panic set in immediately. I tried again to lift one leg, and then the other, from under the blanket, but couldn't move a muscle. Now I screamed. "Mommy! Mommy!" I shouted. "Help, Mommy, help!"

I could hear my mother's rapid footsteps down the hall. She opened the door and rushed into my room.

"What, Cheryl, what is it?" I could see she was trying not to panic too, but her eyes looked scared.

"My legs won't move! Can't move!" I was crying now and thrashing the top part of my body from side to side. The blankets fell away from my legs which lay motionless on the bed.

As soon as she saw my paralyzed legs, Mom ran out of the room and down the hall. I could hear her pick up the phone, dial, and then start talking. Her voice sounded squeaky like she couldn't breathe.

"Please come. My daughter can't move her legs," she said. "Send an ambulance. Our address is ..."

"Mommy," I whimpered. I was so tired. My head hurt worse and worse by the moment and I was beyond terrified. I closed my eyes as tightly as I could. "Mommy." I felt the bed move as she sat next to me.

"Here I am, Cheryl, I'm here."

I don't remember the ambulance ride, but I have a hazy memory of being on a stretcher behind a glass window and looking out to see my mom and later my dad looking in and waving. Then I was moved to a very dark, quiet room. No one else was there.

The nurses came in sometimes to put warm, wet blankets on my back. I remember the blankets felt scratchy. I remember I was in that room for a long time. I don't remember if I slept or ate, but the doctors and nurses later told me that I was there for three days and nights. They told me it was an isolation room, a place where I could get better without making other children sick.

I was three years old when I contracted polio. I pieced together much of the story from what my family told me over the years. My mom told me that they were not allowed to see me during that first week. The doctor ordered that I be put in isolation and the staff was to wear masks, gowns and gloves whenever they entered the room.

They told my mom and dad that the fever, head-ache, and no movement in my legs indicated infantile paralysis, polio. It seems that I caught it while splashing in the water of our neighborhood lake. The polio virus lives in water and attacks a part of the spinal cord that impacts specific limbs or other organs. My legs were paralyzed. And, although I regained use of my left leg fairly quickly, my right leg remained weak. I couldn't move my right foot at all after the onset of the disease, and my leg didn't continue to develop. I left the hospital three months later on crutches and with full leg braces. But my isolation would last long beyond that original seclusion in the contagious disease ward.

I continued in outpatient treatment three times a week after my parents brought me home. I was a small energetic toddler before my illness, but I left the hospital as a prim, determined little girl with her jaw set, dressed in a white, short-sleeved blouse with frill on the sleeves and at the collar. A black, satin jumper, full leg braces. Ugly brown high top shoes completed my look.

The weekly therapy and the surgery helped my body become stronger. By the time I started kindergarten, I wore only a short brace on my right leg. After an operation to fuse my right foot, I didn't have to wear any brace at all. I still walked with a limp, though, and I couldn't run. I could participate in some less vigorous activities by the time I began elementary school, so my parents and doctors were hopeful on my behalf. Compared to other children who contracted polio, I was faring well.

Still, I noticed that I was different from my class-mates. I liked reading and playing board games, though I did try to stay active. I kept up with the neighborhood street hockey the best I could and went to summer camp each year. I even swam the channel which bordered that camp. But unfortunately, the gap between what I couldn't do and what others could do seemed to widen as we grew older. I felt as if I didn't belong, more separated and left behind as each year passed.

Eventually, I left myself behind too. By the time I reached my preteen years, I felt empty inside. There was an outside me who interacted with the world, went to school, and kept up with my daily activities, but the *inside* me grew more and more numb. The more I saw the difference between my peers' ability to engage the world with ease compared to my limping navigation through life, the more I separated from them. I let my mind leave my body as often as I could, until there was nobody home most of the time.

> *I am a Misfit.*
> *There is no place to call my home.*
> *Wandering the world on my own.*
> *Because like the snail,*
> *I carry a shell on my back.*
> *The post cards from my travels*
> *Are written to me alone.*

I took my first drink at 14. Trying to escape my pain any way I could, I drank often. And then I started to cut myself.

> *I rail against you, my body.*
> *Angered by your scars, your too small leg and the limp with which you walk.*
> *I hide in the shadows,*
> *Ashamed to show your too big arms, my intensity, and the rage which fills me.*
> *I feel ostracized from others, separated from you, split and numb enough to seek your destruction.*
>
> *I repeat the mutilation first done by the surgeons.*
> *I mimic the sleep of anesthesia.*
> *I wrap you in plaster cast walls*
> *that works for a while.*

*Until you and I feel the stirring of wakening,*
*See new, green leaves on ancient trees,*
*Shimmering starlight on clear, blue water.*
*The gentle smile of a would-be friend.*
*My yearning to respond, but not wanting to be known.*

*Even so, you walk a thousand miles,*
*Swim hundreds more,*
*Shed forty pounds.*
*And an ounce of blood each month.*
*You care for children, parents and friends,*
*Seek love,*
*Fight for justice and hold each moment in your heart.*

*When will I revel in your beauty, my body?*
*My dear companion,*
*When will we be united?*

When I was twenty-eight, I joined a Catholic community of nuns and traveled to Guatemala and El Salvador where I was an observer at a displaced persons' camp which our community hosted near San Salvador. I was displaced. And they were displaced. I fit in for a while as an ally to the families and a teacher to the children of the camp. However, my sense of isolation and separation from the sisters of the community grew stronger when I returned to the U.S. Over time, I realized that my lifestyle and many of my values and those of the community were not aligned. So, I left the convent at thirty-eight. I wandered restlessly over the next few years seeking a place to call home and some way in which to find peace. But if one cannot find a home in one's self, it is difficult to be at peace.

Eventually, I became the evening and weekend host at a women's retreat center. One of the perks of the job was the ability to attend some of the retreats and workshops offered at the center. I remember one three-day retreat in which we were invited into silent reflection. I took out my sketch pad and charcoal crayon and began to draw. The finished picture was of three ovals, shaded like pearls.

The following Monday, I went to my prescheduled colonoscopy appointment. After my procedure, the nurse told me that the doctor would like to speak with me. My friend, who drove me to the appointment, joined me near the nurse's desk while I waited. Most of the other patients had gone and the clinic was preparing to close when the doctor came out to speak with me.

"We found a mass in your colon. I'm sorry. I'm positive that it is cancer because of its size and shape. But I sent a biopsy to our lab for confirmation."

She handed me a business card.

"I suggest that you make an appointment with our surgeon as soon as possible. She is one of the best."

I nodded and accepted the card. My friend and I stood up. She took my hand as we walked silently through the reception area, out the sliding glass doors and to her car. I remembered the three ovals I had drawn during the retreat reflection, pearls/tumor? Somehow I found the image centering.

*There is no GPS to navigate Cancer's journey.*
*Nothing to say, "Turn left after this MRI.*
*Travel three miles to meet the Doctor.*
*Stop at the insurance desk;*
*Say yes to surgery, ask for further directions,*
*And watch for the dangerous side effects of chemo."*

*There are, if we are fortunate,*
*Those who have travelled this road before.*
*Guides who take our hands and walk with us for a while.*
*We share conversations,*
*Talk about the days when we crave*

*Mom's chocolate chip cookies.*

*We laugh about the crazy mix-up we experience;*
*Putting the left shoe on the right foot,*
*Taking the hospital elevator up, when our destination*
*is down.*
*Chemo brain.*

*There is no universal sign to show us how*
*To say good-bye,*
*To those who do not make it.*
*No definite mile marker for having a body part re-*
*moved,*
*No symbol representing the changes in one's identity.*

*There is only this moment and this place.*
*We stand on the 'X' which marks the spot.*
*The present moment, which tells us:*
*"You are here."*

My new normal? I started teaching preschool while being treated for cancer, and focused on getting well. One day in the midst of this, after years of wandering, I received a newsletter in my email advertising a pilgrimage to "Avalon and Beyond." The newsletter said a small group would visit several sacred sites in Glastonbury, England, seeking healing for those who came along. I was drawn to the idea of traveling to the land of Guinevere and King Arthur, through the ruins of Camelot. My heart needed something and I felt this adventure could offer me hope, though I couldn't see how.

So, I registered, paid my deposit and made plane reservations. Three months later, I joined 13 other pilgrims to Glastonbury, which legend tells us is also known as Avalon, a center of Goddess energy and the isle of priestesses.

After years of feeling reviled and separated from myself, I couldn't have imagined the transformation that lay in front of me, couldn't have foreseen finding my priestess self. By now, I didn't even know what I was missing, only that I'd been gone so long.

We climbed the Tor, an ancient tower believed to be Merlin's home during the time of Arthurian legend. We visited King Arthur's grave, near the Abbey of Glastonbury. We walked the fortress walls, now covered in grass, of what many believe is the site of Camelot. And we stood at the cliffs on the coast of England, a couple of hours from Glastonbury, overlooking the waters of Bristol.

Teacher, author and priestess, Kathy Jones, writes of Avalon on her website In the Heart of the Goddess.

"Lying to the west across the waters, is the Isle of Avalon, where the Goddess reigns forever and the mysteries of women reign."

I and the other travelers had spoken of the spiritual energy and the sense of something beyond our own existence many times during our journeys. I felt this power most strongly on the cliffs, peering out over the seas and into the mist between water and sky.

*I stand at the edge of the cliffs and peer out over the turbulent waters.*
*The dark clouds part for a moment and the rays of the sun shine through.*
*Legend says that just beyond lay the island of the Priestesses,*
*Where the wisdom and power of women is held.*
*I have arrived at the shores of Avalon.*
*I am still for some moments,*
*Holding the posture of a mighty tree,*
*Tall trunk with arm branches stretched toward the Heavens,*
*And feet roots reaching toward Mother Earth.*
*Standing, holding my strength and sustenance,*
*and I give thanks.*

*Mother Earth, bearer of life, I bow to you in gratitude.*
*Father Sky, spirit of freedom, I bow to you in gratitude.*
*Sister Sea, you who hold the mystery of the unknown, I*
*bow to you in gratitude.*
*Brother Wind, you who guides our journey through*
*gentle breezes and fierce storms, I bow to you in grati-*
*tude.*
*All creatures of the earth, sky and sea who share this*
*path with me, I bow to you in gratitude.*

As I stood on the cliffs of Bristol, drawing energy up from the earth through my imperfect legs, filling my heart, I took a moment on our tour and paused in silent reverence. I had a sash with three pouches tied around my waist. Each pouch was tied to the sash with a ribbon of a different color. I had brought the sash with me from Central America, to the U.S., and now to Avalon, the mantel of my long quest for peace. The pouches were filled with ashes, representing the burdens in my life which I had written on paper and burned during a women's gathering in the Pacific Northwest some months earlier.

Now, feeling strong and well-grounded for the first time in a long time—maybe forever, I reached to the sash wrapped at my waist. I undid the first of the three pouches and loosened the silver strand of the first pouch. It must have cut my hand because I began to bleed just a little. I let the blood run freely. The ashes in this represented the burned images of past wounds:

The times spent in the hospital; as a child with polio,
The surgeries following the illness.
The tumor removed when I was 54.
The psych unit at University Hospital.
The drunken follies.
The misuse of over-the-counter drugs.
Cutting my wrists.
The scream of the ambulance.

Waking up strapped to the hospital bed.
The doctor's anger with me for scaring my parents.
The broken relationships and the ones that never came to be.

I cast the ashes upon the sea and prayed.

> *Wind, Ruah, Spirit, Fierce and Tender Healer of Avalon,*
> *Return these embers to me transformed that I may express compassion*
> *For myself.*
> *And for those whom I encounter.*
> *Blessed be.*

Next, I reached to my sash and untied the second of the pouches there. The strand tying this pouch was red. Red for the fierce will to live. Red for the fiery passion burning in my heart to stay alive. Red to enflame my own spark, to inspire the spark in others. This velvet container held ashes representing fear.
Fear of rejection,
Of judgment,
Of criticism and being excluded,
Fear of my own limitations and self-loathing,
Of unworthiness
And being considered damaged goods.
Fear of never being enough
And most of all fear of never being fully seen, heard, and accepted for who I wholly am.
Then I cast these ashes of fear upon the sea too.

> *Wind, Ruhah, Spirit, and our Lady of Avalon,*
> *Fierce/Tender Healer,*
> *Return them to me transformed.*
> *That I may walk with myself*
> *And with others in strength and courage.*
> *Blessed be.*

The red ribbon from the pouch of passion fell loose in my hand now. And finally, I embraced—in myself—and others—the courage to live lives from the heart. I whispered my wishes for those I cared about.

> *Tragedy and hope in El Salvador.*
> *Families fearful of having loved ones disappeared by the army in Guatemala.*
> *The solemn presence in the streets of the Mothers in the community.*
> *Names of those who were dead,*
> *The crowd shouting Presente!*
>
> *The beauty of the Central American countryside.*
> *The kindness of strangers preparing food for refugees returning*
> *From the mountain caves.*
>
> *Returning home to the States and then*
> *To the origins of the Sisters of Peace.*
> *Entering and exiting. Obeying others*
> *And finally following my own call*
> *Toward life.*

I reached for the third and final pouch and slowly untied the yarn of blue to pour the ashes into my hand. These ashes were the last remnants that I carried from the women's ritual back in the Northwest. They represented stagnation, never moving, never changing, smothered growth.

Never risking sharing the depth of myself
Holding those vulnerable parts of myself
Behind a wall of silence.
The times when I remained trapped in fear.
Times when I drowned my feelings through drinking.
Or ran away from conflict and healthy communication.

The times I chose what I considered safe, rather than taking a leap of faith.

I cast these ashes of stagnation and false security upon the sea.

> *May the wind, Ruah, Spirit, the Lady of Avalon, Fierce and Tender Healer,*
> *Return them to me transformed that I may walk in peace.*
> *Blessed be.*

The strand of blue fell gently into my palm.

> *This, the color of the river of passage which*
> *Flows through all. It is the transition and the peace*
> *Which comes while resting upon the waters.*

I gazed again across the dark waters toward a parting in the clouds. It was as if I could see beyond the veils of time and space and there the Fierce/Tender healer, the Lady of Avalon, was my companion. I hadn't expected this, but here we were. Together. I in myself, she in me, and I in her.

> *I shift my focus to the divine within.*
> *The image of the Lady*
> *In my heart.*
> *I look inward and see*
> *In my mind's eye that*
> *The strands of yarn have*
> *Twined. Frayed threads*
> *Of a life,*
> *Woven into*
> *One braided band.*
> *I am whole.*
> *Blessed be.*

# At the Well

## Cami Ostman

I sit on a cold stone bench in front of the Chalice Well. A pilgrim in Glastonbury. My life is undergoing a hard transition, and I'm so weary I can barely keep my eyes open. I've come on vacation to rest—to this spot in England where feminine power is purported to magically infuse and inspire weary souls. As a literature major in college almost thirty years ago, I was introduced to King Arthur and to Glastonbury, and ever since then I've wanted to come.

Here in Glastonbury, in the Roman era, this town was a seaport. Mists rolled in off the ocean and Arthurian legend says that when the land was thick with wet clouds, a passageway to Avalon opened up. Avalon, a mystical island where Merlin's wisdom was welcomed, was ruled by the priestesses of the Goddess, while England, on the other side of the mist, was a Christian land.

The Christian legend says that water flows continuously from this well I sit beside now because Joseph of Arimathea—an uncle to Jesus—buried the chalice Jesus drank from at the Last Supper right here. At this very spot. Now healing waters flow—always and forever. People come to drink this water when they need restoration.

I need restoration. I'm desperate for it, and I don't care if it comes from miraculous Christian water or Goddess power bubbling up from an endless underground spring. But I don't really have much hope the water here at the Well will do any good. What I really need is answers to the questions I'm grappling with. Mostly, I want to know if I'll be okay—if I'll ever feel strong again.

I've just left a marriage to a man I loved. But I felt I *had* to leave it, and I didn't want to ignore what my body was telling me—even though my body doesn't really seem to be any happier now that the marriage is over.

Just a few months earlier I walked away from a home I loved, a community I'd built over the course of a decade, and a geographical landscape that otherwise thrilled and satisfied me. But I knew that if I had to be directed one more time where to walk or how much pressure to use on the gas pedal or how to load the dishwasher, I would implode. If I had to endure one more outburst when I didn't please or comply, if I had to hear another unkind interpretation of my behavior, I would crumble into a shadow of who I wanted to be— who I imagined I *could* be at my core. I was slowly losing myself into an ugly, ingrown cave of self-loathing. And my body began to hurt. My chest tightened and my belly and limbs and lower back ached. I knew I had to go.

But as I sit here on a mild day in April, light breeze blowing from the north, welcome shade from well-tended trees shielding me from the sun, grief closes in, and I wonder if everything was really so bad that I needed to sneak away, surreptitiously leaving my sweet hometown to rent myself a furnished apartment in the big city a hundred miles away. Did I really need to text my husband, instead of telling him in person, that I wasn't coming back? Was I so frightened of his anger that I had to blow up my whole life? Every relationship has trouble, right? Everyone gets mad. Maybe I was being unfair. What did I want anyway? Perfection? Could I have stayed if I'd been stronger? More forgiving?

And did it help to leave? I'm more afraid now than ever. Afraid about supporting myself. Afraid of being alone. Of fucking up my life. I miss who I used to be before I was afraid.

Now I stretch out on the cement bench next to the opening of the Chalice Well, letting its coolness soothe me, and I wonder what I thought I'd find here. What do I really need to recover... or find... or create in order to be someone I like? Someone who moves through the world with joy?

I close my eyes and a recent memory replays in my mind. Traveling through South America. We were sitting at a bus stop. He was asking me to help him read the symbols on a map he was studying, but the map was too far away for me to see. I knew that if I reached over to take the map from him, he would accuse me of taking over, so I simply said, "I can't see it from here."

Silence. A few moments passed.

"How about this one? Can you tell what this symbol is?"

I repeated my statement. "I can't see from here. It's too far away."

And then, without my seeing it coming, like the car that T-bones you from out of nowhere, he snapped. Some sudden imperative to bring me into submission seemed to emerge. A need to make me understand I wasn't doing something he wanted me to do. Read his mind? Make him feel loved? I couldn't guess. He shoved the map to within two inches of my nose. "How about now, huh?"

Fear flooded through me, but I sat perfectly still. He'd thrown things before, pounded angry fists next to me too close for comfort, even badgered me to within an inch of my patience about how to do household tasks, but he'd never violently gotten right into my space like this. This was new. And I wasn't sure how far his rage would take him, so I held my breath and waited. I could feel the eyes of another waiting passenger who sat in my peripheral vision. Shame made me blush. Remaining as calm as I could, I nearly whispered, "Well, now it's too close for me to read."

My statement enraged him further, and he began moving the map forward and backward in front of my face saying, "How about here? Or here? What's the perfect distance for you?"

Eventually I turned my face to look at him—slowly, in a measured motion—and said, "If you give me the map, I can try to help you read it."

This calmed him—I don't know why—and he relinquished the map to me so we could resolve the question of what the symbols represented.

By the time we got on the bus, I had decided to leave the marriage.

Now, with this memory, one I have replayed almost daily for months, I let tears stream out of my eyes into my hairline. I adored this man—who could be as kind and beautiful as he could be aggressive—but I couldn't risk something like that happening again. That's what you call a red flag, isn't it? You should listen to them, shouldn't you? I'd ignored plenty over the years. But that moment was clear.

Still, now I feel adrift. I left because of fear, but I don't have any clear path for my life without him. And, in spite of my resolve never to be treated thus again, I miss him. Terribly. I miss coffee in bed in the morning watching the news, the thoughtful gifts he often gave me, the friends we shared in common. And I miss having a partner who took care of most of the practical aspects of our life together. Maybe that's what he was angry about. I don't know.

The Glastonbury air smells like freshly cut grass. I remember to be grateful that, whatever troubles I may have, I don't have hay fever. That's a good thing because I plan to stay here today as long as it takes for the heaviness I feel to shift—or until the groundskeepers kick me out.

The presence of other pilgrims interrupts my thoughts. A group of about a dozen middle-aged women circle around the well and block my view of it. They arrive singing softly, holding hands with each other. To a person they're in colorful, billowy cotton, and sensible sandals. Old hippies, or whatever the British version is. Older than me by a smidge. I was born in 1967 and came of age in the eighties with punk-rock and a return to conservatism with Ronald Reagan. I don't wear loose clothing. And I don't sing in public. I let myself feel irritated at the group—for intruding on my grief. For being too colorful and lively.

I decide to squeeze my eyes closed and try to ignore them.

When their song ends, one woman speaks up and starts their meeting... or ceremony... or whatever they're doing, with a prayer, "Mother of us all, we are here to honor your presence and power." Her friends grunt supportive affirmations, and sway their bodies in the fresh, fern-scented air—and I feel my ire escalate. I consider moving. I could walk up the hill and collect some of the water from the spring into the plastic container I bought at the gate on my way in. But I'm too stubborn. I was here first. I decide I will just wait them out.

Another woman, someone on the opposite side of the circle, says, "We honor the divine feminine, and commit ourselves to recovering the stories that have been abandoned."

Suddenly my body heats up. Starting at the back of my neck a hot wave of sweat takes over my whole head. Then my face and my shoulders and torso start to burn up. These goddamn hot flashes are new since about a year ago. Sacred feminine indeed. I'm 49 and menopause is happening in earnest—earlier than I expected it. My body is playing a sick joke. I sit up to take off my down vest and my sweater. I'm stripped down to a tank top and shorts.

I lie back down and shift uncomfortably. The heat dissipates eventually and when the sweat dries on my skin, I get a chill—so I sit up again and re-clothe myself. Now, a third time, I lie down on the stone and listen to the voices of the hippies while I look up at the blue sky beyond the foliage and try to moderate my anxiety.

"Now it's time to recount one of the sacred tales," one of the women in the circle says. She's the one standing right in front of me, blocking my view of the Well.

*Great! It's story time.* I sigh with exasperation. Normally I love stories. I'm all about stories in my life—in my work as a therapist and a writer. But right now, I need quiet. Crave it like dry skin craves moisture.

"One day during a great hunt in Ingleswood Forest Arthur wandered away from his companions to find the stag he'd killed with his last arrow," the storyteller begins. I loosen my annoyance a little when I realize she'll be telling an Arthurian story. I even allow that some distraction from my own looping thoughts couldn't hurt me.

"He was stalking a deer in a lonely grove. And as he wandered into a thicket of trees, a man startled him by stepping from behind a big trunk and saying, 'Arthur, lucky for you I don't have an arrow in my hand.'"

I don't recognize this story, don't remember reading it in lit class. The old gals seem to know it though. They make gleeful aspirations when they realize which story is being told. One woman even claps and says, "Oh, this is my favorite."

The storyteller continues. Apparently, Arthur recognized the man as a guy called Sir Gromer, whose land the King claimed in a raid at some point. And although Arthur was afraid for his life, he convinced Sir Gromer that if he killed an unarmed man, the killing wouldn't be honorable. Everyone would scorn him.

"'I'll give you anything you want if you'll spare me,' Arthur said.

"'You don't have anything I want,' said Sir Gromer. 'However, you do make a point.'" The storyteller deepens her voice when she plays the part of Sir Gromer, who seemed to agree that it would be better to get his retribution in an honorable way. "'How about this,' Sir Gromer said, 'I'll give you a chance to solve a riddle. Exactly a year from now, you come back here by yourself without your knights or weapons. If at that time you can't solve this riddle, none will object if I take your life. But if you answer the riddle correctly, there won't be any battle. Swear on your honor that you'll return in one year.'

"'I swear it,' the king said. 'Tell me the riddle?'

"'Answer this: What is it that women desire most, above all else?'"

I almost laugh out loud when I hear the storyteller say this. If I knew the answer to *this* question—knew what I wanted in my life—I wouldn't be in my current predicament. My irritation at the little coven of women interrupting my self-pity fades altogether now. They're telling a teaching story. I'd probably do well to pay attention.

"'I assure you,' said King Arthur, 'I'll come back in exactly a year and bring the answer to this.'

Here the raconteur stops her telling long enough to blow her nose. Evidently, she doesn't enjoy the glorious absence of hay fever that I do, and out of sympathy I decide to forgive her for blocking my view of the Well.

She carries on: "Sir Gromer left, and the king called for his companions who immediately saw he was upset."

On their way back to the castle, Arthur confided in his nephew, Sir Gawain, about what had taken place. And because Gawain loved Arthur, he promised to help the king travel all around the country to find the answer to the riddle.

During the next year, they inquired everywhere. All the people who answered were certain their answers were correct, though each said something different.

Some said women loved money—and to be well supported; others said they wanted large homes. Some said women wanted handsome, strong husbands; others said they wanted a man who wouldn't argue with them.

I sigh again when I hear these, this time because the idea that what a woman wants—deeply and truly wants—is to have money, prestige, or to be right, sounds both too ridiculous and too familiar. Is this what my husband thought I wanted? This time my sigh attracts the attention of the woman just the right side of the speaker. She turns and winks at me, then nudges the woman beside her to opens the circle a bit so I can see the Well again. I smile weakly, mostly in embarrassment that I was so judgmental when the group first arrived.

The story continues, "Back in Ingleswood Forest with only one day left to find the correct answer, King Arthur met a lady. She was covered with gold and jewels, but she was a horribly foul, ugly woman. Her face was red. Her nose was runny. Her mouth was too wide, and her teeth were yellow and hung out of her mouth. And she was shaped like a barrel."

The women around the circle giggle. I join them. We all know what is coming: This ugly hag—Lady Ragnell is her name—is the unlikely holder of the answer Arthur needs.

"The lady rode up to King Arthur, who looked away from her ugliness.

"'Dear King Arthur,' she said. 'You can ignore me if you want, but be sure of one thing: your life is in my hands.'"

The King pays attention to her now, even tries to look right at her.

She tells him she knows the answer, but she wants something from him before she'll give it to him. "'Or go ahead and lose your life. It's your choice,' she declares.

"'What do you want from me?' said the king. 'I'll grant it if I can.'"

The ugly gal wants a particular knight to marry. Sir Gawain, it turns out. Arthur's favorite. I can't see how this is going to turn out for everyone, but I'm all in with the story. I want to know. "'Either I marry Sir Gawain, or you lose your head!' she declares."

Wow! *The gumption!* I think. What a gauntlet she threw down. I lie there on my bench thinking back to my marriage, thinking about how I'd tried to be as resolute as Lady Ragnell in my own ugly last days before leaving, but how in the end I'd slunk away. I'd tried—weakly—to present an ultimatum: Change or I'm out. But what did I want, anyway? To control *his* behavior? For him to be less angry, less resentful? Was it fair to ask someone to change? And if he had changed, would that have done the trick? Would I have felt mollified and agreed to stay? Lady Ragnell had such clarity about what she wanted. Me, not so much.

The story goes on. "The king was upset at the idea of giving his nephew to marry such a woman. So he said, 'Then I'll have to die, Lady.'"

When the king returned to his castle, he met Sir Gawain and told him everything except Lady Ragnell's request to marry him. Arthur said simply that the lady would share the secret only if she could have the promise of a husband. Of course, Sir Gawain—too good to be true—offered to marry her. The two rode back to tell her the news and to ask her for the answer to the riddle.

"'Sir,' said Lady Ragnell, 'now you'll know what women desire above all else. Men say we want to be beautiful or to have attention or money. But they're wrong. What we desire above everything is to have sovereignty—to rule our lives as we see fit, to not be beholden to anyone. So go, Sir King. Your life is safe now.'"

There is silence around the circle of women as the storyteller pauses for us all to take this in. I feel my own heart jump into my throat as the words hang in the air. I've been asking myself all these long months—since my decision to leave—what I was expecting, what I wanted from him. And here it is. Somehow, I'd wanted to be in a relationship where, even though I was part of a couple, I still belonged primarily to myself. I wanted to make my own decisions and guide my own way through the world.

*But,* I think, *Lady Ragnell already belonged to herself.* She lived in a cave in the woods where no man told her what to do. Why did she want to get married? The silence in the circle of women now might reflect their own similar questions.

The story next takes us to Arthur's confrontation with Sir Gromer, who turned out to be Lady Ragnell's brother. He was pissed off, of course, that his sister gave Arthur the answer but he had to keep his word. Arthur was free.

Now Arthur sped to get Lady Ragnell to bring her back to his castle for the wedding. Unfortunately, my storyteller reports, she was so ugly that the prospect of a public wedding was deplorable. But the ugly old bag insisted she would have a full wedding feast with all of the kingdom in attendance.

*Good for her!* I silently applaud.

Now the story comes to its zenith and by this time the circle of hippies has opened up to include me as if I'm one of them. The storyteller takes a deep breath.

"Here's the thing. On the evening of the wedding, Lady Ragnell carefully watched her groom to see if he would avoid her in the wedding chamber. Strangely, he didn't do this. The knight behaved as if he cherished his bride.

"The Lady Ragnell said, 'Sir Gawain, now that we're married, show me your courtesy with a kiss. If I were beautiful, you wouldn't delay our wedding night activities, would you?'

"Sir Gawain gallantly replied, 'I'll come to you at once!' As he turned around to kiss his bride, he saw in front of him not the ugly creature he'd married, but the most beautiful woman he'd ever seen."

I don't know why, but I didn't see this coming—didn't foresee that the Lady would turn pretty.

"'What! Are you a witch?' Gawain cried.

"'No!' she said. 'But I have to tell you something, my husband. Several years ago, I was deformed by an enchantment my brother, the terrible Sir Gromer, placed on me. My beauty, as you see it now, isn't permanent. You need to choose whether you'd like me to be fair by night and foul by day, or else have me fair by day and foul by night. With the enchantment, it can't be both. What do you choose?'

"'Oh no! The choice is too hard,' Gawain said. 'Either *you* suffer during the day or we suffer together at night. I put the choice entirely in your own hands since you're the one who is most affected. Whatever you choose, as your husband that choice will also be my own.'

"Lady Ragnell bowed her head in gratitude. 'Mercy,' she said. 'Thank you. Because you left the decision in my hands, the evil enchantment is released completely! Now I will always appear just as I am at this moment. The only thing that could release me from Gromer's spell was if a husband granted me, of his own free will, sovereignty to choose what I wish for myself. And you have done just that. You have granted me sovereignty, that thing which every woman wants above all else. Kiss me, Sir Knight, now, and let's both be glad!'"

In spite of my numb weariness, I feel my heart swell. Lady Ragnell found a man who respected her, who agreed with her that she was a sovereign being! I am happy for her. But the women in the circle with me are oddly quiet. Since I don't know better, I think this is the end. These women know the punch line is still to come. The narrator clears her throat, the pollen is thick this afternoon, but she's determined to make it to the end of her narrative—hay fever be damned. She finishes with a grave tone.

"And so the Lady Ragnell remained beautiful all day and all night, and she and Gawain the Knight lived happily for seven years. Then, one morning Gawain awoke to find that she was gone. Taking nothing with her except what she came with, she disappeared and was never seen again."

"What the hell," I say out loud, and I sit up to look at the group. "She leaves? After all that?"

The woman who'd nudged the storyteller aside so I could see the Well, the one just to my right now, nods slowly. "Isn't it extraordinary?" she asks. "She takes the sovereignty he gifted her with and uses it to go her own way!"

"But why?" I ask.

A woman across the circle waves her hand to catch my attention. "I think I know. You have to claim your sovereignty. No one can really give it to you."

The group is quiet for a long minute. Then they begin singing again. A soft song. And as they sing they file away from the Well, leaving me alone. Some of them acknowledge me as they go. Some don't. Like the mists of old, they rolled in, and now they roll away. But they leave me with a gift: a passageway. A portal to my own sovereignty. Permission to cross the void between fear and the strength I feel beginning to bubble inside me.

# Birds, Bees, and Bucket Seats

## Cheryl Perry

I squirmed awkwardly, trying to make myself comfortable in the folding chair while my mom stared intently at me from hers. We sat facing each other on the back porch, so named because it had once been the actual back porch when my grandmother ran around there as a child. Now, I sat inches from the washer and dryer on my right with my great grandma's old yellow table bumping my elbow on the left. With my four younger brothers and sisters always nosy about my seventeen-year-old life, it was challenging to find space for a private conversation. I found myself wishing for one of them to burst in and relieve me from the interrogation room.

"You and Scott seem to be getting a bit more serious," my mom began, her hazel eyes boring straight through me.

"Maybe, I guess so?" I mumbled, staring down at the yellow linoleum and shifting my butt to the side against the metal seat.

"Your father wants me to talk to you about how we behave with boyfriends. You might find yourself under pressure to do things."

It was always "your father" this or "your father" that when she wanted to address something uncomfortable without taking responsibility for feeling that way herself. But I was curious. What kind of conversations were she and my dad having about my developing relationship? I imagined her chatting at my dad with her speculations and him grunting in dismissal, uncomfortable with the idea that his baby girl could even be considering such things.

I stared at her feet while my mind flooded with images of the night before.

*Slinking off into Scott's room to "play Nintendo®" after visiting with his mom. Lying on his velvet blanket while he massaged my naked body. His lips slowly and seamlessly replacing his hands, softly kissing my shoulders, my neck...and eventually finding my own mouth.*

"It's wrong to do some things before you are married...and you are too young to be married."

*Bracing himself, right arm next to my cheek, his left hand tracing its way gently down my body, pausing briefly to stroke my breast before making its way to the soft place between my legs. His fingers finding their way inside me, his tongue wrapping itself around mine. Both of us moaning with muffled pleasure so as not to awaken his mom. His hard cock replacing his fingers as he slid himself inside of me, feeling myself come again with the soft rocking of his lovemaking sending waves of ecstasy throughout my entire body.*

"Your dad wants to make sure that you know to say no if he ever puts any pressure on you." She stared at me intently, the force of her words turning my stomach into a knot. Our love was anything but pressure. His touch brought my body to life. I felt more comfortable with him than I'd ever felt with anyone. Ever.

"He's never been anything more than a perfect gentleman, Mom. There's no need to worry."

*He lay briefly on top of me, our shared fluids glued to our skin, our bellies pressing together in synchronized breath. He rolled onto his back and I nuzzled my head into the safe warmth of his chest, savoring the gorgeous awakening of my body as a place where pleasure happened.*

"Ok, but if that ever changes, I want you to talk to me. I know his parents are divorced," she practically whispered the word as though it were a disease, "and they're not as involved as we are. I talked to another teacher at school about you two and he said that Scott was a challenging kid. He said we could let him date you but that we should never let him marry you."

"Why would he say that? Scott has never been anything but nice to all of us."

"I know, but that's just what he said."

"Mom, did you and Dad wait until you were married?"

She looked me right in the eyes and lied, her eyelids wide open as if blinking would give the truth away. I had read their love letters. The ones they'd written on their summers apart. The ones where they'd reminisced about their lovemaking in romantic subtleties. The ones they never knew I'd found.

"Yes. We waited." With those words, I knew I'd never be able to talk to her. I'd never be able to tell her how sweetly my boyfriend loved her baby girl. I'd never be able to tell her how his touch sent ripples of pleasure up and down my spine. I'd never be able to tell her how I knew he was my forever.

"Ok," I replied. I stood slowly and found my way back to my bedroom. I lay down on my little girl quilt and placed my hand on my belly, remembering how softly he'd kissed me there not even 24 hours earlier.

*I ran my fingers across his chest and rolled onto my back. He reached for the towel and gently removed the remnants of our sex from my skin, and then his. He leaned over and kissed me softly right below my navel.*

Every day after school, I hurried through the cold out to my car, The Big Brown Boat as my friends affectionately dubbed it. I drove out to Scott's dad's shop, a giant barn that lived on a large piece of farmland near his father's old double wide, and sat on the concrete next to the woodstove while Scott tinkered away on his race car. I'd diligently finish all of my calculus homework while periodically catching a glimpse of his round bum highlighted by the pockets of his Levi's® jeans. Never mind the ache in my bones from sitting on that hard floor. Never mind how I huddled next to the stove to stay warm. I loved just being in his presence. As soon as I'd answered the last problem, I stowed my books in my pack and stood to watch what he was doing.

He held a spark plug in his hand and slid the metal tip over a metal coin-shaped thing. The engine hung from a yellow stand, completely outside of the car while he worked on it. Before Scott, I'd ever seen the insides of a motor before.

"This coin is a gapping tool. It sets the gap on the spark plug to the right spacing. And then they go inside of these holes here," his fingers pointed toward the series of circles on the side of the engine block. My skin tingled. I had never given two shits about anything to do with motors. I was not the least bit mechanically inclined. But with the way his eyes lit up when he talked about what he loved, I couldn't be anything other than entranced.

His hands moved toward the front center of the engine and he pulled out a long cylinder-like thing with different offset bumps around it.

"This is the crank," he said.

He held it up and pointed toward the large holes in the block, removing another large cylinder from inside one of the holes.

"And these are the pistons," he said, indicating toward the cylinders. "The crank spins around and each of these bumps pushes up on the pistons. They all go up and down and create the compression to light the spark plugs, all in perfect timing."

I felt the familiar awakening in my pelvis as I listened to his low voice.

He moved through all the parts of the engine...the cam shaft, the valves, the heads. I didn't fully get it all, but I understood his love for this car. He was sharing a part of his soul, part of what made him happy—with me. And I loved to see inside his heart like that.

Over the next several months, I watched him rip apart that engine. It belonged inside of a 1970s Chevy Vega that he intended to drag race up at the tracks across the border in Canada. Sometimes I did my homework and watched him, sometimes I stood hip to hip with him and helped him clean parts. Sometimes, we'd become so turned on in each other's presence that we had to run off for a "Nintendo" break. We'd drive down the road to his mom's place and make use of his bedroom or the shower. Or we'd sneak off to some other part of his dad's farm.

One of these times, he was tinkering with something on the engine. I set down my calculus book and hopped up from my station beside the woodstove. The Vega was just poking its nose inside the shop door. I squeezed my way around its front end and came up behind Scott, wrapping my arms around his waist, running my hands up and down the front of his body to entice him into distraction.

"I feel the need for a quick game of 'Nintendo'," I teased.

He turned from the car motor and kissed me, wiping his greasy fingers on a shop towel as he did so. Dropping his towel, he filled his hands with my ample buttocks and pressed me into his body.

"C'mon," he whispered, grabbing my hand. "I know just where to go." Dragging me with him, we slipped around the side of the car and ran out the door of the shop.

We ran through the gravel, dodging his stepmother's geese as they pecked the ground looking for tidbits.

I had never been into the other parts of the barn. He led me over to some old, rusted pieces of equipment, behind a stack of hay bales that came up to my elbows. He pulled me towards him and we hungrily unbuttoned each other's pants while our tongues traced the insides of each other's mouth. When we'd finally freed ourselves from the confines of denim, pants pushed down around our ankles, he spun me around and bent me over. I rested my forearms on the stacks of bales, raised myself up on my toes so he could pound into me at just the right angle. Waves of pleasure began to build as he slid himself hungrily in and out of me.

"Cheryl...? Scott...?" I heard his younger sister call. I looked up across the stacks of bales directly into Nicole's eyes. She stood maybe 30 or 40 feet away from us, her long ponytail highlighted by the sun coming in from the open sliding door. There was no doubt she was close enough see what was going on. Her eyes widened and she hurried away, continuing to call our names as though she'd never seen us fucking. I was so embarrassed to have been caught that I lost the building orgasm.

"It doesn't matter," Scott tried to dismiss my concern, "Nicole doesn't care."

"I care," I said. But I bent back over and let him finish. He pulled out of me, and I felt the familiar warmth of him ejaculating on my back. He took a corner of his t-shirt and wiped it off of me. We pulled up and buttoned our pants, and he grabbed my hand. Then we wandered off to find Nicole.

We crossed back over the old farm implements, squinting a bit as we stepped out of the dark barn. He led me around the corner toward Nicole's voice, where she stood in the shadow of the open door.

"Oh, there you are!" She feigned surprise as we came up behind her, an unspoken offer to forget what she'd seen. "I made some soup if you guys wanna come in?"

I looked toward Scott, ready to follow his lead. "Sure, that sounds good," he accepted both of her offers, a sly grin in my direction, his eyes twinkling with the naughtiness of our afternoon delight. Even amidst my awkwardness, I felt that familiar tingle in my loins when he looked at me that way. I just couldn't get enough of him.

As we wandered back to the house through the maze of tractors and plows and engine blocks scattered about the expansive gravel, long blades of grass popping up between them, Nicole chattered on excitedly about a plan she had to build a fence for her horses, hopeful to enlist our help.

Bit by bit, Scott's race car took shape. One sunny, spring Saturday, his dad's neighbor Tom came across the road to help with the car. They wrapped a strap around the engine, hoisted it up and slowly, carefully dropped the completed engine into the front compartment of the hood. Then the two friends spent the next few hours connecting wires and hooking up knobby things and whatsits.

"Go for it, bud!" Tom announced as he slid out from under the car belly up.

Scott slipped into the bucket seat, a crooked grin on his face. He turned the key and the engine roared to life with a rumbling that stirred a strange vibration in my chest. Scott climbed back out of the car, his eyes sparkling at his hard earned success, and continued poking and prodding engine bits while it ran.

"I think she's ready to take for a spin!" Tom announced. Scott hopped back in and threw the transmission into reverse. Tom and I followed him out to the empty country road, watching as he drove off. Scott had given me his video camera for the occasion and I pointed it in his direction, hoping to capture his inaugural quarter mile. The roar of the engine grew louder and, within seconds, he'd flown past us, the exhaust breeze moving my curls just enough to tickle my face and offend my nose. We watched him slow down and pull into another neighbors' driveway, the Vega slowly rumbling back toward our station near the mailbox before turning into his dad's gravel driveway.

"Ten seconds! Pretty fucking fast!" Tom exclaimed, holding his stop watch in the air. "How was it?"

"So amazing!" Scott shouted over the engine noise, his toothy smile evidence of the pride he felt. "You try it now!"

Tom took Scott's place in the driver's seat, and Scott took his place by my side. He slung his arm over my shoulder and we followed the car out to the road. Tom performed an instant replay of Scott's previous drag race action while we watched. Scott and I wandered back to the shop and stole a quick kiss while Tom turned around. He held me tightly, proudly. This was the first racecar he'd built entirely on his own—and I'd shared it with him.

Tom rumbled up to the shop door in the Vega.

"Woohoohoo!" he hollered over the loud chuckle of the engine. "This is better than fucking!"

"*I'm pretty sure it's not,*" I thought to myself. I noticed Scott did not agree with him.

Later that evening, I pulled the Big Brown Boat into the driveway, maneuvering it into place between my dad's truck and my mom's car. I opened the door of the back porch, the familiar scent of my great grandmother still lingered in this space years after she'd moved on. I moved between the yellow table and the laundry across the yellow linoleum, the reminder of my mother's words still lingering in the room. I moved quickly through the door at the opposite end of the room, careful to keep the cats from escaping and crossed the hallway into my bedroom. I dropped my backpack on the floor and tossed my letter jacket on the end of the bed before laying down on top of my little girl quilt and relishing the brief moment to myself. I could hear my mom in the kitchen making dinner and my sisters and brothers bickering about the TV in the living room. I could picture my dad reading his latest novel tuning everything out from his recliner in the corner. Everyone was completely oblivious to my arrival.

"Dinner is ready," my mom yelled minutes later, followed by the shuffling of hungry bodies into the kitchen. I stood reluctantly to join them, my mind still on the events of the day. I made my way down the hall, through the living room and into the kitchen.

"Cheryl!!" my youngest sister cried out, always the most happy to see me. "I missed you all day long!" she sang, throwing her arms around me. She chattered about everything that had happened that day and all of the injustices of sibling interactions while we dished up our tuna casserole. My mom waited for everyone else to dish up before making a plate for my dad and taking a small scoop for herself. We all made our way out into the living room. My mom perched at the end of the couch near my dad's chair while everyone else spread around the room, making sure to be in sight of the TV. Ben, the older of my younger brothers at about 18 months behind me had been spending a lot of time with Scott recently. Scott had taken him under his wing, mentoring him in all things mechanical. He was anxious to hear about the progress on the Vega.

"Did Scott get the motor running today?" he asked between bites of casserole.

"He sure did," I replied with a grin.

# The Invisible Man

## Dana Tye Rally

We grew up lucky, my middle sister and I—lucky by anyone's standards. Lucky to live in a large, two-story house. Lucky to spend most of our childhood in a sprawling new neighborhood on the west coast of Canada filled with kids our age or younger. And perhaps, luckiest of all, to be children, with nimble feet and strong legs that leaped and stretched and sidestepped through the tangled woods in our back yard, and—once we'd reached the unmarked property line between the base of a tall cedar and somebody else's green grass— with sturdy imaginations that swept us farther still. It was daytime, always daytime. Our minds roamed free, then, unbound by walls or indoor structures with their dark, cobwebby corners, where cold wind clawed at our lungs but sharp words couldn't cut us, where taking up swords to defend horses and moats and castles made us forget the weight of our father's derision, which even outside we carried around in our coat pockets.

As we grew, hovering around adolescence, I reveled, in particular, over living across the street from our elementary school. Every lunch hour, soon as the first bell rang, my friends and I would skip across our quiet street with barely a glance before charging up our steep asphalt driveway. These visits, friends in tow, were never planned, but my mother was almost always there to greet us. With my doctor-father at work, the house was peaceful. She would smile and haul out the frying pan from the cupboard of our sunny orange-and-yellow kitchen, cooking up extra grilled cheese sandwiches and doling out glasses of milk to groups of five or six girls. We'd cluster around our shiny maple table until the school warning bell blared, then dash back, slumping into our desks exactly as the teacher arrived.

At twelve, my obsession with boys—fueled by a longing for male attention—became research, research I longed to share with my girlfriends from school. On days my mom's station wagon was missing from the carport, my friends and I would eat the contents of our lunch bags at recess and then race up our driveway when the lunch bell rang. We would huff with breath, giggling and clattering up and over the raised threshold of the carport door, lock the door inside the downstairs bathroom, and take turns poring over Jacqueline Susann's *Once Is Not Enough*, a novel I'd snuck from my mom's personal bookshelf. Racy movies with nude ladies or the word "sex" in them were off-limits in our household back then, but no one kept tabs on what I read. One or two of us would plunk down on the pink plastic toilet seat, while others pressed against pink-flower-patterned walls and peered over shoulders to see pages I'd folded over at the corners.

We read about orgies—lots of people having sex together I'd inferred from studying my dad's medical books on reproduction—and about the main character's disappointment with her lover's small penis. This latter bit raised questions (why big was so much better, when bigger for a man meant something wrinklier and saggier and harder to tuck into his pants). We liked pages with the word "penis" on them. Most of us had only seen a quick flash of our father's or brother's, and the sexy lady in our book seemed equally interested in talking about them and in seeing them as often as she could.

I'd never really talked about sex much with my mom or dad—none of my friends had spoken with theirs on the topic, either. But the thought of approaching my father with any of my burning questions made my insides twist in protest, though as a doctor he would have been the obvious parent to quell my curiosity. I rarely spoke with my dad unless it was to tap on the upstairs den door on evenings or weekends so I could hand him his requested glass of rum and Coke®, or pretend to care about the third-period hockey score on TV, or tell him our dinner was ready. Sometimes he didn't come out for dinner at all. My father preferred to go straight into the den from work, and Mom was content to make him a second dinner—something like curried eggs on rice, which my mom later told me she gagged over while making, but which I still crave to this day: all that rich cream sauce slathered over velvety hardboiled eggs, sweetly spiced with an exotic sprinkle of curry powder, all the more exotic since it was only served to my dad, while the rest of us made do with hearty casseroles that might stretch a day or two thereafter.

My friends in the pink bathroom wouldn't have thought much of my dad's absence either. It was the mid-'70s, at least a decade before sensitive new age guys bothered to tote around their babies or wear t-shirts extolling the virtues of being a parent. My friends' dads were typically off working during school hours or, as we were to learn later, fooling around with their secretaries—a sport a few of the fathers pursued in the entitled circle in which I grew up. My father waited years before having an affair with his secretary. As a family physician, the keeper of special healing powers and bodily secrets, my dad availed himself first of all to nurses or nursing students, wide-eyed over this darkly handsome man and his thick wallet, at his sense of fun and adventure, and eyes that crinkled at the corners when he laughed. Which he occasionally did, even with my mother. His deep staccato laughter and devilish sense of humor were no doubt two traits that first attracted my mother to him.

I say these things now because the story of my dad's unfaithfulness was hidden from us then, but poured from my mom like hot lava when I reached my 20s. I took in her stories, and by my 50s they were hardened into my own anthropological layers, each one smoothed solid by repeated heartbreak, chiseled and laid flat by therapy. I rarely saw the man, our father, who lived in our house while we were growing up. Childhood friends who came to our house, friends whose fathers I'd met and shared dinners with, friends I learned to invite over because their presence buffered the hostility that lurked inside our walls, usually didn't get a chance to meet my dad.

One such frequent visitor was my good friend Sophie, who'd spent a year playing Monopoly and badminton at our house and in our yard, who'd sat on my yellow-checkered bedspread to play Truth or Dare, and who one day looked at me all of a sudden and asked a question I wasn't expecting. *D'ya have a Dad?*

Sophie's blue eyes were solemn, her back pressed against the wall and hands tucked in prayer position between her legs. We were perched at the bottom of our beige, shag-carpeted staircase—me at the bottom, her one step above.

*Or is he...dead?*

She spoke the last words with a gulp between them, like she'd been saving them up for weeks, like maybe her mom had wondered as well, and she needed to spit them out so she could run back to her own nearby house and share the news.

*Course I have a dad*, I said, standing up to point toward the closed room at the top of the stairs. *He's up in his den, watching football or something.* I laughed nervously. *Why d'you think my dad would be dead, silly?*

But Sophie didn't laugh back. Her face remained skeptical. And my living, breathing father never did come out of his den to meet her, never did get up from his falling-apart brown leather chair to prove me right.

I was embarrassed, but in a way, I was glad. Whenever my dad did emerge, usually intercepting me in the kitchen to replenish his drink or TV snacks, the air felt heavy around him. I wasn't sure I wanted to introduce this man to my friends, not face-to-face at least, where his sharp words could come out suddenly, without context or provocation. Or where his slurred speech might give away what a nice time he was having on his own, without the forced interplay required for companionship. My dad was always exhausted from work, mom would explain. He needed to be left alone to unravel his hard day, after enduring hours of strangers—mostly middle-aged women—whining about their cramps and their kids and their loneliness. I would witness these things firsthand as a medical office assistant for him during my first summer job at 14, and I would feel the first stirrings of empathy. People truly thought doctors were gods. They never saw them at home when they were feeling cranky or inept, or yelling at their children to stop slurping their soup, or knocking back three or four sludgy black morning coffees to erase the queasy sorrows of the night before.

By the time my baby sister, the last of three daughters for my parents, arrived on the scene, my mother had become an expert at playing both Mom and Dad. On weekends, once my sister was out of diapers, mom would take the three of us to the park or community center swimming pool, stopping en route for quarter-pound bags of candy from the mall candy counter. We could ask for whatever we liked. She would take us home and let us spread our crayons and paints and construction paper across the maple dining table, never complaining when the paint leaked permanent purple or green or blue stains onto the lacquered wood, while she busied herself making Heaven-scented lemon loaves or chocolate chip cookies. Sometimes while we made art, she pulled weeds from the garden, or even mowed the lawn—one of the many manly but tedious tasks my father refused to do. We built a life around and despite the invisible man upstairs, staying out of his way when he did make an appearance. My daytime memories are a mix of warm and inviting smells from the oven, aimless chatter and occasional squabbles with my middle sister, mom's long and gossipy chats on the phone with friends, one leg straddling the stool by the phone, the other foot braced against the wall, my mom chuckling and twirling the phone cord around and around her fingers as she talked.

And when night would fall, around dinnertime, our shoulders would tense up and our chatter would turn to whispers, or so my mother tells us now. We were never really conscious of the ragged split between one state of being and another, between the sense of day yawning before us like our long and unwieldy shag hallway carpet, and then the day's abrupt end, with my father arriving home and slamming the carport door, his anger aimed at wresting it from its hinges, the vibrating walls a signal to still all of our childish and therefore unseemly impulses.

Over time, when the rum and Coke®s turned to straight vodka and the den door stayed closed into the night, I gradually grew to anticipate my father's absences more than his arrivals. Perhaps that's why I was surprised one night when he happened upon me on the family room couch making out with my then-boyfriend Craig, an affair that lasted all of two weeks. I was fifteen and my tall, dark, muscle-shirted guy was eighteen. I had vague illusions of true love and promise rings, while Craig's thoughts lived in his hands, groping for whatever skin he managed to expose. We got caught, and after we finished fumbling over buttons and zippers, my introductions to Dad hastier than my boyfriend's retreat, I was shocked when my father's response was to sit me down at the kitchen table to bestow a bit of fatherly wisdom.

*Got a minute, Peaches?* he said gruffly, standing at one end of the lacquered kitchen table and motioning for me to sit straight across.

*Um...yeah, sure.*

I sat on the bumpy edge of the wooden seat, my toes flexed against the floor for a quick exit. Dad never sat me down to talk. He rarely weighed in on anything personal, really, much less topics outside of my marks at school or when dinner would be ready. All I knew were Mom's inquisitions—*Who is this Craig? Where does he live? Do we know his parents?* Stuff that made the undersides of my legs stick to the seat.

But instead of pulling out the chair across from me, my dad kept walking around, shuffling around work papers he'd scattered across the table and gathering up pens and calculators like he was planning to work elsewhere on his office budget. When he talked, all I could see was one side of his black-whiskered face.

*So*, he said, still pacing, words tumbling out like he was ordering around his office nurse. *You need birth control? You know, pills, whatever. Come to me, okay? I got tons of samples at the office I can pick up for you, no problem.*

*Uh... okay, Dad*, I mumbled back. In some ways, I was unfazed. Dr. Dad kept a drawer full of free pharmaceuticals in our upstairs bathroom for all of us to help ourselves.

But I was also embarrassed. I was a virgin who'd never even seen a condom wrapper.

I never got the chance to profess my innocence, though, because Dad's next words felt like he'd crammed a popsicle in my mouth.

*Just, for Crissakes—don't get pregnant. And if you do, we don't want to see you again, he said. Don't come home.*

Before Dad went back to his den that night, I probably stared through him with the eyes of a cow ambling across a country road. I didn't know what to think or say in reply. But after that, I carted his command around for years like a bruised elbow that I'd absent-mindedly hit against the stair banister one too many times, occasionally relieving its sting by turning it into a funny story to tell friends. I was never really certain if my dad meant what he'd said. Yet I think those words registered in the recesses of my brain somewhere, where they remain to this day, in a part of me that still feels homeless, still abandoned and shivering on a street corner somewhere.

*I was lucky.* I whisper to myself when I end up on that street corner in my mind, again dodging the dark clouds, always trying to forget my father's words. *I am lucky. I know how to let the cold wind claw my lungs. I know how to keep those words from cutting me. Don't I?*

# Roommate Grandpa

## Morgan Steele

The story of how my grandparents fell in love is a legend in our family. Bubba would often recount the story to us grandkids and we'd hang on his every word despite the fact that we'd heard it all before.

"We were neighbors, you know," he'd say, straightening his back, feigning a mock-serious facial expression and folding his thick, wrinkled hands on the table in front of him.

He'd never tell the tragic backstory of how they came to be neighbors, but he didn't have to. Our parents had whispered that dark tale to us as kids when we were too innocent to know that there are some questions you aren't supposed to ask. They told us how Bubba's mom died of a heart attack when he was three; how Bubba's father remarried quickly before he also died, when Bubba was nine; how Harry's new wife, the guardian to my orphaned grandfather, was the quintessential stereotype of a wicked stepmother. She sent Bubba 200 miles away to live at military school before the dirt on his father's coffin could even settle.

Bubba didn't tell us about any of that, keeping to the silver lining: on holidays, the academy would close and put him on a greyhound bus to Farmington, Michigan, a GI Bill suburb of Detroit, where his stepmother lived three houses down from where my grandma grew up.

On a visit home, he went out his back door to escape a tongue-lashing from his stepmother. He sat on the cement stoop overlooking a half-acre patch of grass identical to all the other yards behind the cookie-cutter Craftsman homes in the neighborhood.

Out of the blue, he heard laughter.

"I heard these voices," he said, his face lighting up with a boyish sense of devious wonder, "and I looked to my left and three houses down I saw these dark-haired goddesses hanging laundry on the line! My jaw dropped, I was like WOW!"

At this point in the story, he always makes a wide-eyed face like he's been hit on the back of the head with a frying pan. I interpret this to mean he thought they were hot, and honestly, it's gross to think about your grandpa having such thoughts.

It was love at first sight. They eloped with a bun in the oven when they were both 19 years old. That bun was my dad. They spent 50 years together before she died, but it wasn't easy. A few decades in, Nannie developed alcohol and drug abuse addictions. It was hard on Bubba. He drove her to the emergency room each time she overdosed. She often fell and injured herself, racking up medical bills. Like most couples of their generation, she did all the cooking and cleaning even when she was so drunk she could barely hold herself upright. There were eggshells in the food she made and used coffee grounds sprinkled throughout the kitchen. She often drove drunk to go shopping and spent thousands of dollars buying brand new appliances they didn't need. She was fired from the prestigious hospital where she had once been a world leader in her field.

Plus, she wasn't always a nice drunk. She blamed her sickness on him and bullied him into believing it was his fault.

In her late-sixties, Nannie was diagnosed with liver and kidney failure. In the few months surrounding her diagnosis and her death, Bubba went through a wild identity transformation. There he was in April, facing the impending death of his wife, and he began talking about himself in the past tense as though he was already dead. In May during the immediate aftermath of Nannie's bodily departure, he seemed lost at sea. Even though their marriage was fraught and lacked joy, she was the only family he'd ever known.

And yet, by June something shifted and he began to focus on the future. He rented a dumpster and threw away almost all of his earthly belongings. He put his house on the market and signed a month-to-month lease for a house in Seattle down the street from where my aunt and uncle lived.

Coincidentally, I was also moving to Seattle that summer. I had dreamed of a west coast escape for years. As if by fate, a career opportunity fell into my lap that I couldn't turn down. The only catch was that I was broke and Seattle had one of the most expensive rental markets in the country.

I called Bubba after I accepted the job, and he knew why I was calling before I could even say hello.

"Of course you can stay with me," he said. "That's what grandpas are for, right?"

That was how my grandpa became my roommate, and that's where our true story begins.

When I arrived a few weeks later, he was already settled in. He was thrilled to have someone else around. I always knew Bubba was a creature of habit, but it only took a few days of living in the house to realize how disciplined he was at sticking to his daily routine. Every day was the same. He'd wake up at 5 AM and sit at the table and type away at his sociology projects—he was a sociologist by trade. Breakfast was a multi-hour affair of never ending cups of coffee and one serving of Greek yogurt. The very second my bedroom door creaked open in the morning, he sprang up from his makeshift desk, scraping the legs of his chair across the linoleum. I'd hear the padded steps of his ancient white New Balance shoes.

"Hey Darlin'," he'd say as I descended the staircase. Every day the same: creak, screech, plod plod plod, hi Darlin. It seemed that without his first love, Nannie, to take care of, and without his second love, work, to keep him busy, he didn't know what to love. So he loved me.

He resisted my efforts to coax him into trying new things, so eventually I gave up and followed along with his routine. However, in the midst of bumbling about our day to day, I missed an important cue. I assumed he was working at his computer each morning on a sociology project harkening back to his working days. I wouldn't have known any different until one morning something changed.

I creaked open my bedroom door as usual, trying to keep quiet so that I could have a few moments to breathe before he smothered me with attention. To my surprise, the cursory screech of his chair didn't come. I stopped on the third stair and listened. No tap-tap-tapping away at his ancient keyboard. My heart seized up. What was happening? Was he dead?

When I reached the bottom of the stairs, I slowly peered around the corner, worried about what I would find.

"Bubba?" I said. He was hunched over the kitchen table and fidgeting with something.

"Oh!" he said, startled. "Hi Darlin. How'd you sleep?" It was his usual line but I could tell he was reciting it more out of habit and less out of interest.

"I'm fine," I said quizzically, peering over my shoulder as I poured myself a cup of coffee, walking around to see what in the hell he was doing. His cup of coffee was untouched. His yogurt was unopened. His laptop full of graphs was nowhere to be found. He was bent over his phone, swiping feverishly through his photo library, squinting through his thick lensed glasses.

"What are you doing?" I asked.

"What do you think about this picture?" he said, shoving his phone towards my face.

It was a photo of him as a professor, maybe twenty years ago. He had a thick swath of black hair swept across his forehead, which was wrinkled in thought. He was mid-sentence, thin lips open and jawline defined. He was wearing gold rimmed aviator shaped glasses, a white button down shirt, and a paisley tie, always incorporating his hippie attitude into all aspects of his life.

"That's really nice, Bubba," I said. "I like it! When was that taken? I don't think I've ever seen it before."

"Hmmm," he said, retracting the phone and resuming his swiping. "No, it's just not right. What about this one?"

He showed me another one, this one from several decades before the professor photo. I was familiar with this one. It was the sepia toned school portrait from his senior year at the military academy. He was wearing his school uniform: a thick wool jacket and a thick sash across his chest, adorned with golden pins.

"Oh Bubba," I said, always a romantic for old shit, "I love this picture. Can you send it to me? Can I have a copy?"

He turned his phone back towards him and relaxed into his chair as a weight seemed to lift from his shoulders. He nodded slowly. "Yes, I think this'll do." He said. He leaned back in his chair, reached for his coffee mug, took a sip, frowned as he realized it had gone cold, and put it back down again.

He withdrew his laptop from a bag beside him, opened it up, and started typing.

I put his mug of coffee in the microwave, eyeing him quizzically. "What are you going to do with that photo?" I said.

"There's this website I found that does online datting, but for seniors." He made the same face as he made in the professor photo: analytical, focused, scheming. He held laced his fingers in front of him. "It's been about 3 months. I think I'm going to try to get back in the game."

I turned toward him, frozen in the act of setting the time on the microwave. "Uhhh what?" I said. Of all the possible futures I'd envisioned for this man of routine, online dating was not one of them.

"I've been carefully constructing my profile," he said thoughtfully, stroking his chin. "I've analyzed my audience. Who are the women who would be interested in a 70-year-old widower? Well, I logged in and it turns out there are plenty of divorced women out there. It really doesn't feel fair, actually, because for every man like me there are dozens of women pawing for him. It's like shooting fish in a barrel."

I was flabbergasted. All this time I thought he was writing some sort of presentation on the practical applications of sociology and really he was applying a sociological analysis to get a geriatric hook up. My jaw dropped. My grandpa, humble man of reason and modesty and data, was using his Ph.D. to game the online dating system and score himself a hot elderly date.

He rambled on about the statistical probability of finding a second soul mate online and I felt like I was frozen in time. To my horror and disgust I tuned back into the conversation just in time to hear him say:

"I'm looking at a one-to-ten scale of attractiveness in finding a mate, you see," again with the professorial earnestness, "and a prospective mate can earn extra points for non-physical traits, but really it's a buyer's market, so to speak..."

"Uhh," I said hoping to stop him from finishing this sentence which would require that I acknowledge my grandfather had a sex drive. "I've gotta go to work!"

I fled the situation, leaving the room before the microwave could even ding.

I was not prepared for this, I thought later as I walked through the rain to my bus stop. As I waited for the bus, I started to laugh. Bubba was dating! Hadn't I thought all along that such a kind, compassionate, thoughtful family man should have a partner in life who would care for him the way he cared for his family?

Knowing him, he wasn't going to take dating lightly. He would enter with calculation and trepidation into the dating scene. With his profile photo selected, he had the cherry on top of his algorithmically perfect dating profile. I decided to refrain from spoiling his good mood by telling him that there was a bad word for putting misleading photos on a dating profile—catfishing.

I, having never actually used online dating myself, wasn't sure what to expect for Bubba, and once he had finalized his profile I forgot that he was even dating.

That was, until I came home from work one day in October.

I opened the door and listened for his greeting but it didn't come. I poked my head in and looked left and right. I was alone. I took out a book, settled on my bed, and fell asleep. When I awoke it was dark and still he hadn't come knocking. I went down to make myself dinner. As I was stirring my veggies on the stove he came in the front door. I rushed over.

"Where have you been?!" I asked, like a concerned parent catching their teenager in the act of sneaking out.

He took off his raincoat and put it on the hook.

"Hey Darlin," he said, chuckling. He paused for dramatic effect before revealing, "I was on a date."

My jaw dropped.

"What?!" I said, waving my spatula around wildly, slinging olive oil everywhere. "With who?!"

He went on to explain that he had been matched with a woman online who seemed "motherly" from what he could tell from her profile, which was a quality he was seeking. I suppressed my gag reflex at the Oedipean thought. Her profile picture had a photo of her with her two adult sons—surely a sign, Bubba thought, as someone who also had two adult sons—but when he showed up to the date, she was much older than her photo, which he thought was distasteful. I thought his distaste was ironic for a 70-year-old who was using a photo from age 18 on his dating profile.

"On a 0 to 10 scale of attractiveness," he said, "she was about a four, and I'll go down to a six but not lower."

He said she was nice enough but that he probably wouldn't see her again.

His evening absence became a trend. Every few days I'd come home and he wouldn't be there. I noticed that a pair of weights appeared beside the front door. When I asked Bubba what they were for, he said he was going on walks around Greenlake, a loop near our house, with the weights so that he could build up some muscle for the ladies. This, I thought as I threw up in my mouth, was too much information.

I was simultaneously happy for Bubba for getting out there and weirded out by the process of watching him learn how to date for the first time. Because he fell in love with Nannie when he was 19, he had never dated the way we think of it now. He might as well have thrown a rock from his doorstep and married the nearest warm body it hit.

One day, I was on my laptop at the kitchen table when Bubba came through the front door like he was walking on air.

"Hey Darlin," he sang as he waltzed over and kissed me on the forehead. He hummed as he poured himself a glass of water and then sat down across from me, tapping his foot.

"Someone seems like they had a good day," I teased.

"I was on a date," he said, "with a stewardess."

"You mean a flight attendant?"

"Well, yes," he said. "She doesn't do that work anymore but back when she did they were called stewardesses, and oh boy! If you could go out with a stewardess back in my day, it was a big deal, they were a real catch, the real deal. I always wanted to date a stewardess."

I resisted the urge to roll my eyes.

"Well that's great, Bubba," I said, playing the good sport. "So you had a good date?"

He went on to tell me that not only was this stewardess pretty and kind, but she was a mother with adult kids and young grandkids in the neighborhood. She was a hippie type like him and they had a great conversation.

He saw her the next week and the week after that, and then more than once a week, and then they were going on walks with weights in hand together. She liked to go on long walks, this stewardess, which was good for Bubba who was always an active person but had become sedentary while Nannie was dying. This new woman liked aimlessly wandering consignment shops browsing for bargains, something completely foreign to my goal-oriented Bubba. I still hadn't met her, but I could tell she was having a good influence on him. He seemed lighter in spirit, more relaxed, happy.

One day, I came home from work, tossed open the door and flew inside from the rain. I heard wet noises to my left, looked over and screamed. Bubba was making out with someone on the couch. I was horrified.

"Um, hi," I said, and quickly tried to run up the stairs and burn the image from my retinas.

"Hi Darlin," Bubba said, catching me before I could get to the top of the stairs. "Come down, I want to introduce you to someone."

I groaned internally. Meeting the person who was just swapping spit with my grandpa was the last thing I wanted to do. I descended the steps and stood away from the couch, keeping my distance.

"This is Susie," Bubba said. She was small-framed, slight like a bird. She had long silver hair and a soft smile. Her eyes seemed thoughtful but she was obviously embarrassed.

"Hello," she said. "I've heard so much about you. So nice to finally meet you."

"Likewise, I've heard a lot about you," I told her, leaving out the part where Bubba said he had a fetish for stewardesses. "Really nice to meet you, have a good night."

I turned to run back up the stairs but Bubba caught me again.

"No, wait!" He said. "Come sit down, tell us about your day."

My cheeks burned, but I couldn't say no to Bubba. They were seated almost on top of each other, arms around one another. The lights were dim, "mood lighting," I assumed, so I flicked them back up full blast to break up any romantic tension in the air. I sat on the couch farthest away from them.

"It was fine," I said, keeping things short in hopes that Bubba would let me escape this awkward situation. Susie seemed just as uncomfortable as I did. Bubba was the only one who didn't seem to realize that having your granddaughter sit with you and the person she just caught you making out with was weird.

I saw Bubba less and less after that. They would go babysit her grandkids, go on dates, go for long walks. Sometimes he was gone in the morning when I woke up or he slept in having stayed out late on a date. His "Hey Darlin" became a distant echo and our living situation became more like college roommates and less like family.

One day, Bubba was still in bed when I woke up for work. I heard deep hacking coughing coming from behind his closed door. He said he was fine, but when I came home that night he wasn't home. He still wasn't home by 9 p.m. and I started to get worried.

I called him and my Uncle answered the phone. Bubba was in the hospital, he had pneumonia. He had to go into surgery that night, I couldn't come visit until the next day.

I pulled up to the hospital first thing the next morning. Expecting to see my dad and uncle wringing their hands by Bubba's head, instead I found Susie. It was only the third time I'd ever seen her, and here she was, showing up for my grandpa in his time of greatest need. It wasn't just Susie. There was a couple a little older than me, and two solemn looking toddlers. I knew they must be Susie's family.

I said hi to them, and then quickly in those first moments of conversation, I realized what an impact he'd made on their lives. He was already a part of their tribe.

My relationship with Bubba changed as he incorporated this new love into his life. I saw that our family was like a mobile hanging on a tenuous thread: one piece had fallen away, and the mobile had rocked in chaos for a while. When it settled, though, it found a new balance that wasn't exactly the way it was before. Bubba and I had figured out a new way to relate without Nannie. And now that he'd found Susie, the mobile of our family shook anew. Now it had to find a new balance yet again, different but still tied together by love.

Love You!!
I wouldn't be
here w/out you!
Amanda

# Nowhere Men

## Amanda Stubbert

Picture it. You walk up to the shop only to find the door locked and the windows dark. It should be open. The hours listed on the plastic sign filled in with Sharpie add up to an unlocked door and employee at the ready. But no. You can't even ask why. Though you cup your eyes and peer through the glass, you are faced with nothing but the swaying cardboard announcing the obvious, that they are closed. It could be the dry cleaners holding the uniform you need in the morning or the ice cream shop that was meant to be your reward for a week on the treadmill, but whatever the genre, the consequence is the same. You won't be getting what you need and there isn't anything you can do about it.

My father's "store" was closed so much of my childhood that finding it open was the surprise. Remember those goofy signs business owners can buy that say 'open' on one side and 'shut' on the other? These rang strangely true for me in my relationship with him.

Hearing this, you may picture a sad after-school special. The one showing a small child wearing a coat and backpack, poised at the window, waiting for a car that will never arrive. The phone eventually ringing to explain why her father had, yet again, been unavoidably detained. This does not represent my experience. My father was either there or he wasn't. There was the time, for example, when he paid for five years of braces with one check, and then the time the electricity was nearly cut off because his checks didn't come. There was a time he took us to Europe for three weeks and a time we didn't know where he lived for three months.

In between appearances there were no plans abandoned because there were no plans made, no promises broken because there weren't any promises. There wasn't anything.

Unfortunately, my old man wasn't the only one who I would find 'shut' for no apparent or pre-arranged reason. Paul did the same thing.

Starting with our friendship in junior high, through the all-night undefined phone calls, and into the hot high school romance, we lived in symphony or silence: all or nothing, together or apart. The words "regular," "normal," and "steady" weren't in our vocabulary which made our time together so focused and intense there was no room left for anything or anyone else. Have you ever been to a concert or movie so good that, for a moment, nothing else exists? Together we were a forest fire burning quick and hot, engulfing everything nearby. But the off times, the times apart, left me with nothing but silence and ash. A loud, cold silence.

Paul's exits came without warning. I would lay on my waterbed, holding the yellow headset. Ring... Ring... Ring... Then the click and, "You have reached..." I would hang up. Having left a message yesterday and one the day before that, I wouldn't leave more. The usual cycle of questions would begin: *Did his mother erase my messages? Had no one played them yet? Was he mad about something? Or just not interested in talking? Not interested in me?* My mind became a Petri dish in the silence. Thoughts grew and multiplied when there was no evidence to refute them. *Had I said something wrong? Was he bored with me?* And my worst fear: *Was I merely one of many girls he was seeing and no longer an ultra-special only?*

It could be a day, a week, or more before he returned a phone call or appeared on my doorstep signaling, he was ready to be with me again. All in.

Perhaps I accepted this bizarre and selfish form of non-commitment because it was familiar to me. I did know how to wait. *And Paul was worth it,* I told myself. *All good things come to those who wait,* I repeated over and over. *Good things come at a price. Nothing is ever perfect.* I had dozens of these Farmers' Almanac lies at the ready. The question I never did ask was, if he was worth the wait, perhaps I was worth more than the waiting?

My old man met wife number four at an AA meeting the summer before my junior year in high school. She was about my height with a helmet of burnt-red hair and didn't appear to like me very much. She would smile and be polite, but the lack of warmth was easily detectable. They moved to Ashland, a small town in Southern Oregon famous for the Shakespeare festival which flooded the area with tourists in the summer and the active Wiccan community which flooded the town-folk with urban legends year 'round.

My siblings and I went to visit the newlyweds over Christmas break that winter. This was the first time the five of us had shared a holiday since I was four years old, so I had equal amounts of excitement and appre-hension. These new circumstances had the potential to bring about a new era in my relationship with my fa-ther. Dare I hope? New house, new wife, new tradi-tions, why not new interactions? Expecting a sudden change was the definition of crazy, but I just couldn't help myself.

I knew for sure there would be good moments, there were always a few. If my brother or sister picked up a guitar, Dad's ukulele would appear as quickly and smoothly as a sneeze being met by a "bless you." And a three-part harmony picked up like the Kleenex®. And I was right. That first night in Ashland the talent show was humming along like an episode of *The Partridge Family,* when someone asked me what I wanted to sing. I stared back dumbly, suddenly unable to think of even one tune. They never asked *me,* so I wasn't prepared! I felt like an Algebra teacher had called me to the black-board instead of a well-meaning sister asking for a request. "Anything from Simon and Garfunkel!" I blurted out. *Ah...relief.* I knew every word to every song on their Greatest Hits album so whichever they picked, I would be safe.

They began to play and within a few bars, five of the inhabitants of the small, stuffy house were crooning away. But I didn't know that one. I don't mean the lyrics escaped me, I mean I wasn't sure if I had ever heard it before. I stayed quiet.

Somewhere in the middle of the chorus my new step-mother noticed my lack of participation. "Why aren't you singing? You picked this song?"

Everyone stopped. "I thought you said anything Simon and Garfunkel?" Half-Sister asked.

"She meant anything off of that *one* album she has." Whole-Sister explained to the group in a tone that implied a pat on the top of my head.

"OK," I tried again, "how about 'Bridge Over Troubled Water'?" We dove back in. Of course, this melody included multiple notes entirely too high for me. I couldn't have reached them with a step-stool.

"What's the matter now?" called the oh-so-observant stepmother over the musical din.

"Too high!" I called back, wishing for the voice of Julie Andrews or, if not that, the superpower of invisibility.

"Sing the alto harmony..." offered my brother.

And we cycled back to my recurring nightmare where four singers attempted to teach me how to intone different notes than the ones I already had ingrained in my head.

"No! You're singing my note again!" someone would call out as I inevitably fell back onto the melody. This was supposed to be fun.

After one disappointment too many I snuck into the tiny kitchen and used the wall-mounted phone to call

Paul, the one person who might actually care exactly what I was going through—if he were in the mood to answer. This would be a long distance call I hadn't asked permission to make. I didn't care. The odds of him answering were slim, but worth a shot at a sympathetic voice, one that could make me laugh.

Ring... Sweet relief as I heard a click and a "Hello?"

"Got a few minutes and a shoulder to cry on?" I asked without preamble.

"You can cry on any part of me you want." See? He was making me laugh already. "What's wrong?"

"Oh, the usual. I keep expecting to be included or taken seriously or anything that *doesn't* make me feel like I'm adopted and a disappointment." I began in fake cheery voice. And then returned to my normal timbre. "I don't know why I looked forward to coming here. I'm counting hours at this point." When there was no response, I added, "This is the part where you cheer me up."

"What if I come and see you tomorrow?" he offered.

"Be serious."

"I am being serious. It's on the way to my grandparents' in Medford and I was headed there anyway."

With a tone implying *Oh, you will not* I said, "You would really come here?"

And with absolutely no tone at all, he replied, "Yes, I really would."

"I love you!" I exclaimed one decibel too loudly, then whipped my head around to see if I'd drawn attention. I lowered my voice, "I really, really, really love you."

"See you tomorrow, Kid."

I hung up the phone, offering up a silent prayer of thanks to Mr. Alexander Graham Bell. How did girls with daddy issues manage before telephones? Ride a horse to the telegraph office? I returned to the living room with a new sense of joy and stamina, not to mention an I-have-a-secret grin on my face. Which, of course, no one noticed.

The next day, I loitered in the front room making up one reason after another for being there. I didn't want to be caught staring out the window waiting for Paul, but I didn't want to risk being in the other room and having my family descend upon him like a pride of witty lions on an unsuspecting zebra who's been conveniently separated from the herd, either. Of course, I needn't have worried. If there was ever anyone who could take care of himself in the wild, it was Paul.

I heard the tires on the gravel driveway moments before his mother's light brown sedan—known as "The Boat"—appeared around the bamboo bushes. My stomach zinged something akin to stage fright, not all-out fear, but something awfully close.

I rushed to be the first at the door, calling, "Oh! Did I forget to mention that my...um...boyfriend was going to swing by on the way to his grandparents' house? Well, he's here."

This declaration brought all six of the little house's inhabitants into the smallest room therein. I flung open the door and my mouth to start a barrage of explanations I had not yet practiced, but the look on his face clearly communicated "I got this," and both were quickly closed.

Paul greeted my father and brother with his own name and a firm handshake, then waved to my sisters and stepmother, all crammed into the kitchen doorway, before saying anything to me. He then gave me the longest hug allowable with my family observing us like we were an exhibit at the primate house. My back facing the wall, Paul put his hand on the small of my back, fingers outstretched, somehow suggesting without a word that he would have grabbed my ass if no one was looking. I choked back a nervous laugh.

"You've been driving for a long time. Do you want to go for a walk to stretch your legs?" My not-so-secret code for "let's get out of here."

"But I just got here." He turned to my dad with an easy smile, "Can you believe those Blazers?"

The entire motley crew migrated as one back into the living room and took up every couch, chair, and ottoman around the Christmas tree and the miniature potbelly stove. The two of us shared the overstuffed chair that was almost big enough for two. Paul talked fishing, golf, and basketball while he held my hand, steeling me with strength. He laughed at my dad's dad-jokes. He asked my sisters questions about their guitars and listened attentively to their answers. This was approaching Norman Rockwell territory. I suddenly couldn't remember why I had been nervous.

All too soon, the clock bid him go, grandparents were waiting. Everyone kept their seats and allowed me to walk him to the door solo, for which I was grateful. I wanted to say thank you in a way that conveyed what I meant, though the actual words *thank* and *you* were the only two that came to mind. With a chaste kiss and a quick hug, he returned to 'The Boat' to backtrack across the highway and back to his own life. My hero.

But what was this? My father and brother simultaneously rose to their feet and slowly crossed to the front window. What was happening?

My brother mumbled something like, "Can you see?"

"Buick," replied my old man. "Looks like late 70's/early 80's."

What were they doing? Why did they care? Then, as they continued to guess at the make, model, and year, I saw it. They were checking up on him like fathers and brothers are supposed to do, by checking to see what kind of car he drove and if he drove said car responsibly. If he could take care of a car, if he had chosen safety over flashiness, then possibly he could take care of a daughter and a sister. They watched him drive away. Did he peel out, take the corner too fast? These were, apparently, true signs of his character. I didn't have the heart to tell them the character trait they were assessing (i.e. "The Boat") belonged to his mother (and he hated it). I didn't bring up the fact that I was quite certain he had not only driven drunk on multiple occasions but had also held on to the bumper of The Boat while a drunk friend pulled him behind on a skateboard. That particular act of irresponsibility had resulted in a broken collar bone and his parents' decision to move to a new neighborhood where Paul could make 'nicer' friends.

My father and brother's manly (though completely misguided) way of checking him out didn't matter to me. The fact that they had meant everything. I didn't know whether it was the way he looked at me or the confidence with which he spoke that made them take Paul seriously. Maybe it was the holiday or the fact that he'd driven so far out of his way? I didn't care. My father was acting like a dad. And this time for something I was happy to claim as my own—a boyfriend who was acting like a boyfriend. For this one moment in time, both shops were open for business and I got what I needed when I came to the door.

# Baptism by Fire

## Renee Linda Thomas

*I came to explore the wreck...*
*I came to see the damage that was done*
*And the treasures that prevail*

From *Diving into the Wreck*
—Adrienne Rich

I was determined to not let my fears of what Donald Trump's election might mean for those of us who don't conform to traditional standards get in the way of my plans for personal transformation. I'd already contacted Planned Parenthood and enrolled in their Transgender Services program. Then, I'd begun a regimen of "Hormone Replacement Therapy" and applied for a court-ordered legal name change. Step by step, I would follow through with the hard work of changing every single legal form of identification—driver's license, social security card, everything—to my chosen name, Renee Linda Thomas, in my attempt to begin to heal the deep wounds of nearly seventy years of living on the razor's edge of gender ambiguity.

Starting on my birthday on November 14, 2016, I began the process of "officially living full-time as a woman," in spite of the fact that I had precious little idea of the true meaning of those words. I was incredibly excited by the prospect of future birthdays holding the promise of true celebration instead of being the dreaded signal of the cyclical return of painful memories.

My final decision to become a woman had come to me less than a month earlier, on October 21. I'd stepped out of the shower in the early morning with a

firm commitment. I had already developed an exten-
sive wardrobe of feminine attire over the span of fifteen years or so. Nestled between dress-folds were all
my childhood daydreams of shifting from the handsome prince charming to the lovely Cinderella prin-
cess-to-be, dressed in white satin—all the while waiting
and longing for the other (glass) shoe to drop, for
somebody to find me out and crush me.

But by my birthday on November 14, afraid though
I was, I decided to combine a celebration of my 68th
birthday with a coming-out party commemorating my
rebirth as a woman. This was also the day when I
marked my long-delayed transition into the 21st Century by setting up a Twitter account and openly declaring
that I was a proud, bold, and beautiful transgender
woman. I posted a selfie just to prove my point. It was
the first time that more than one person at a time had
seen me dressed in "full feminine garb."

There were only two guests at my birthday party.
There was Michelle, an intersexed and, dare I say, veteran, transgender woman I had met at my favorite sec-
ond-hand clothing shop. It had taken many weeks for
me to work up the courage to speak to her, to ask her if
she were, indeed, transgender. I was afraid I might insult her if she wasn't. I was also afraid that she was
transgender. Then I would have to come out to her and
to myself as well! The other guest present was a lovely
transgender woman named Aoife. I had met her at the
Washington Gender Alliance support group just the
week before. Mary Lou, my wife of thirty-years was our
beautiful and gracious hostess and my inveterate ally
through all manner of trial and triumph. She provided
the cake with sixteen candles, stand-ins for the sweet
sixteen birthday I had missed so long ago.

That same week I'd begun to see a counselor named
Miranda, who specialized in seeing clients with "Gender Dysphoria." Each time I thought of her name, I was
reminded of "Miranda Rights." From the beginning of

our relationship she was meticulous about presenting my rights as a client, presumably to announce up front that she fully understood the many pitfalls and perils of transition. I had always maintained the right to remain silent, on the grounds that speaking my truth might incriminate me. This therapy was the first time I had spoken openly and freely to anyone about being transgender. Now, I was no longer left completely alone in my longstanding gender-based sufferings. For the first time, in Miranda's presence, I felt fully accepted, and even admired for my persistence and my survival as a gender non-conforming person. From the start, Miranda worked to educate and enlighten me, as well as to normalize and reassure me about virtually every aspect of transition. She affirmed for me that she had lived through and understood the trauma and the drama that growing up transgender had inflicted on my life. She also honored my longstanding efforts to educate and liberate myself from the prison of my past. She listened to my tales of childhood abuse without flinching and expressed respect for my courage and persistence through many years of prior therapy.

Most importantly, Miranda acknowledged that deep trauma, particularly the wounds flowing from gender non-conformity, required one to heal the wounds again and again as each new situation of transition presented itself. I could tell from the soft glow of recognition in her eyes that each of us might be in the presence of bravery and greatness. Once when I asked her how I would know when I had reached the sweet spot when I could step forward bravely as a woman, she said, "You will take it all for granted and not think twice about being a woman. When it's time for lunch, you'll just eat lunch without wondering if you're doing it properly— as a 'real' woman would do it."

I so much wanted to believe her that such a day would come.

If being with Miranda and her warmhearted, hard-scrabble empathy was my Balm in Gilead for my lost but now not-so-lonely transitioning soul, then joining the Washington Gender Alliance Support Group was my "baptism by fire" into the wild, raw-and-ragged world of "real-life" transgender and gender non-conforming people.

While there were those who came to a meeting once, poured out their heartbreaking stories, and were never seen again, there were also others whose courage in just getting themselves in the door was overwhelmed by a paralyzing fear that left them speechless. To see these frightened people smiling and talkative by the end of our meetings told me that I was in the right place. I attended meetings religiously in those early days and held a special place in my heart for the young people who came—whose mistreatment in the hands of an uncaring world, at such tender ages, left them so bitter and angry that they saw the world as a hostile unjust place. I understood. I'd been such a young person.

But even as I empathized with the younger members of this group, I learned a lot from them, too. They showed a sharp intelligence, sense of confidence, and a readiness to pounce whenever I asked a question or made a statement that betrayed my own ignorance. Their expressions of anger and rage against injustice badgered me and kept me honest. Still, I was there with my own perspective and wisdom as an elder who had failed to create the world they were brought up to expect. We were in this together.

There were other elders in the group, too: the veterans of transition. A woman, just one year older than myself, had helped found the Washington Gender Alliance in 1996 and had not missed a single meeting. She was our anchor, our port in a storm, who could recall every step of her transition, from her early years of hiding out as an overcompensating super-masculine Nascar® race driver and as a rock and roll roadie for an all-girl band, all the way through every gruesome detail of Gender Reassignment Surgery—not to mention hundreds of hours of painful electrolysis. All of that adding up to joyously living the life she always felt she was meant to live. Just being in her presence gave me hope.

At one meeting, I met a young transgender man of 19 who seemed so much more confident in his new body than I had ever dreamed of being when I was an imposter man. This young man displayed such a genuine sense of irrepressible fearlessness and bravery, mixed with kindness, and acceptance, that I intuited his stance could have only come from his previous life as a girl. I was expecting to hear a painful story of his "coming out." Instead, I nearly fainted when he said simply, "I'm stealth. I pass so well as a man I haven't had to come out to anyone. I took a semester off from college to have top surgery, and I just don't care what anyone thinks." He said those words without a trace of the usual false male bravado that had always left me thinking, "Yeah right." He spoke without bitterness or anger, and I believed him.

I was dumbfounded. To me "going stealth," meant hiding out in the shadows, going through the motions of being a man, enduring repeated, unspoken trauma, biding my time for 68 years, hoping nobody would notice me, all the while not even daring to explore an alternative life for myself. Here was a young man, sitting right across the room, who seemed miraculously free of such experiences.

He saw going stealth as an adventure to be embraced. He seemed free of the feelings that he was an alien, a stranger, living in a strange land. Instead he was comfortable in his own skin, confident that the world would provide whatever he needed. And I felt a strange sense of pride that by "simply living to tell the tale" I had somehow paved the way for this young man.

In contrast with the swagger of the young man who lived his life in stealth mode, there was a deeply wounded Iraq war veteran in our midst laying claim to being the first Marine Corp officer to successfully transition while in the service. Listening to her heartbreaking story of childhood abuse was like holding a mirror up to my own life. My heart ached for both of us whenever she spoke, though I was growing more and more comfortable with even my own pain.

But it was the non-binary folks who scared the living shit out of me—in a good way. Their raw courage to celebrate and boldly thumb their noses altogether at outdated notions of gender identity astounded me. I was old enough to be their mother, yet my new status, coupled with their openness, seemed to confer upon me a rough equality, perhaps even a grudging respect, across the generations. I admired these young people. They were so much more confident of their own reality, their own abilities, their sense of safety in the world, than I had ever imagined possible for myself.

Every week these beautiful, tender, brokenhearted, strong folks provided a kind of solace for me as I marched forward in my transition process. Whenever I began my weekly check-in, I was often moved to tears. "So good to be back again among my people," I'd say. A six-foot-four trans woman across the room, in a flowery summer silk mini dress, with long, shimmering auburn hair down to her waist, and roman sandals with long leather straps winding elegantly around a set of knock-out gorgeous legs would wink at me, "Love ya babe," she'd say in return.

I'd found a home.


On January 21, 2017, at precisely 1:30 PM, at the same moment Donald Trump was being sworn into office, my wife Mary Lou, my friend Aoife, and I walked into the municipal courthouse in Bellingham, Washington. I raised my right hand and duly swore that I was not in any way changing my name for fraudulent purposes. How strange it seemed. I wondered why, in two hundred thousand years of human history we had yet to figure out that "gender" matters as a legal concept. I could change my name, yet there was no provision in law for changing my gender. I was among a dozen or so petitioners that day, most of whom were there for the same purpose. They were surrounded—as I was—by loved ones, life partners, husbands, wives, friends, mothers, and fathers. They offered high-fives as we tentatively approached the bench and the black-robed judge. Once the judge's signature was procured, we danced in joy and tears, returning to the hugs and kisses and applause from those arrayed along the wooden church-like pews. Even the judge, who just happened to be Aoife's next-door neighbor, seemed to enjoy the festivities—the simple fact that once a month he got to preside over a birthday party instead of sending someone away in handcuffs.

As we waited in the hallway for certificates to be printed, a nice woman who served as "the clerk of the court" appeared. She congratulated each of us, handed us our walking papers, and offered us chocolates. My crew celebrated over drinks and imaginary cigars, and stuffed ourselves with appetizers at a café on Railroad Avenue. The lovely waitress addressed all three of us as ladies. I left a very generous tip.

I was afraid that precious moments like these might slip away in the face of overwhelming concerns for safety and protection in a hostile post-election world. I was not a little worried that our collective, ever-expanding joy and courage might soon be obscured by the politics of division as the fears of losing ground would be sown anew in the Trump era. But even so, the very next day I appeared shaking but defiant at the Washington drivers' licensing office and presented two required letters. One was from Planned Parenthood, the other from my counselor Miranda. Both I offered as "proof" that I was indeed transitioning to become a woman. When my temporary "enhanced driver's license" printed out the bearer's gender as "M," I reminded the clerk to correct the "mistake" and braced for her resistance. "By the way, I wish to be an "F" instead of an "M," I said, hoping the quiver in my voice would not betray my fear. "Oh yes, so sorry," she replied matter-of-factly, rather unclimactically, in fact. "Here is your new license to be a woman." After all those painful years of living in the shadows, I stepped into the bright sunshine and thought, *Well, that was easy!*

As I left the licensing office, a middle-aged man made a great flourish of holding the door open for me. "After you ma'am," he said with an exaggerated bow. My first thought was, *He's mocking me. Yeah, he's right, I am a poor excuse for a woman.* But my next thought was: *What the fuck do I care?!* Then I started to giggle, just like a silly schoolgirl, and could not seem to stop. I had never giggled before. Could it be the hormones? It must be the hormones. I glanced at my new driver's license with the letter F in place of the letter M and thought: *I cannot pretend that changing from M to F will ever begin to make up for a lifetime of gender-based pain and misery, but it is a start.* Still, halfway across the parking lot I stopped in my tracks, *WHAT THE HELL HAVE I DONE?* I looked at the new photograph and wondered if I was in fact nothing but a fraud in a dress.

Afraid I would lose my nerve, I drove across town to the Social Security Office where a sweet kindly blue-haired grandmother, fresh from a gender sensitivity training no doubt, completed the paperwork to officially reinstate me in the government records with my new name. Within a few minutes it was clear to me that the US government did not think I was a fraud. Then, because there were rumors that Trump was planning to deny passports to Transgender folks, I raced over to the courthouse again and applied for a passport.

In my entire 68 years I had never travelled outside of the United States. Perhaps my fear of travel outside familiar territory was linked to how I'd lived my life in constant fear of being stranded, banished, exiled, or left to die alone. But now, here was the prospect of, at long last, after so much hard work, being just free enough of all the old familiar pain to press the reset button. Maybe unfamiliar didn't have to mean dangerous. I would get a passport and decide what I wanted to do with it.

My application for a passport was denied. Apparently, my birth certificate was so old that the official State of Connecticut seal had worn completely off. Several weeks later "my ticket to ride," a replacement certificate, came in the mail. Nobody at the passport desk seemed to notice the contradiction in the words "baby boy" with my physical presentation or the "F" on my driver's license. I was now free to move about the cabin as a woman.

That night after my passport application was accepted, back at home with all of my official paperwork put right and knowing I had a community of people scattered around town who loved me, I giggled that schoolgirl giggle again. My eyes welled up with bittersweet tears of joy. Why not just enjoy the ride? Why not, from this moment on, honor every moment as an opportunity for celebration, every day as a new day? One thing was clear: There was no turning back! THERE WAS NO TURNING BACK. I had finally, at long last, declared myself a woman. However strange and imperfect, and wounded, I would embrace the journey into this new country.

And now I am a woman. AND NOW I AM A WOMAN. And now what do I do? I'll start with lunch.

# So You Want Change?

## Molly Noelle Ware

*My response to racism is anger. It has served me as fire in the ice zone of uncomprehending eyes of white women who see in my experience and the experience of my people only new reasons for fear or guilt. And my anger is no excuse for not dealing with your blindness, no reason to withdraw from the results of your own actions. We welcome all women who can meet us, face to face, beyond objectification and beyond guilt.*

—Audre Lorde

I'd been teaching at the University for ten years, working to make our teacher education program more equitable and attractive to a diverse student population, and struggling to get tenure as someone who'd made a lot of waves working for change. I'd also been waiting for a group of students who were as passionate as I was about changing the public educational system for the better. But the students I'd worked with in our program were mostly a lot like I had been as a student in college. They'd done pretty well, played by the rules, been recognized as good students, and wanted to make a difference in others' lives. Oh, and they were mostly white. Just like me.

So, imagine my delight when one Saturday morning, two weeks into a new term teaching prospective teachers, I realized I had a group of change-maker students (just like the ones I'd been hoping for) in my class. I was at home and sitting cozily in my light-filled bedroom. I was still in bed with a cup of herbal tea and my laptop open, checking messages, when I came across this note: "Thank you," the email from my students read, "for your focus and patience around social justice concepts in our work." The note was written by four students in my new methods class who were earning their minors in Education and Social Justice (ESJ). Three were students of color, one was white. Since almost day one they'd been complaining to me about how, during class discussions I'd been facilitating, the other students in the class were refusing to see the implicit racism built into our educational system. I felt their pain, but because I knew that change happens slowly, I wasn't as worried as they were that the rest of the class was permanently stuck in a blind spot.

"The four of us have been discussing our frustration at length," their email went on to say, "and today we have decided to move from 'critique to create'!'"

This was a phrase I'd never heard, but it struck me as exactly what I wanted for my students—to move out of criticizing and to begin to think about how to create change. I felt a tingle of excitement that I might not be the only voice in the room asking us all to look at power dynamics and inequities. Still, though I couldn't put my finger on why right away, my body tensed when I read their words. I'd known these four were frustrated—just last week they'd cornered me after class to share their agitation—but I didn't know they were meeting outside of class to discuss their feelings with one another. I tried to slow my breathing and relax. *It's good the students are galvanizing their energy*, I tried to tell myself. But something ate at me.

The cohort, only 15 students and a couple of weeks in, was already on the verge of teetering off a cliff. The cultural divide between the critical, resistant, activist students from ESJ and the more idealistic, compliant "good students" who comprised the majority of the class felt immense. I'd already designed several class activities to get them all thinking about how teachers' biases and assumptions often create inequities in the classroom, but the quarter had just begun. And apparently, we weren't moving fast enough for the ESJ students.

The tone of the email turned demanding, "If you choose to support us," I continued to read, "your current plans for Monday will be postponed." *Postponed*?! I felt the blood rush into my face as I moved instantly from anxiety to anger. I hadn't expected a coup. They didn't have the right to take over my classroom. And while I supported both the passion and goals of these four students to open the minds of their peers, I wasn't interested in having their frustration hijack the class. To be honest, I was rattled.

Because it was Saturday, I only had two days to ponder this strange situation and figure out how to manage their request to take over and teach class. I started to panic. If they led class on Monday, our progress in terms of the content we needed to cover would be completely waylaid. The readings and other assignments I'd given for the weekend were actually important to our work with public-school students on Wednesday. Had this group even considered how their plan might affect their own learning? Or the middle school kids and teachers we would be working with locally? Or the cohort as a whole? Or me? I read on, "We realize this means we'll need to communicate with the rest of the cohort...this is why we would like your response as soon as possible so we can draft a letter explaining the new plans."

I was livid now. Scrolling quickly through the students' closing words, I lost my temper entirely when I read, "We would like these activities to be fully student-centered...we ask that you come to class only as a witness."

I slammed my laptop shut.

So, I was supposed to just hand over the class to a group of frustrated students who basically wanted to force their peers to comply with their understanding of social justice? My brain started whirring. I couldn't catch my breath as I spiraled. Privilege and social justice were important topics, but it didn't work to teach them in the abstract! It also wouldn't work, I suspected, for part of the class to shame the rest of the class. There was a reason we were going to be learning through teaching kids! The reason was that we would have practical experience to use as context. My brain kicked into high gear. When exactly did these students imagine we would get to the assignments they needed to complete before seeing real public school students in only a few days? *No! Absolutely not!* I thought.

Somewhere inside, I had an inkling I was more reactive than the situation warranted. I knew a different professor would pull back and find a sensitive way to navigate the situation. But I was suddenly—too suddenly—on system override. And there was no slowing me down once I got there. Which meant it didn't occur to me that *I* was the one feeling obligated to respond immediately. And *I* was the one now fuming in response to students' request. As I rode the wave of my reaction, I didn't even imagine I could just ignore the email for the moment and talk to the students about their message in class on Monday. This would have been perfectly reasonable. I also didn't think of some way to work *with* the students to meet all of our needs. This might have served us all, as well. Instead of staying calm, somehow, the mounting crisis my students perceived created in me an almost frantic desire to take control of the situation.

I stared at my ceiling, feeling another flash of fiery rage, knowing on some level that this reaction was too big, but not yet curious about why anger was my primary response. If an email from a group of diverse, change-maker students was throwing me into such a tizzy, clearly there was something driving this reactivity. Somehow my rage felt familiar. It reminded me of stories my mom had told me about my grandfather's volatility—which he masked well underneath the twinkle in his eye, his full-fledged belly laughter when telling funny stories, and his ongoing justice work in his community. But that familiarity didn't give me much insight into my own agitation. Throwing back the covers, I pounded my fist on the bed before re-opening my laptop. Then I kicked into action and wrote my response to the students—an overlong and overwrought email explaining why I couldn't support their request. After hitting send, I stared down at the orangish-red hues of my comforter in a mound underneath my laptop and screamed with all my might. That scream seemed to come from some place I didn't have access to and it unsettled me.

Monday morning with my students came and went. The rage I'd felt on Saturday still lingered under the surface, but I held it together. The four who had emailed me sat in stony silence with arms-crossed and icy stares all class. I desperately wanted things to feel better. But after meeting with the group of four in my office later that week and making no headway, the impasse felt hopeless. And as the weeks wore on with students refusing to open up, I began wondering whether my own rage and reactivity, rather than their overstepping of boundaries, had created the standoff we now faced. The last thing I wanted was to create an environment that prevented students from learning. Or that squelched my students' desire to change the educational system. But despite these desires, my attempts to make amends with the students and explain my reasoning wasn't working.

I wasn't sure *what* to do. And every time the thought of letting students be pissed all year came to mind, I felt a gnawing feeling of guilt rear up in me hard. Clearly, I was failing at preparing these young people for their calling as teachers—a feeling I hated more than anything. The guilt became even more painful than the original anger had been, and I felt a despair and a pressure to do something. I just didn't know what that something could be.

A few weekends later, still stewing in painful bouts of disappointment in myself and frustration at my inability to connect with my students, I realized I needed to so some serious soul searching. I could see I'd overpowered and discouraged my four change-maker students, even as I could see they wanted to take over the class and make their classmates—who already held privilege and power by virtue of the fact that they were white and unaware of systemic injustice—see the error in their thinking. I remembered a friend's story of a breakthrough she'd had using a process called Family Constellation to overcome stuckness in her life. After looking online, I discovered a monthly open group session on Family Constellation work and decided to attend. I didn't know anything about this sort of work other than what my friend had told me and what I'd read online about how the process used a systemic approach to heal multigenerational pain. But something in me sensed my reactivity might be connected to my family, compelling me to attend the upcoming meeting.

A few days later, spitting rain accompanied me as I entered our local historic Fairhaven library through the back door. I wound my way down the stairs and through several old rooms until I heard voices around the corner. Through a walnut-stained wooden door with twelve panes of glass, I saw the facilitator, a woman named Lisa, sitting in a circle with about 25 other people.

A small, round drum in hand, Lisa, a tall woman with dark chocolate hair and a serious smile, chatted with the woman sitting next to her while waiting for the last participants to join the group. I cut across the room to one of the few remaining wooden folding chairs.

No sooner had I removed my damp wool clogs and folded my legs crisscross than Lisa rose from her chair to begin the session. After introducing herself, she began drumming quietly, inviting the group into a meditative state. Drumming meditation was unfamiliar to me and I felt totally out of place at first. Uncomfortable, I reminded myself this wasn't so different from practicing yoga—just a way to focus.

After a few minutes of dropping into the space with the drumming, Lisa spent a few minutes describing family constellation work to the group. "We carry our families with us like a hologram," she said.

Her words drew me in because this was why I had come. I needed to understand my own guilt and anger as a first step to repairing the situation with my students. Still, not knowing what was about to happen, I was uncomfortable, albeit intrigued, by Lisa's declaration that our families live with us, virtually like ghosts.

"Does anyone have a situation they want to work with tonight?" Lisa now asked the room.

I paused just a second or two before raising my hand in the air. *I came for a reason*, I thought, *I'd better put myself out there.* "I'd like to try." I said it quietly, unsure about volunteering in a room full of strangers. Lisa invited me to come forward.

Nervous now, I got up to sit next to Lisa. Her deep brown eyes, intense and wise, focused intently on me as she asked me what was going on.

*I might as well be honest*, I told myself. I wanted to understand my reactivity. Where had it come from? And why did it feel so out of control and unstoppable? I hated so much that my process and choices were negatively affecting my students. I was motivated. "I'm working with a group of students this quarter," I said, "who are really angry with me and the rest of the class. They're focused on their frustration, and I feel totally reactive when they try to get me and their classmates to listen. I'm ashamed, but I can't find a way out of this." I could feel my face becoming red and heated as I spoke. My guilt, tinged with the original anger I'd felt when I'd gotten their email, threatened to come bursting out even now as I shared examples of my students' litany of judgments against me, and mine of them.

Lisa looked me in the eye, soothing my reactivity, and refocused me with a question. "Does this remind you of anyone in your family?" Her eyes stayed with mine in a way I felt unusually able to tolerate.

I responded right away. "Totally! This reminds me of my mom. She's in so much pain but hates hearing about anything painful. Anytime I'm in pain she tries to make it better but never really even hears it." The words came out with an emotional flood. I hadn't seen it coming. After asking me another question or two, Lisa surprised me by directing me to select people from the circle to represent me, my mom, my dad, and my sister to create a tableau of my family in the center of the circle.

"Let's start with just these four family members," she directed. I stood up and walked slowly around the circle, pausing in front of each person trying to sense who to select for each family representative. After physically moving the representatives into the middle of the circle, into positions that made the most instinctive sense to me, I took my seat.

I didn't know what to expect, but my pain made me open. I waited and watched.

Lisa began with a question to the four representatives now inside the circle. "What are you noticing in your bodies?" Immediately, the younger woman representing me began moving quickly from one spot to another inside the circle, her arms waving in the air and head shaking wildly. Eyes darting back and forth, she loudly exclaimed, "I can't get comfortable anywhere. I've just got to get out of here." Her beige, shoulder-length hair flopped from side to side as she continued moving in a chaotic pattern, skittering herself as far as possible from the rest of my family representatives in the circle.

*How did she know?* I wondered. But she was spot-on. I felt deep relief as I watched my representative reveal a truth I'd always felt but never consciously acknowledged quite this clearly. I'd never felt like I belonged with my family—or anywhere, really. And I'd spent most of my life frantically trying to escape and distance myself from them—even my choice in career was an attempt to escape, to create a different dynamic in my classroom than the dysfunction I'd known growing up.

Sitting next to Lisa I felt exposed. I wasn't sure I wanted to continue watching family truths reveal themselves to a room full of strangers. But somehow what was happening in the room felt bigger than me— like what was happening wasn't just about my story but was actually part of a shared, collective story. A story my students were a part of, too. I would stay for them, if for no other reason—stay connected to my own vulnerability.

Perhaps fueled sheerly by intuition, Lisa suggested I invite in my mom's dad and mom, Grandma and Grandpa Sieber. I wondered immediately what might happen once my Grandpa Sieber joined the group. Gramps was a force to be reckoned with in our family— a World War II Navy Cross winner who had courageously helped sink the Japanese battleship *Yamato* and flown over 40 successful dive-bomber missions in the Asian theatre. As my grandparents' representatives joined the group, my nuclear family quickly rearranged itself. The woman representing me settled down and began focusing her attention on Gramps. Lisa asked me if I noticed what had just happened.

"Yes. My representative seems fixated on my grandfather. It's like they are mirroring each other somehow." I felt shudders down my spine as I spoke the words. What was I seeing? I couldn't wrap my mind around a budding insight that was happening with a group of complete strangers. My body understood something in that moment. I viscerally understood there was some connection between my grandfather and my experience with my students. But what?

Lisa rose from and crossed to the center of the circle and explained, "If a family member is unacknowledged in some way, often someone in a later generation will feel systemic pressure to represent the excluded person. Usually families exclude something or someone when they can't process the pain of grief, guilt, or tragedy."

Her words landed with a thud. Of course. Gramps' parents and extended family had prohibited him from ever talking about the war once he returned home. Before I had much time to think about how my grandfather's unacknowledged guilt and trauma might be influencing my reactivity with my students, Lisa continued. "Do you know how many Japanese men were killed in the battleship your grandfather helped to sink?"

Tears welled up in my eyes. My throat clenched as I tried to choke back a sob. *What a question!* "I don't really know. He's never talked about it. All he's ever described is the sinking of the battleship, not what happened to the people after it sank."

Eyes were glued to me as I spoke. After several seconds, Lisa said, "I'd like you to select five people to represent all the men who died when the *Yamato* sunk."

People around the room spontaneously burst into tears. I was instantly very shaken by this outpouring of grief and I began crying, too. Still, I identified five new representatives. As they entered the circle, they began lying on the ground in front of my family—one by one. I watched in silent curiosity—a curiosity, I noted, I'd been lacking when relating to my students over the past few weeks. Lisa seemed to know something else was needed in the tableau. "It's good to bring in the families of the fallen soldiers," she said. "These men need a chance to say goodbye to their families." This made sense to me, of course, but what did it have to do with me? I was taken aback by what she said next. "And I think your family needs to honor the loss of *their* families."

I looked at Lisa for a moment when she said this. There it was—the deep guilt and pain of war—the pain that one group of people inflicted on another group of people with no outlet for processing the inevitable regret, guilt, and grief. I wasn't sure I could go there. This was so vulnerable and touched on my own transgressions with my students. But I'd come this far and wouldn't stop now. "Why don't you identify five more people to represent the families of the lost Japanese soldiers?"

I watched as the soldiers' families entered the constellation. Now, most people who had been sitting in the circle were participants in my story—my four family members, Grandma and Grandpa Sieber, five soldiers, and five family members of the soldiers. The soldiers now rose to their knees and began standing as they saw their families enter the circle. My family representatives began shifting uncomfortably at this outpouring of emotion, distancing themselves. Their shoulders and bodies became more rigid.

Tears flowed freely among the participants. Lisa now asked my grandfather to acknowledge the loss of the soldiers to their families. The rest of my family representatives watched intently. I watched, too, as my grandfather's representative repeated the words Lisa suggested, honoring years of loss and pain for the soldiers who had died in the sinking of the battleship and their families. As he did, the constellation began to readjust. Almost immediately, family members of mine who had wanted to stand further apart began shifting position, speaking up with phrases like, "I now feel like I want to move closer to Dad." And, "I want to stand shoulder to shoulder with my wife instead of off to the side." My own body relaxed, releasing deep grief.

Tears began drying up and sobs quieted in the room. In response to the shift of energy, Lisa began bringing the constellation to a close. "Why don't you take one more moment to take in what you're seeing?" she asked me. I nodded, feeling an unusual sense of peace.

"And now," Lisa directed me, "take each representative by the hand, thank them, and say, 'I release you.'" I rose and did as Lisa directed.

By the time everyone was back in their original spots, my spirit was quiet. I breathed in. Deep exhaustion. And then breathed out. Unexpected catharsis. Emotional release.

Lisa began beating the drum one last time as the group sat in silence. As she did, I took in the sense of connection and vulnerability with the group in the reconfigured circle. We were no longer strangers. And my family's unacknowledged guilt hadn't scared them away. Instead, it had revealed the inextricable link between us as human beings.

When the drumming stopped, I left the library. Later that night I would reflect that the suffering my grandfather had inflicted on the Japanese on the ship and the rage he felt at never being able to put words to his guilt and trauma, was the same rage I felt when students tried to take over "my" class. And I could now see that my guilt as the white woman struggling to teach class in a way that engaged students of color had trapped me in waves of anger when students expressed their anger at me for pulling rank on them. The guilt I felt at shutting down any possibility of making change with the very students who were most driven to make a difference was driving our stalemate.

As I climbed in bed that night, I knew that I probably had a hard year in front of me. But I hoped I could now move forward in a new way—with just a little more curiosity and a little less anger and guilt. I would wonder what stories brought each of my students to their stances. I would attend to my own agitation with new tenderness, too. And, maybe—just maybe—as I became able to approach my work in this way, my students, too, would learn to bring this openness and curiosity to the public school students they would serve in their careers one day.

# The Warm Glow of Community

## Wendy Welch

My husband Jack and I started our used bookshop in
three steps: 1-3-2. We wanted one, opened it, and then
learned how to run the place. Part of our back-of-the-
envelope "business plan" included fostering cats at
some point, and another vague future detail involved
putting in a coffeehouse or café on the second floor.

About five years in, the book I'd written about our
bookstore was out in the world, the foster cats were
one of our main attractions, and we kinda maybe sorta
knew what we were doing—most days. Time for the
next adventure.

We'd talked about that café off and on over the
years, but neither of us really wanted to take on the
day-to-day minutiae of running it. I was busy teaching
at the college and writing; Jack was knee-deep in customers and kittens. We decided to hint on Facebook
and Twitter that we were "exploring options" for opening an eatery, and then sat back to see what might happen next—more or less hoping someone would emerge
from the crowd and wave, yelling, "Pick me, pick me!
I've always wanted to run a restaurant!"

Which is what happened. A woman named Kelley
messaged that she'd wanted to cook professionally
since high school and had vast experience preparing
wholesome foods for cheap because her household of
seven people required a tight budget. Her cooking style
could be best described as "mountain fusion," she
wrote. Plus, she was looking for a new adventure.

Already intrigued, we remembered Kelley for do-
nating six dozen handmade Scotch Eggs to the annual
Celtic festival Jack directed. (If you've never eaten a
Scotch egg, consider yourself lucky. My husband says I
can't write that. I say a writer is honor bound to tell the

truth.) Kelley had managed to make even those horrid things taste good, so we had immediate confidence in her abilities.

We invited her over to talk, she came that night, and the next day Kelley quit her stable but boring job and became owner and operator of the Second Story Café. Ecstatic, she was. Terrified, we were. Had we just screwed up this woman's life?

"Of course not! This parallels our own story." Jack tried to be brave, pointing out how we'd fled a horrible work environment to create (and be created by) the community surrounding our bookstore, learning the ropes as we went and braving near-starvation as we figured out how to make our dream into a sustainable business. In our chat, Kelley had said practically the same thing about getting away from "soul-destroying" work and making her dreams of a restaurant come true.

"The low-budget, high-flying life has been good enough for us all this time. Could you imagine doing anything else?" Jack said, just before downing a large gulp from his Scotch. He was scared, too; I recognized that tightness around his eyes.

Sure, we kept our lumpy low-flying (no matter what Jack said) cow of a bookstore from crashing each time it attempted to jump over the moon, but the place only had to feed two dogs, two humans, and whatever foster cats were passing through. Jack's retirement pension stood between us and financial ruin, plus we owned the bookstore as well as lived in it, so there was no rent to pay.

Kelley and her partner Sam had a mortgage and five kids bound for college. There's personal fulfillment, and then there's a full stomach. Both have hidden costs.

And what about the cats? Would a café one flight of stairs above mean we had to stop fostering with a local cat rescue?

Jack fixed me with a firm gaze. "If we do...."

"Then I will," I said, meaning it.

Jack cocked his head at me.

"No, I've been thinking about this, and if we have to quit fostering, I can just fundraise for a spay and neuter program and still be involved. There's more than one way to spay a cat."

My husband of 15 years, who had seen a couple hundred feline guests come and go, guffawed, but then his face grew thoughtful. "Perhaps we're adopting Kelley and her family in place of cats. After all, if this goes wrong, we'll be responsible for them."

In the dim light of the upstairs landing, standing in our home-about-to-become-restaurant, we looked each other in the eyes, and shivered. Maybe we weren't up to this challenge after all. The best we could do was offer Kelley free space in return for taking our meals in her café: will rent for food. That seemed a good deal for everyone involved, but flying without the benefits of a safety net still made us nervous on Kelley's behalf.

Yet this snowball was already careening downhill at breakneck speed. Inspector number six at the health department (aka Ben) had checked regulations regarding animals in the bookshop; cat cafés were operational in Virginia now so no problem. Ben showed far more concern with the actual restaurant set-up and equipment when he visited. Jack had installed a spring-loaded gate at the top of our stairs to keep the cats out; Ben said that looked fine, all we needed now were an extractor fan, another sink, an ice machine, a refrigerator thermometer, a splash guard, and separate cutting boards for meat, fish, chicken and vegetables.

"Oh," said Kelley, smiling with tight lips as the list grew. "Is that all?"

"Of course you know people will call in complaints even when you have everything perfect," Ben added as we finished jotting down renovation plans.

Yes, we knew. Small towns are places where people use the civic laws to be uncivil; businesses made anonymous complaints about one another based on family feuds that came and went. As a steady source of agitation, Angry Old Family members reported upstart incomers for anything and everything. From their point of view, it broke the law to start a business without asking them in the first place.

That's how Jack and I first met Ben, right after the bookstore's one-year anniversary, when some conscientious citizen called in an anonymous complaint that we served meals without a license. (We weren't serving meals, period.) He stopped in and said hello again when another do-gooder insisted we needed an elevator to have a two-story business, after we bragged on Facebook that our inventory had expanded to the point we were moving Classics to the second floor; Ben and his friend the town planner dropped by, and without further ado had us sign something that got our 1903 house grandfathered out of the elevator requirement.

We joked during Ben's pre-café visit that both those complaints had followed big successes for the bookstore, celebrated by community members. The first had been our store's two-year anniversary, the second the publication of my book.

Ben smiled as he started down the stairs. "All the inspectors pretty much assume, anytime a certain type of complaint rolls in, that something nice has happened for the target, and someone else is mad. That turns out to be right in more cases than not. Lotta nice people in the world, and a few bitter ones." At the door, he saluted. "Until next time something goes well."

With the health questions resolved, plans got underway at the speed of desperation. Kelley's two-week notice at her old job was almost up. She couldn't afford to live without a salary, plus in typical *modus operandi* we'd blared all over Facebook, community flyers, and everywhere else we could think of via free advertising that the café would open October 8.

We started shifting furniture October 5.

Jack had just finished renovating our cobweb-bestrewn, damp-proof basement into a comfortable three-room caretaker's flat. Since our bedroom was about to be Kelley's dining room, we needed to move our stuff down two floors over the same weekend that Kelley set up shop above—all while keeping the bookstore open. She and Sam brought their brood of five children over for slave labor and we sent fifteen-year-old Brook, the middle child and acknowledged mastermind of the tribe, to mind the store. The rest of us set to, some moving kitchen equipment in the front door and up the bookstore steps as the rest carried bedroom furnishings down the outside staircase and across the yard to the basement. We looked like an M.C. Escher painting come to life. Or maybe an ant colony.

I can still see nine-year-old James, their youngest, proudly struggling up the bookstore's staircase with determination and a smile, hauling a 30-pound bucket of cooking oil after him. (We kept the kids' heavy lifting inside so no one reported us for child abuse.)

Three days of non-stop labor let Kelley open on time, a smile on her face, black circles under her eyes, the new equipment in perfect working order. Perhaps the ghostly odor of fresh paint lingered on the landing, but the reek of disinfectant had dissipated by then. I'd sluiced down the stripped-to-its-bones kitchen with a famous vet clinic cleaner so strong, you are advised to use a face mask and gloves while mopping. I wore both, but as Jack pointed out after snapping a photo, working barefoot probably negated these safety factors.

The pain of prepping melted in the warm glow of success. Customers warmed to Our Good Chef Kelley right away. Hers was the only healthy eating place in town. Through the changing weather, she kept soup and salads coming. In November, we warned her that from Thanksgiving to February would be lean times; customers dried up as the weather grew cold but would return with the robins in spring. Feeding her kids café leftovers and delirious with joy at owning a restaurant at last, Kelley assured us she was in for the long haul.

In mid-December, the weather went crazy, temperatures plummeting so low that schools canceled because children couldn't safely wait for their buses. Instead of down time, Kelley's $1 delivery fee became the hottest ticket around; she ran vat after vat of made-from-scratch soup to local businesses and individuals too cold to get out and eager to stock up. Bundled in her scarf and fuzzy hat, glasses fogged, she hauled so many take-out containers through the door, our furnace went into overdrive to cope.

We congratulated her on remaining successful in a hard month, and thought things looked good. Not so fast: during that cold snap, and unbeknownst to us, the pilot light went out on Kelley and Sam's ancient furnace. They relit it, but the pilot went out again. And again. And again and again and again....

The family lived two miles away in the tiny town of Appalachia, where they'd purchased a ramshackle bargain of a 1900s house with wrap-around porches on both floors and cracks in the walls. They began waking to ice inside the windowpanes. The children slept in hats under sleeping bags; Kelley and Sam tried to scrape together funds for a repairman. Kelley hid this from us as long as she could, cooking and worrying at the same time.

The day we heard about the furnace, our friend Mark Cooperstein was in for breakfast. Mark and Elizabeth, nearby owners of an ancient farmhouse and therefore familiar with the vagaries of old homes and antique furnace care, were long-time friends of the bookstore and among the café's best customers. Mark didn't know Kelley all that well—yet—but when he heard her telling us about the flickering pilot light that morning, he offered to ask his buddy Rick to take a look at the furnace.

"Rick does heating and cooling repairs cheap, honest, and well. He'll tell ya exactly what's wrong with it," Mark promised, already dialing.

That was as much of the story as we knew until that evening, when we came upstairs to shelve some Classics after the café closed and found Kelley crying into the sink. Between sobs, she told us Mark brought Rick to her house that morning. The latter spent two minutes with the monstrosity in the basement and bounded up the stairs.

"Get the kids out of here and I mean now," he said in a voice that left no room for questions. Mark bundled the startled children and family dog into his truck and took them to Chez Cooperstein. Rick called him later with a sordid tale of toxic fumes, open flame, and dangerous gases. The pilot light was a mere symptom. Short version: the furnace was not only irreparable, but dangerous.

"What kind of money are we talking?" Jack asked, cutting with perhaps more concern than tact to the heart of why we assumed Kelley stood so ashen-faced, still clutching her phone.

She sniffed. "A whole new furnace. Rick says he'll install it for cost, but we have to wait until he's done with his regular jobs. Plus we have to get the new furnace shipped here to put in—he got us a deal someplace—so it will be January before we can go back to the house."

Neither Kelley nor Sam had family in the area; Kelley's were gone save for a sister in Indiana, while Sam's parents lived in England. How they would pay for the furnace in the first place we had no idea, but adding housing costs to that number was beyond the pale.

Jack and I didn't look at each other, but I could feel him doing the math. Kelley had quit a well-paid job to start her own business inside our business. She had responsibilities, and she was ours. So, how would we fit five kids, two adults, their cats and a dog into the bookstore for at least three weeks, and come out friends?

Jack spoke with gentle firmness. "It will be tight and I don't know what we can do about your dog getting along with ours, but of course you will move in here. We can make it work."

Kelley shook her head, crying harder now. "Mark and Sam went back to pack up clothes and stuff for the kids. He says we're staying with them until the furnace is in."

Jack and I expelled breath we hadn't known we were holding; the family had better housing than we could offer.

The Cooperstein farmhouse became the epicenter of our holidays. Everyone joined in as Mark remembered the miracle of the Maccabees with latkes and applesauce; Kelley and Sam celebrated the returning sunlight of Winter Solstice; and Elizabeth, Jack and I thanked God for Mary giving birth to Jesus.

The kids made out like bandits.

We baked homemade bread in the kitchen: rosemary, apple clove, even spicy jalapeno. Our jokes ran heavily to *Little House on the Prairie* references; Mark became "Pa" and the women went so far as to plan matching aprons. (Thankfully, these were never completed.) The young'uns piled onto the sofa with Mark to watch 3-D cartoon movies on the big screen TV, and roamed the hilly pastures clearing brush when the winds lifted. The two oldest boys, Tom and Ciaran, midwifed the baby goats Elizabeth raised for milk; these got named Ron, Harry, and Hermione. School started again and Mark announced he would be driving the youngest boys to school each day.

"Our house is too isolated, and it's too cold for them to stand outside waiting for the bus," he said. "They're kids. I'll get them there." Sam and Kelley didn't blink when their youngest child James ran past during this discussion, grabbed an apple from the basket on the table, and called Mark "Grandpa."

Rick drafted Tom to help install the new furnace, and afterward offered him a job. "Best worker I've seen in a long while," he told the lad's beaming parents.

Finally, Our Good Chef Kelley's family settled back home with the new furnace about two months after the adventure started—just in time for the arrival of a new phenomenon weather reporters announced as the Polar Vortex. (If we thought December was cold....)

Snug in their house, Kelley's clan weathered winter just fine. More than their furnace created new warmth. The two youngest boys invited Mark to Grandparents' Day at school, and he went with such undisguised glee that we teased the buttons would burst off his coat. Meals continued to be shared between all our old houses, and normalcy more or less settled in. Jack and I went to the Cooperstein's one night for dinner when Kelley and company couldn't join us, and the couple seemed bereft.

"It's so quiet." Elizabeth lamented as we sat crocheting and knitting. "I miss the elephantine pounding of little feet."

No mess, no fuss. Life had thrown Kelley a curve ball, and someone caught it for her. A friend of mine has a sign in her kitchen that says: "What are we put on Earth for, if not to help carry each other's packages and eat each other's cooking and say it was good?"

Yep.

## Kelley's Scotch Eggs

Hard-boil the desired number of eggs. When boiled, pop them into cold water to cool quickly; this prevents a black ring forming around the yolk.

You will need three shallow plates: beat a raw egg in a shallow plate; put a few tablespoons of flour in the second, seasoned with salt and paper; and in the third place a generous amount of breadcrumbs, seasoned if you prefer with garlic. (Jack doesn't like to season his.)

Add a couple tablespoons of mixed herbs (we like parsley, sage, rosemary, and thyme, and yes, Jack thinks that's funny) a wee pinch of nutmeg (or mace or allspice) and chopped spring onions (one large or two small) to sausage meat. One pound of sausage will do eight eggs, give or take. Mix this well with your hands.

Next, shell the hard-boiled eggs and roll them in the seasoned flour. Divide the sausage mixture evenly into as many pieces as you have eggs. Flatten these and then shape them around each egg; don't leave cracks or gaps. Roll this in the beaten egg to coat it, and then in the breadcrumbs. Make sure the meat is well-covered in crumbs.

Heat about half an inch of oil in a small, deep frying pan or saucepan; the oil is hot enough when it can brown a small bread cube in 60 seconds. Fry the coated eggs, turning them until they are brown all over and the sausage meat is cooked—usually eight to ten minutes. Drain them and let them cool. Scotch eggs freeze well, and are easy to transport. They usually keep for a good week in the fridge—although not at our house. Jack devours them.

# Contributors

Maggie Andreychak is driven by a narrative voice that has nipped at her heels since she first stepped into the woods as a child. Raised in the Appalachian foothills, she has a powerful love for mountains, water, and the wonders of nature. Her upcoming memoir, *Melodies of Mist,* explores her experience of incest, divorce, and rebellion, and the God that pursued her relentlessly through it all.

Jessie Blair is a gender fluid person of Mohawk and Celtic descent. They have several published articles, including interviews, in *Western Living Magazine* and *Vancouver Magazine. Peace Arch News* published their article about an LGBTQI storyteller project and their short fiction stories have appeared in anthologies created by Filidh Publishing. In their spare time, they play the ukulele and sing off-key to their cat.

Sarah Buel is a cat lover, a dog lover, a horse lover, a goat lover, a pig lover, a rabbit lover, a deer lover, an otter lover, a seal lover, a whale lover, an eagle lover, a heron lover, a pika lover, a marmot lover...

Nancy Canyon's writing has been published in *Raven Chronicles, Water~Stone Review, Fourth Genre, Floating Bridge Review, Able Muse, Main Street Rag,* and more. With Pacific Lutheran University's MFA in Creative Writing and University of Washington's fiction certificate, she teaches writing at Whatcom Community College and coaches for The Narrative Project. *Saltwater,* a book of poetry, is available at nancycanyon.com.

Cathie Collins is a professor of Nursing and an ardent ally of the Transgender Community in Virginia. Fiercely proud of her children, she looks forward to spending time watching them change the world just by being themselves.

Saskia Davis devoted forty-one years to the care and guardianship of her beloved sister, as well as advocacy for others with intellectual developmental disabilities, before her sister passed away. Her essay provides a small window into the memoir-in-progress tentatively titled *Adventures in Grace*.

Wendy DiPeso's first gig was a humorous column called "Wendy's Windows" for her High School newspaper in Hawaii. She later became editor-in-chief. She's a regular contributor for the Open Mic nights at Third Place Books in Ravenna. Married with four children and six grandchildren, she draws inspiration from her colorful family history.

Lula Flann, a devotee of head-turning ensembles and brilliant broads, writes Cozy-Noir from her Cascadian bungalow by the bay. A mad sketcher of clothing inspirations since the advanced age of eight, Lula is drawn to patterns that make for clever clothing collections as well as desperately colorful characters.

Ingrid Roeske Good is a mother, daughter, caregiver, wife, genealogist, business owner, travel enthusiast, filmmaker, photographer, humanitarian, pet lover, musician, dreamer, and writer who resides in the beautiful seaside community of White Rock, Canada. Her anthology piece is adapted from her developing memoir, *I Would Die for You*.

Lynn Goodman is a writer, sculptor, and biologist. She spent three years working as a fisheries observer on commercial fishing vessels in Alaska. She currently resides in Portsmouth, Ohio, with her husband and two dogs, and is at work on a memoir.

After 70 years, Mary Lou Haberman, a sojourner, finds sanctuary when penning memoir, family stories, poems and essays. She spends time putzing and pondering and delights in her kids' and grandkids' authenticity. Her upcoming memoir weaves her life search for peace, while living with bi-polar disorder, with the journey of women in her family who came before her.

Colleen Haggerty is a writer of memoir and personal essay who has been published in various anthologies. Her memoir, *A Leg to Stand On*, a finalist for the National Indie Excellence Awards, recounts her journey into motherhood as an amputee. An inspirational speaker and coach, Colleen gave a TEDx talk, "Forgiving the Unforgiveable."

Anneliese Kamola is currently writing a coming-of-age memoir that braids together family history, travel writing, and climate change. She lives in Bellingham, WA, and works as a freelance developmental editor and as a coach for The Narrative Project. Anneliese has previously been published in TNP's *True Stories: Volume 1*.

Nicki Lang is an artist and writer living in Bellingham, WA with her husband, two sons, and two dogs. You can follow her visual work on Instagram @nicki.lang.studio and her thoughts on life and death on her blog: everybodydies.home.blog.

Emerson Lee is a creative non-fiction writer and poet who explores themes of self-love, self-care, and self-determination, especially as they relate to trauma and mental illness. They live in Tucson, Arizona where they work with memory-impaired seniors and they enjoy desert adventures with their two dogs.

Rebecca Mabanglo-Mayor's non-fiction, poetry, and short fiction have appeared in print and online in several journals and anthologies including *Katipunan Literary Magazine, Growing Up Filipino II: More Stories for Young Adults, Kuwento: Small Things, Beyond Lumpia, Pansit, and Seven Manangs Wild: An Anthology,* and TNP's *True Stories: Volume 1.* Her collection of poetry and essays, *Dancing Between Bamboo Poles,* was released in 2019.

A native of New England, Linda Morrow relocated to Bellingham, WA in 2013. Her Memoir, *EXCEPTIONAL: Redefining Boundaries for My Son and Myself,* will be published by She Writes Press in October, 2020.
"The Wedding" is an amalgamation of sections from several chapters in her book.

Cheryl Nelson is a retired preschool teacher. She is also a polio and cancer survivor, and former Catholic nun. Cheryl earned her BA in Early Childhood Education from Western Washington University and her Masters in Counseling at Seattle University. Cheryl currently lives in Bellingham, Washington with her two dogs. She looks forward to pursuing her interests in writing, travel, and lifelong learning.

Cami Ostman is the author of the memoir *Second Wind: One Woman's Midlife Quest to Run Seven Marathons on Seven Continents* and the editor of several anthologies. She's one of the founders of Red Wheelbarrow Writers in Bellingham, Washington and the CEO of The Narrative Project which supports writers in getting their books done.

Cheryl Perry is a writer whose interests include natural birth, mountaineering, clairvoyance, sports, farming, food, architecture, natural building, peaceful parenting, improv, thru-hiking, weight lifting, and anything that involves authentic connection with other human beings.

Dana Tye Rally is a former award-winning newspaper journalist and magazine writer for *Flare, Elle Canada, More,* and *Costco Connection* magazines. Her anthology piece whispered itself to her one sleepless night as she shared two hotel beds with four women in Manizales, Colombia. The piece has since inspired her first memoir-in-progress, *Lessons in Reverse.*

Morgan Steele wields irreverence and vulnerability to craft weird true stories about her adventures and mishaps. By day, she manages legislative affairs for a statewide advocacy organization. She lives in Washington with her husband, dog, and three dozen houseplants. When she's not rallying or writing, you can find her buying more houseplants, to her husband's great dismay. Her work can be found at www.morgantic.com

Amanda Stubbert published several poems and articles in her college days, wrote and performed a one-woman show while working as an actor, and penned a dozen stories for her own children as a mom. She is now committed to publishing her memoir, *Norwegian Wood,* a coming-of-age story set to the music of the Beatles.

Renee Linda Thomas lives just north of Bellingham, Washington ("our little paradise") with her beloved wife Mary Lou Phillips. Her contribution is a segment from her upcoming memoir *And Now I Am a Woman* which traces the story of her liberation from the lifelong traumatic effects of gender non-conformity.

Molly Noelle Ware, a lifelong educator fascinated by how systems change, works as an entrepreneur, education professor, and leader at Western Washington University, where she explores how change-makers within systems survive and thrive. In addition, she founded We Evolve, a consulting company focused on facilitating systemic change and innovation.

Wendy Welch is an ethnographer and author of *The Little Bookstore of Big Stone Gap, Fall or Fly: The Strangely Hopeful Story of Foster Care and Adoption in Appalachia, Puddledub to Paradise,* and *Public Health in Appalachia.* She directs the Graduate Medical Education Consortium of Southwest Virginia.